Citizenship, Work and Welfare

Searching for the Good Society

Julia Parker

Lecturer in Social Administration
Department of Applied Social Studies and Social Research
University of Oxford

First published in Great Britain 1998 by
MACMILLAN PRESS LTD
Houndmills, Basingstoke, Hampshire RG21 6XS and London
Companies and representatives throughout the world

A catalogue record for this book is available from the British Library.

ISBN 0–333–67360–3 hardcover
ISBN 0–333–67361–1 paperback

First published in the United States of America 1998 by
ST. MARTIN'S PRESS, INC.,
Scholarly and Reference Division,
175 Fifth Avenue, New York, N.Y. 10010

ISBN 0–312–21259–3

Library of Congress Cataloging-in-Publication Data
Parker, Julia (Julia R.)
Citizenship, work, and welfare : searching for the good society /
Julia Parker.
   p. cm.
Includes bibliographical references and index.
ISBN 0–312–21259–3 (cloth)
   1. Citizenship—Great Britain—History.   2. Political science–
–Great Britain—History.   3. Industrialization—Great Britain–
–History.   4. Great Britain—Social policy.   I. Title.
JN906.P37 1998
323.6'0941—DC21
                                                    97–38693
                                                         CIP

This book is printed on paper suitable for recycling and made from fully managed and
sustained forest sources.

10   9   8   7   6   5   4   3   2   1
07   06   05   04   03   02   01   00   99   98

Printed and bound in Great Britain by
Antony Rowe Ltd, Chippenham, Wiltshire

For my Family

Contents

Acknowledgements

The idea for this book arose out of conversations with students, colleagues and friends. I am grateful to all of them and to the writers on whose work I have relied, most of whom are listed in the bibliography. My special thanks are to Susan Field for her care and patience in helping to prepare the drafts for publication.

J. P.

'the city is built
To music, therefore never built at all
And therefore built for ever'.

Introduction

Citizenship is a status that represents a collection of rights and duties conferred by political authority rather than stemming from economic power or social position. The group of citizens may be large or small and will have different entitlements and obligations at different times and in different places. In classical Greece citizenship was the privilege of a small minority. In modern democracies it generally includes the whole adult population, though particular groups – women, the very poor, people without work or belonging to ethnic minorities, the old and those with disabilities – may find their rights limited by discrimination or neglect. Discussion of citizenship may be empirical or normative – analysing existing political and social rights or debating what they should be.

This study is concerned with attempts to define citizenship in the latter sense and to describe the kind of society in which it could flourish. It claims no special knowledge of political philosophy or history or economics. The central interest is in the ideas and values and aspirations that lie behind developments in social policy; in the tradition of critical writing on social reform and the quest for the common good. It is necessarily very eclectic, ignoring some of the most famous utopias – that of Sir Thomas More, for instance, or Plato's Republic – and confined to British writing of the nineteenth and twentieth centuries. The most familiar recent discussion is T. H. Marshall's historical account of the development of the civil, political and social rights of citizenship and his attempt to assess the effects of the increasing equality of status on the inequalities of class. But while Marshall was interested in the rights of citizens, others have placed more emphasis on obligations. T. H. Green and the young men at Oxford who fell under his influence saw good citizenship as imposing a duty on educated and privileged men and women to devote themselves to advancing the welfare of the poor. This meant a persistent endeavour to bridge the stark social and geographical divisions which had become more evident as industrialisation advanced. It led men such as Arnold Toynbee, Henry Scott Holland and Samuel Barnett to pioneer university extension lectures on social and .economic questions for working men and women in their clubs and friendly societies and co-operative associations. And it also led them to the East End of London and other industrial towns to live among the poor as friends

and neighbours – as they hoped – and fulfil their civic duties as poor
law guardians or members of school boards or other public bodies in
efforts to strengthen the fragile structures of democratic local government. There is, of course, another strand in approaches to citizenship
that stresses the rights as well as the duties of the rich in emphasising
repression and control of the disorderly poor, rather than compassion
for their lot. Often the two responses mingle in the same person, but
the instinct to repress and to punish is very evident in such contemporary figures as Charles Murray and Michael Howard.

In the writing and 'lay sermons' of Green and Toynbee the idea of
citizenship is endowed with a strong moral imperative. It is a call for
individual action to help the poor and to create social harmony. For
such men the responsibilities and entitlements of citizenship were not
solely a matter for government. They also depended on and required
voluntary effort – a mixture of philanthropy and self-help. Rejecting
the 'old liberalism' of extreme *laissez-faire* of Spencer and Mill,
Green's followers were yet suspicious of the state and ambivalent
about the ability of government to establish the wider opportunities
for all classes that they sought. It was left to the New Liberals at the
end of the century to argue that the state was an acceptable and
indeed necessary instrument of welfare.

In the meantime more emphasis was placed on the many manifesta-
tions of voluntary action. The poor should strive for their own betterment, individually and collectively, in trade unions, friendly societies
and co-operative associations. This is a kind of 'active citizenship'
beyond the bounds of government that has become prominent again
in the exhortations of politicians at the end of the twentieth century.
Just as 150 years ago admonitions to the poor were coupled with calls
to the rich to perform their civic duties, so in 1988 the Speaker of the
House of Commons appointed a committee to consider 'how best to
encourage, develop and recognise Active Citizenship'.

The aim of this study is to distinguish the different elements in the
various conceptions of citizenship; the dependence on statute or on
volunteering, the emphasis on rights or on duties, the importance
attached to philanthropy or self-help or co-operative association,
and the implications for democratic or authoritarian forms of government. Ideas about citizenship reflect the economic, social and political
environment and it seems likely that expectations would expand in
times of prosperity and diminish in leaner years. But the reality is
more complicated, for demographic developments and changing political ideologies and values influence the significance accorded to

economic circumstances. The debates about citizenship revolve around the three great principles of social organisation – liberty, equality and community; about the importance to be attached to each of them and about the nature of the compromises that have to be made when they conflict.

In the following pages the debates are traced through the writing of some of the famous social critics of the nineteenth and twentieth centuries. The first chapter sketches changing approaches to citizenship over the past 200 years and the growing emphasis on the idea of 'inclusion', the freedom to enter fully into social life. At the present time notions of inclusion and exclusion are commonly used to signify the rights and duties of citizenship. The second and third chapters contain more specific discussion of the views and teaching of T. H. Green and his disciples that emphasised the moral obligation of the privileged to work for the common good.

The middle part of the study focuses on work; the impact of a rapidly developing factory system on the lives of labourers and the efforts of men such as Robert Owen and John Ruskin, shocked by the social consequences of industrialisation, to find ways to rescue some remnants of citizenship from the devastation. Work, they argued, was central to the well-being of individuals and of society, and it must be made enjoyable, educative and useful, sentiments repeated in 1997 by the newly appointed Secretary of State for Social Security when she declared that 'the best form of welfare for people of working age is work'. Successive chapters describe different visions of the good society and prescriptions for realising it, tracing the tendency of the Fabians and New Liberals to put more faith in government and demand more from the state.

The third part, and final chapter, of the book changes perspective to consider the problems that confront governments in Britain which may wish to establish and guard the rights of citizens at the close of the twentieth century. The problems are those of a country rich in world terms, but going through a second industrial revolution that is transforming the nature of work, and threatens to remove the chance of any employment from substantial numbers of people. At the same time an ageing population increases the need for economic and social support.

The debate about citizenship has particular relevance in Britain in the 1990s as the relationship with the rest of Europe is negotiated and a new government comes to power proclaiming a commitment to social justice. A few days after his appointment, the new Foreign

Secretary announced the government's intention to sign up to the European Social Chapter: 'We do not accept that the British people should be second-class citizens with less rights than employees on the continent.' The formidable, though familiar, political task if citizenship is to have any substance is to find ways of diverting the national wealth away from the dwindling number of those who produce it to everyone else. Economics is the study of production and 'provisions'; politics is about the social distribution of resources. Efforts to develop citizenship have to move from the economic to the political problem and find ways of turning provisions into entitlements.

I Approaches to Citizenship: The Social Question

1 Rights and Duties

Ideas about citizenship – its rights and duties, privileges and obligations – have lain at the heart of political debate through the centuries. It is a status that expresses the relationship between government and people, defining those who are accorded a collection of 'entitlements', but also excluding those whose claims are not acknowledged. Himmelfarb has remarked that the natural, unproblematic poverty of one age becomes the urgent social problem of another. So, too, people without particular rights but also, perhaps, with little sense of deprivation at one period may come to feel themselves and be seen by others as deprived at a later time. Thus, women's political and social expectations and opportunities have been transformed over the past hundred years. And young and old people, homosexuals, ethnic minorities and people with disabilities have all gained wider citizenship status.

The extension of citizenship is no automatic process, of course. T. H. Marshall has traced its development in Britain over three hundred years and more.[1] But as governments in industrial countries have tried to control social spending through the 1980s and 1990s some groups, notably the unemployed, have seen their social rights diminish. Economic and demographic trends, as well as changing conceptions of the appropriate social roles for women or old people or those out of work, all play a part in determining who shall be regarded as citizens and what that status shall entail.

Discussions about the rights and duties of citizenship often find only a pale reflection in social and political reality. Opinions about the proper relation of state and people are generally controversial, and social change needs strong interest groups to back it, as well as a government powerful enough and with the resources, knowledge and administrative machinery to bring it about. Some of the prescriptions of the more utopian writers, moreover, call for a transformation in human character and behaviour that may be beyond the power of governments to effect. Notions of citizenship, however, like the objectives expressed in much social legislation, are of interest, and to be judged not only in so far as they are reflected in social arrangements at any given time but in terms of the vision that they represent of a society towards which people may strive and which may be more fully realised in the future.

3

During the nineteenth century ideas of citizenship were closely linked to the increasingly evident poverty and squalor and disorder of the growing industrial towns. The movement for political enfranchisement was well under way by the 1850s, a movement that later extended to women as well as to men and to claims for economic and social rights as well as for the vote. The developing interest in social citizenship was more complex in its origins and more difficult and controversial in its application. For some who, in an increasingly scientific and rational age, had lost their evangelical religious faith, the 'impulse of self-subordinating service was transferred consciously and overtly from God to man', as Beatrice Webb put it.[2] It was, she claimed, the passing of the Kingdom of God and the coming of the Kingdom of Man. The transition is vividly portrayed in Mrs Humphrey Ward's *Robert Elsmere*, whose anguished rejection of belief led him to social work in the East End, and whose story reflects the real life experiences of many young men in Oxford exposed to and taking part in the religious debates of the middle of the century.

For such men, urged by Benjamin Jowett, Master of Balliol, to go and find their friends among the poor, citizenship was primarily a matter of their own moral obligation, arising from their own social privileges, to do something to alleviate the misery of urban destitution This could mean social work in the poor districts of the large towns, or serving on the public bodies administering the poor law or public health or education acts, or working for social change through new parliamentary legislation.

Often these various strands of endeavour intermingled. But by the end of the century the division seemed to have hardened between those who believed that social advance depended on philanthropy and individual effort and those who preferred the agency of the state, a division reflected in the majority and minority reports of the Poor Law Commission of 1909 and which has again become prominent in the 1980s and 1990s. This bifurcation in ideas about the meaning of and means to citizenship is unfortunate and misleading and it is to a great extent an artificial dichotomy, perpetuated in the heated debates of the opposing factions, the Fabians and the Charity Organisation Society sympathisers, on the Poor Law Commission. It is unfortunate and misleading because it falsely suggests that individual and state action represent alternative rather than complementary ways to social advance. It also neglects the further and equally important element in the understanding and practice of citizenship, the joining together of men and women in trade unions, friendly societies, co-operatives, working men's clubs, local statistical, literary and philosophical societies and other associations for mutual advantage. Sometimes association was for protection or self-help, sometimes the outcome of benevolent 'do-gooding'. But whatever their origin, such movements demonstrate the way in which people may find opportunity and satisfaction in civic activity that allows them to develop social or cultural or economic interests in voluntary association with one another but independently both of the state and of private charity. This kind of association does not necessarily give rise to any widespread desire or pressure for greater equality or for the extension of political rights. Many Christian Socialists were opposed to adult suffrage and thought that the working class would better prepare for citizenship by joining friendly societies and co-operative organisations.

A different approach to citizenship that put more emphasis on the need for greater equality was to insist on the rights of the poor rather than on the duties of the rich. This was also a view that tended to prefer state action as more reliable than philanthropy as a means to that end. It reflected a preoccupation with social injustice and distress and the conviction that extreme poverty required the systematic attention of government and should not be left to the chance ministrations of compassionate members of the upper classes moved by a sense of moral obligation and social responsibility. Thus the secular way out of Darkest England led not only through farm colonies but through state schools and higher education, decent public housing and a reformed poor law, through more interventionist central government and more efficient local administration.

The one conception of citizenship in terms of moral obligation and the other in terms of social justice shade into one another and have their common meeting place in the plight of the poor. In the first case the striving towards perfection – the moral end of human existence – imposes a duty on the rich not only to perfect themselves but also to try to make sure that others do the same. The struggle is one of individual wills, conducted to a large extent independently of material circumstances. This individualistic approach requires the poor to work for their own betterment as well as the rich. Changes in physical conditions engineered from outside can never in themselves bring progress and may indeed be damaging in undermining independence. The idea of citizenship involves the pursuit of intellectual and moral improvement, which it is assumed can take place within a very unequal society. The social rights approach, by contrast, stresses the significance of material circumstances in encouraging or limiting spiritual and moral growth and attaches great importance to substantial social and economic inequalities, insisting that poverty is a problem of the rich as well as of the poor.

This does not mean that either definition of citizenship has a monopoly of altruism. The charitable befriending and instruction of the poor might fulfil a moral duty and might be socially and culturally uplifting, but it was also seen as a way of preserving public order and bridging the dangerous rift between the classes that caused growing alarm in the later part of the century. In the same way the expansion and reform of state education and of the public health and poor laws might be an acknowledgement of social rights, but they too were also seen as a way of softening the discontents of the potentially rebellious working classes. Fear of the mob was as important as compassion for the unfortunate in shaping ideas about the appropriate relationship between rich and poor and government and people.

The debate about citizenship and social justice developing with the changing economic and social circumstances of the industrial workers in the nineteenth century and inspired by the teaching of T. H. Green and his disciples has its parallel in the closing decades of the twentieth century. This later period also has witnessed a sharp and visible increase in inequality between social classes to produce such a contrast between wealth and deprivation as to move some observers to point to the reappearance of Disraeli's two nations. The political turmoil described in the pages of *Sybil* is not so evident today, muted no doubt by the political rights that have been already won, by the public welfare benefits that alleviate the harshest poverty and by the wider opportunities for personal, social and economic advancement. Nevertheless, the gulf between rich and poor and their increasing geographical separation, with poor families concentrated in poor areas with poor houses, poor schools and poor jobs, and with the propensity to disorderly or violent behaviour, has aroused enough alarm, compassion and indignation to provoke renewed discussion of the 'social question' and how it may be resolved.

As with the older debates, the arguments turn on how far the welfare or well-being of individuals should be a public or private responsibility, how far government should or can provide security and opportunity and how far such matters should be the province of other institutions – the family, charitable effort, or the market. The discussion centres on the well-known problems: the proper limits of individual liberty, the desirability of social and economic equality, and the degree of 'moral hazard' in generous public provision for misfortune that may remove the spur to independence and self-help.

But while the old problems of the rights and duties of citizenship remain the same, the societies within which they have to be resolved have been transformed over the past hundred years. The industrial countries are all richer than they were, but economic advance is uneven and falling rates of growth arouse fears about the possibility of maintaining relatively high levels of welfare spending and about the impact of that spending on economic performance. Perhaps more significant, the changing character of production is raising doubts about the possibility of ever reaching the kind of full employment that Keynes and Beveridge took for granted that governments could arrange. More people are out of work, more in part-time jobs and more on short-term contracts. The significance of work as a moral duty, as a determinant of personal satisfaction and material living standards, and as the source of entitlements to maintenance during interruption of earnings all come in question. Jobs are harder to find and harder to keep.

As well as economic trends, demographic changes bringing increased longevity and dwindling fertility have produced a larger proportion of old people who must depend on more substantial transfers from the young. The ability or desire of government to achieve its welfare objectives in eliminating poverty, providing decent dwellings, equal educational opportunities and equitable health care are in doubt. And, finally, increasing prosperity and the seductive enticements of ever higher living standards fuel individual aspirations and inhibit the impulse to redistribution. It is not surprising that in these circumstances the nineteenth century distrust and distaste for government intervention in domestic affairs should reassert itself and find its expression in the 'old' liberalism of the Conservative administrations after 1979. But the New Liberals have also raised their voices to reassert the unique role of the state as a guarantor of individual welfare, the only institution that can defend the freedom of individuals against the incursions of other individuals and rescue some measure of common good and common interest from the conflict of individual goods and individual interests.

Thus the old battles are fought over again on new battlefields. But there are also new protagonists. When T. H. Marshall wrote his essay on citizenship and social class he was writing about Britain and about a particular historical tradition whereby civil, political and, most recently, social rights had grown to include the whole adult population, conferring a measure of social if not economic equality. Since Marshall was writing demographic trends, population movements, changing ideas about the appropriate relations between men and women both in work and family life, and keener awareness of the interests of a variety of minority groups have brought new claims to citizenship. Quite apart from the economic, demographic and social changes of the last fifty years, however, there has emerged in Europe a new political order that undermines the usefulness of citizenship as a way of examining people's circumstances. Citizenship understood as a status defining social rights and duties is no longer entirely determined by independent nations for their own populations. In the first place, international bodies such as the European Parliament are increasingly legislating across the boundaries of member states so that citizenship relates to the European Union as well as to particular countries. Second, there has been increasing movement across European national frontiers since the Second World War, with migrants leaving their citizenship rights behind them. The status of immigrants in their place of settlement must then be decided anew, partly by the host country but also, in Europe, by the European Union.

This need to develop fresh definitions of citizenship as national boundaries dissolve and reform and, as people move backwards and forwards across them, to consider what limitations or exclusions should apply to newcomers, has led Bottomore to suggest that some conception of human rights rather than citizenship rights would be a more appropriate way of thinking about people's entitlements and obligations. Such an approach widens the debate. While it is always possible to argue about what the proper rights of citizenship should be, the question of what they actually are at a given time and in a given place is a matter for empirical inquiry and the examination of statutes. But human rights have no such tangible expression and are not to be found in legislation. They reflect value judgements, and opposing definitions may represent irreconcilable moral positions – even though the formulation of a set of basic human rights by the United Nations and by non-governmental bodies such as Amnesty International may command widespread agreement.

Thus any study of citizenship in late twentieth century Britain must take on new dimensions. It must have regard to political and social developments beyond this country, and also to alternative conceptions of rights and duties beyond those that appear in the edicts of government legislation. These wider issues influence changing definitions of the social rights of citizens and the way they have accommodated to high and perhaps continuing long-term unemployment, a substantial proportion of elderly dependants and a growing number of young dependants without reliable connections either to the labour market or to stable families. In this complex and insecure social environment the enduring questions remain about the level and nature of public support for people who cannot look after themselves, about how far and in what respects government should attempt to impose obligations on citizens, about the kinds of freedoms that should be defended and how best they can be protected, about the desirability of greater equality and, fundamental to all these matters, the question of how to reconcile the individual and the common interest.

The answers to the old questions, expressed in particular conceptions of citizenship, continue to reflect the nineteenth century conflicts of interest and ideology. Then, the individualistic political economy, 'A creed of Murdstones and Gradgrinds that suited mill owners and merchant princes', in Sidney Webb's words evoking Dickens' infamous characters, was first challenged by the 'nest of singing birds at the Lakes' who would have none of it.[3] Coleridge, Robert Owen, Carlyle, Morris, Kingsley and Ruskin all attacked the middle class doctrine, Webb continued. But he also recognised, in spite of regarding the century as an almost continuous record of the progress of socialism, that social change is slow and must carry the assent of the people. Utopian ideas were unhelpful, Webb asserted, because they implied some kind of revolutionary change to a new order which was essentially static, whereas human societies must constantly change and adjust to new circumstances. Webb's faith, in 1889, in a century of progress that would stretch into the future may be in doubt. But the insistence on gradual evolution is amply justified by the continuing opposition between approaches to the social rights of citizens that spring from the individualists, now termed the New Right, and those that are founded in more collectivist sentiments.

There is also the third strand in the citizenship debate that goes beyond the right to receive any particular standard of living, the preoccupation of the Left, or the freedom to choose between alternatives, the traditional preoccupation of the libertarian Right and recently of increasingly sceptical statists. It emphasises, in addition, the right of people in a democratic society to have a hand in determining the kind of provision that is to be available for them. In Tory language 'active citizenship' commonly means some form of voluntary work, so children in schools, for instance, are encouraged to take part in community service. But the term may also refer to the contribution of people outside government in planning services and developing policies. The language of the Left is about 'enabling' and 'empowerment', which denotes not only the ability to use services that already exist but also the chance to help to develop new ones. It is an aspiration that refers back to the nineteenth century struggles of trade unions and co-operative associations and friendly societies to fashion social arrangements and social relationships after their own choosing.

Citizenship, then, describes the rights and duties that govern social relationships; it defines the way people behave to one another and their obligations and entitlements or expectations in relation to the major social institutions, the state, the family and the market. It is a normative as well as an empirical term, expressing different conceptions of the good society. Thus it shares the characteristic that Marshall attributes to social legislation; it represents an ideal to be striven for as much as a state of affairs already existing. Ideals, however, are informed by different values and shaped by different interests. It is not to be expected that any particular conception of citizenship will command universal approval. So argument continues about what the status of citizens should involve, and government legislation and administrative practice subscribes more or less to contending definitions.

The argument, however, is heavily influenced by knowledge. The nineteenth century saw a huge increase in the collection of national information by government. Reports from poor law commissioners, factory and public health inspectors, and the Registrar General's Office provided a wealth of facts and statistics that allowed social problems to be precisely measured. At the same time advances in professional knowledge suggested ways of dealing with them.[4] Doctors and sanitary engineers were crucial in halting the spread of disease. The medical profession has been and remains a powerful advocate of measures to improve public health, but other professions, especially those concerned with education, have played a vital part in uncovering problems and proposing remedies. More recently the emerging professions of social work and social research have been amassing data about the extent and causes and consequences of poverty and inequality.

This is not to suppose that knowledge necessarily leads to action, but it may alter the understanding and perception of problems and the formulation of concepts. While argument about citizenship continues, the idea of inclusion is fundamental in much recent writing. To be a citizen implies the ability and right to join in the customary activities of society on terms which preserve individual dignity and self-respect, and win the respect of others. Such a definition underlines the distinction between attempts to formulate human rights and citizenship rights. The first are intended to have universal application and pertain to all human beings. The latter, while acknowledging the primacy of human rights, would add the entitlements and responsibilities specific to a particular society and which would be a condition of full membership.[5]

The distinction here is analogous to Amartya Sen's discussion of absolute and relative poverty. There are certain conditions where people are without adequate resources for physical survival that represent absolute poverty wherever they exist and which permit no argument. But, beyond such destitution, there is another conception of poverty which represents the inability through lack of resources – material, physical, social or intellectual – to take part in social life. The necessities for social survival will vary in different societies and in this sense poverty becomes relative. But, as Sen insists, it also retains an absolute character in so far as people without the requisite 'capabilities' are excluded from their communities.[6]

To maintain that citizenship involves the ability to join in social life raises many questions for those who wish to use it as a guide to policy. There are questions about ends and means, about the categories of experience that are essential for community membership, and about the weight to be given to conflicting interests and values. Is work essential as well as income, health and education to enable people to enter fully into social exchanges and social relationships? How much of these various experiences are to be regarded as social needs or rights? There are also questions about how far such needs should be met through state action and how far through individual effort or non-government agencies. What place has voluntary effort or altruism in a society that wishes to develop citizenship? Finally, the search for answers to these questions inevitably raises further questions about the meaning and importance to be attached to freedom and equality, and how far the pursuit of one may jeopardize the achievement of the other. Here the distinction between negative and positive freedom is relevant. If freedom is understood as absence of coercion – freedom from interference or constraint by government or other individuals which threatens personal security or property – then government interventions might be restricted to maintaining public order and national security. But the idea of positive freedom, implying the ability to choose between alternative courses of action, opens the way for substantial government activity. Rational choices require a minimum of education, health and material well-being. The price of greater government responsibility for such matters, however, is the limitation of the freedom to dispose of their personal incomes of those who must pay for it. So discussions about the importance of freedom can only properly be in terms of whose and what kinds of freedom should be preferred.

The distinction between negative and positive freedom is matched by the different interpretations of equality. There is equality of opportunity and equality of outcome, the first obtaining when different population groups have similar chances of access to schools or medical services or jobs, the second where different groups have similar educational, health and employment experiences or achievements. The same distinction is sometimes formulated in a slightly different way by reference to 'formal' and 'substantial' equality. The first admits of no official exclusion from a given activity or institution on the basis of age or sex or class or religion but, nevertheless, places people without the requisite social or material resources at a disadvantage.

Whatever the definition of equality adopted, it is attacked by some as indicating a dull uniformity and by others as requiring an unjustifiable sacrifice of freedom. The first criticism was dismissed by R. H. Tawney in the 1930s when he pointed out that to wish for greater equality was not to hope or suppose that all men were or might become equal, but to desire that the inequalities stemming from the organisation of society might be removed, so providing equality of conditions which would allow individual talents and differences to flourish.[7] The second criticism relating to the unacceptable interference with freedom must meet the alternative contention that equality does not threaten liberty but is essential for its existence. People are only free to develop their potential and realise their opportunities if they start from positions that are similar. And no one has a legitimate claim to great personal wealth as the amassing of fortune owes more to luck and to the education and skill and cultural traits learned from and supplied by society than to individual contribution and effort.

These preoccupations with the appropriate definition of citizenship rights and obligations, the proper strategies for establishing them and the conflicts of values to be resolved are apparent in the arguments which have become more vociferous over the past twenty years. But what is remarkable is the failure to develop any coherent set of attitudes about the significance of work or strategies for providing it. The citizenship literature places far more emphasis on the entitlements and duties of people who are out of work – through age or youth or disability – or who suffer discrimination on account of race or sex.

The position of dependents and of people encountering different forms of prejudice is of course very important and is obviously associated with high risks of exclusion from the life of the community. But if citizenship is about community membership, opportunities for work are absolutely central. For most people it is not only a critical determinant of material living standards but also a means to self-respect and an opportunity for social intercourse. This is the significance of Bottomore's observation that approaches to citizenship must be about 'societal' policies not just social policies; about arrangements for the provision and distribution of employment not just for welfare. Perhaps the preoccupation with welfare of writers about citizenship reflects a common distaste for the market as a satisfactory mechanism for distributing opportunities and rewards, and a preference for thinking in terms of a political distribution founded on moral principles and conceptions of social justice that find no reflection in the operation of markets. But such distrust, however well founded, must not deny the critical importance of people's jobs for their well-being. In this study of approaches to citizenship in *fin de siècle* Britain and through the last two hundred years the discussion of work is a central theme.

NOTES

1   Marshall, 1963.
2   Webb, 1926, p. 143.
3   Webb, 'Historic' in Shaw, 1889, p. 45.
4   See Roberts, 1960 and also M. W. Flinn's 1964 introduction to Chadwick's Report of 1842.
5   Harris, 1987.
6   Sen, 1983, 1985.
7   Tawney, 'Inequality and Social Structure', in Tawney, 1964 (I), p. 57.

2 T. H. Green 1836–1882 and Arnold Toynbee 1852–1883: 'Best Selves'

The debate over 'the social question' and social reform, and the ideas about citizenship that emerged out of it in the later part of the nineteenth century, were heavily influenced by the life and work of T. H. Green. Born the youngest of four children of the rector of Birkin in the West Riding of Yorkshire in 1836, Green spent his adult life writing and teaching in Oxford until his early death in 1882. His interests were not only academic; they extended also to active participation in public life as a local city councillor and as an Assistant Commissioner for the Schools Enquiry Commission of 1868. The conception of citizenship that Green developed was rooted in religious belief, offering a wide-ranging diagnosis of economic and social ills and a philosophical definition of true freedom that carried a powerful and far-reaching prescription for civic behaviour for both government and people. Green's ideas provided and reflected the stuff of political argument and the inspiration to social action in his own time and for those who came after him, so a study of citizenship over the last two hundred years can properly take his thought as a reference point. This is not to claim that his ideas were new, but they acquired vivid meaning and peculiar import as a response to the economic and social problems of a rapidly changing industrial society, and defined the controversies that were to continue through later years.

In his memoirs of T. H. Green, Nettleship describes him as 'a man to whom reason was faith made articulate, and for whom both faith and reason found their highest expression in good citizenship.'[1] Faith and knowledge, Green asserted, were not in conflict. Knowledge, or science, was about understanding the world; faith, or the moral life, about how to make it better.[2] Green rejected dogmatic theology and the miraculous aspects of Christianity. There was no evidence, he insisted, of the existence of God; the history and miracles of the Bible should be seen as symbolic, and Jesus as the best example of a Christian life.[3] A religious life meant constant striving for perfection and self-realisation. God could be understood as the best possible self;

14

faith could be understood as a disposition of man's mind. For the man who had it, the certainty of God was inseparable from the certainty of himself.

Green's conception of citizenship meant that it was a moral duty for everyone not only to strive to realise his own 'best self' but also to try to make sure that others could do the same. The search for personal goodness was not enough as the true good was a common good which required that all be free to develop those human powers and abilities which might contribute to the common wealth, individual freedom being limited only by the claims of others to pursue similar ends. There was no competition nor exclusion in the pursuit of the common good, which was an activity, not a possession. It required that all be treated as ends, not as means to a good in which they had no share.[4]

This represented a denunciation of utilitarianism; self-denial and self-sacrifice might be required in acknowledging the rights of others, and it was the realisation of the 'powers of the human spirit' rather than pleasure or the greatest happiness of the greatest number that was the object of the good life. The recognition of other people's rights also led Green to reject personal piety as a proper end of moral striving:

True citizenship 'as unto the Lord' (which includes all morality) I reckon higher than 'saintliness' in the technical sense. The 'superior young man' of these days, however, does not seem to understand it, but hugs his own 'refined pleasures' or (which is but a higher form of the same) his personal sanctity. Whence, and not from hetero-doxy, ruin threatens Christian society . . . It vexes me to the heart to think of a fine nature being victimised by a system . . . I hold to be subversive of the Family and the State, and which puts the service of an exceptional institution, or the saving of the individual soul, in opposition to loyal service to society.[5]

This insistence on social responsibility, familiar in Green's writing, is linked to a distaste for the monasticism of the Catholic church:

Just so far as ordinary religion, 'catholic' or 'Protestant' is governed by it, it loses its interest for the fully-educated citizen of the European commonwealth. To lapse into it seems to me, at best, a piece of spiritual invilidishness [*sic*]. Catholicism embodies the antithesis in its most objectionable form, in as much as it fixes the Divine, falsely opposed to the human, . . . and represents the 'objective presence' of the incarnate God as a sensual presence in the sacraments instead of a moral one in the Christian society, and makes Him speak authoritatively thro' the priest instead of rationally thro' the educated conscience.[6]

True citizenship 'as unto the Lord' thus expresses itself, for Green, in social action to benefit mankind – but social action directed by moral fervour. Richter suggests that the doctrine of citizenship and social reform developed by Green is best understood as a 'surrogate faith appealing to a transitional generation'.[7] Evangelical Christianity brought dedication to a cause and a calling to self-sacrifice, but the religious grounds of belief were increasingly challenged through the middle years of the nineteenth century. Green's philosophical idealism gave conscience a political and social meaning, and offered Evangelicals a chance to transfer their sense of duty and obligation to the improvement of this world rather than the search for salvation in the next.

For Green, then, citizenship is an idea that rests on the possibility of human perfectibility through the development of those qualities and abilities that contribute to the common good, and that requires men to strive to that end for themselves and for all members of their society. It also implies freedom, for moral advance can only come about through an effort of individual will and choice. Men cannot be made good by public edict.

The insistence that social progress depends on the morality of individual human beings as much as on the material circumstances of their lives is a continuing aspect of the political debate about the rights and duties of citizenship. Green's idealism opened the way both for arguments favouring private philanthropic work with individuals in distress to strengthen moral character, and for government action in sanitary reform and education necessary if freedom to develop intellectual, physical and moral qualities and sensibilities were to have any substantive meaning. A further strand in the continuing discussion of citizenship, and just as firmly rooted in Green's thought, is the idea of active participation. A multitude of organisations outside the state – trade unions, local government bodies and co-operative enterprises – are seen as opportunities to learn and develop habits of community and mutual aid as well as self-help, an idea and a belief expressed in the teaching of the Christian Socialists as well as in the writing and social experiments of Robert Owen and in the growth of co-operative associations and friendly societies.

The conception of citizenship and the way to social advance involving men working together to realize their own and others' highest natures, stands in dramatic contrast to the Marxist view of progress as the outcome of exploitation and of class struggle and the consequent dispossession of the bourgeoisie by the proletariat. Richter observes that Green, contemplating widespread poverty and degradation, did not denounce the religious values of charity and justice professed by the middle classes as conventional hypocrisy but reaffirmed their validity and enlisted them in the cause of reform. In so far as this message was heeded, and in one way or another it can be seen as the inspiration of the many men and women associated with the Christian Socialist movement, it perhaps helps to explain why the continental assumption that Christianity and socialism were incompatible never took root in England.[8] Green, Richter continues, saw the strongest motive for social reform not in anger, but in guilt. His call to social citizenship was directed to those members of the middle classes whose guilt about their ebbing faith could be turned into guilt about their privileges.[9] Marx believed only the underprivileged would act. Green, a clergyman's son brought up in the traditions of evangelical philanthropy, knew that reform could come from above as well as from below if Christian values were applied to social and economic life.

The sense of mission, the anguished search for a social purpose that could be identified as the will of God, is an outstanding characteristic of women, including Florence Nightingale, Mary Carpenter and Octavia Hill, who made their way into public social service in the later nineteenth century.[10] Beatrice Webb observed rather acidly that many of them, and especially those connected with the Charity Organisation Society (a body tending to favour voluntary action and suspicious of government), lacked 'the sense of collective sin' that might have shifted their attention away from fecklessness or misfortune to 'the way in which society is organised' as a primary cause of social distress. Even so, it was the 'new liberals' among the middle class reformers, rather than manual workers, who were mounting the more effective challenge to the 'old liberalism' of Mill and Ricardo at the end of the century, and developing fresh arguments in support of state intervention in social affairs.

Discussion of the role of the state in regulating social and economic life immediately raises questions about individual freedom – a matter of central importance in Green's philosophy as it was the pre-requisite of morality. Actions could not be moral unless they were freely willed.

Citizenship meant seeking the highest moral development, of others as well as of self. It therefore also meant attempting to promote individual freedom to the utmost compatible with similar freedom for all. Law could not make people moral so could never be a sufficient means to social advance, though legislation might be needed to give men the freedom to realise their true nature. Such principles could be used to support the arguments of both individualists and statists that social progress must be based on either voluntary or government action, according to their particular prejudices. But it is common for principles to be in conflict and their implications unclear, so that their import for behaviour has to be worked out in relation to specific questions.

Green attempts to define his own position in his essay, *Liberal Legislation and Freedom of Contract.* Here he notes and rejects the familiar objection to laws that offer some protection and security to workmen – that they interfere with free bargaining, weaken self-reliance, and thus in seeking to do good do harm. Undoubtedly, Green concedes, school and factory legislation represented 'a great system of interference' with freedom of contract. But freedom does not only mean freedom from constraint or compulsion, the power of men to do as they like irrespective of what they like; nor does it mean freedom enjoyed by one at the cost of a loss of freedom to others. Rather,

> When we speak of freedom as something to be so highly prized, we mean a positive power or capacity of doing or enjoying something worth doing or enjoying, and that, too, something that we do or enjoy in company with others . . . a power which each man exercises through the help or security given him by his fellow men.[11]

The wandering savage, Green continues, may appear free because he has no master but though not the slave of man he is the slave of nature. True freedom means submission to law which permits the full exercise and development of human faculties. But the development of an individual or class at the cost of another denies the true freedom which requires 'the liberation of the powers of all men equally for contribution to a common good'. Freedom of contract is only valuable as a means to this end.[12] Contracts involving work that damages health hinder the freedom of the workers to make the best of themselves, which should be the object of civil society. Factory and sanitary acts to regulate working conditions are therefore justified. While it is the job of government to uphold fair contracts, so also it should restrict those which, because of the weakness of one of the parties, become an instrument of disguised oppression rather than a security for freedom. Government was entitled to limit freedom or stop men doing as they liked if by so doing they lessened the power of other men to make the best of themselves.

For Green the justification for state intervention was not only to protect the weak by constraining the strong. It was also a legitimate way of enforcing the sort of behaviour that might be needed to realise freedom. This was the argument for compulsory education.

> Without a command of certain elementary arts and knowledge, the individual in modern society is as effectually crippled as by the loss of a limb or a broken constitution. He is not free to develop his faculties.[13]

While it was not the business of the state directly to promote morality, 'for that from the very nature of moral goodness it cannot do', it was the responsibility of government 'to maintain the conditions without which a free exercise of human faculties is impossible'.

Views such as these seem to offer boundless possibilities of legitimate state intervention. If government is responsible for securing the conditions which allow the free exercise of human faculties, this could imply policies of positive discrimination in health and education in favour of the poor. It could also imply more radical redistributive measures to equalise incomes and living and working conditions to provide similar opportunities for all. This view is echoed and developed by Tawney in his insistence on equality of condition, on a 'social income' guaranteeing high standards of collective well-being in regard to health, security, amenity, environment and culture.[14] If freedom is impaired by unfavourable circumstances, and if the freedom of each individual is equally valuable, it follows that government must work for greater equality among its people.

However, although collectivists and egalitarians may claim Green as an ally, he himself qualifies his interventionist position by asserting that the state should not necessarily do all that he thought it justified in doing. There are, he observes, dangers in 'grandmotherly government'. This looks like acknowledgement of the risks of undermining independence but such risks are discounted by Green in a later passage where he points out that relief from some responsibilities may free people to assume others; that the security of safe housing and sufficient schooling for his family may make a man more careful of their well-being in other respects. There can be no fears of ill effects of legislation, he continues, on those who would have done what was required anyway, and for those who would not, intervention is by definition necessary.[15]

The many strands in Green's theory of citizenship lie uneasily together. Subsequent writers have been able to develop his views to emphasise either state action or voluntary effort as the more appropriate, legitimate and effective way to social advance and moral improvement. Greengarten claims to detect a fatal flaw in Green's thought in his failure to recognise the incompatibility between his theory of the true good and the working of a capitalist market economy. The common good – the moral end of individual and collective action – requires that all be similarly free to pursue it, but men have different talents and abilities, and freedom will lead to inequalities which in turn will hinder the weaker in the search for self-realisation.[16] Such criticism is echoed in present-day questioning of Marshall's thesis that social rights of citizenship conferred by government can bring significant social equality even within a capitalist society where economic inequalities persist.

The arguments about the respective roles of government and individual in fashioning the good society are entangled with the debates about entitlements and obligations. Earlier nineteenth century writers tended to emphasise personal responsibility and the duty of rich and poor through philanthropy and self-help to enable everyone to realise to the full the 'powers of the human spirit'. At the turn of the century the emphasis shifted to rights and entitlements as Fabians and New Liberals began to argue the case for more state intervention. But the insistence on individual responsibility has come to dominate public debate once more at the close of the twentieth century.

For most, of course, saving the more doctrinaire members of the Charity Organisation Society or of Mrs Thatcher's administrations, it is a matter of more or less; not of all government or no government but of where the lines should be drawn. Definitions of citizenship are not exclusively about rights nor only about duties; they include a mixture of entitlements and obligations. Such a conception appears in the writing of Arnold Toynbee and in his lectures to working men delivered in the 1870s and 1880s. Toynbee went to Balliol to read history but, influenced by Jowett and Green, his interests and enthusiasm soon shifted to political economy. His approach to social reform and to citizenship arose out of a profound religious faith that yet remained 'indifferent to dogma and incredulous of miracles'. In Milner's words, he was a man 'on fire' with the idea of improvement in material conditions not as an end in itself but as opening up possibilities of a higher life.[17] Jowett, writing to Miss Toynbee on her brother's death, described him as one of the best persons he had ever known.[18]

Toynbee saw the 'Condition of England Question' as arising out of the social dislocation of an emerging industrial society and the character of industrial work that degraded working people. Milner wrote of Toynbee's enthusiasm for social equality and his desire to bridge the gap between the educated and the wage earning classes. Philanthropic work he thought an individual duty of citizens. But social equality also required action by a democratic state to control the excesses of competition, and action by the municipalities to assure all citizens a healthy life – air, light, water and decent dwellings. Most of all, it meant the voluntary association of free men in trade unions, co-operatives and friendly societies – potent instruments for material welfare and for the moral development of their members. The end of all social organisation and of all material improvement was, for Toynbee, the higher life of the individual.[19]

The effects of the Industrial Revolution proved that free competition might produce wealth without well-being.[20] Toynbee pointed to the growth of huge factories that destroyed the links between employers and men and led to mutual antagonism. The gulf widened as machine tools displaced skilled mechanics and as trade unions, necessary for negotiating labour questions, obliged workmen to act through delegates and 'tore away the last remnants of personal ties between individual workmen and employers'.[21] The gulf widened further as employers, having appointed managers, came to know less of their men. Work was insecure, short-term contracts and yearly hirings common, and workers might leave or be discharged without notice.

The slowly dissolving framework of mediaeval life was suddenly broken in pieces by the mighty blows of the steam engine and the power-loom. With it disappeared, like a dream, those ancient habits of personal affection which had lingered on in the quiet homesteads where master and apprentice worked side by side at the loom and in the forge. Industry was dragged from cottages into factories and cities; the operative who laboured in the mill was parted from the capitalist who owned it; and the struggle for wealth which machinery promised withered the old bonds of mutual trust, and made competition seem a new and terrible force.[22]

The alienation of the workers and the antagonism between the classes were not, however, cause for despair in Toynbee's view. The social divisions, the competition, the miserable living conditions of the labourers, were all problems which could be resolved by a mixture of democracy, state regulation, association among workers and education. The outcome was within the power of the human will to determine; and human will might modify human fate for good or ill.[23]

While Toynbee deplored the precarious position of working men, robbed of the supposedly benevolent protection of their employers, he did not believe that the old relationships should or could be re-established. In any case, they had not always been honoured and were often destroyed by migration of labour. The future lay in developing better relations between employers and workmen, recognising the 'independence of both as citizens of a free state'.[24] The way to the future was already open. Toynbee pointed to crucial pieces of legislation which had extended the franchise in 1867, legalised trade unions in 1871 and abolished the law of conspiracy in 1875, so that the workman had at last 'reached the summit of the long ascent from the position of a serf, and stood by the side of his master as the full citizen of a free state'.[25] This shared citizenship, Toynbee trusted, bringing employers and workmen together on political committees and school boards, would lead to mutual respect and understanding. Democracy bridged the gulf between the classes; law had given equal rights; and education bid fair to give equality of culture. Thus workers and employers might become inhabitants of a larger world:

> no longer members of a single class, but fellow-citizens of one great people: no longer the poor recipients of a class tradition, but heir to a nation's history. Nay more, we are no longer citizens of a single nation, we are participators in the life of mankind . . . Strengthened by this wider communion and ennobled by this vaster heritage, shall we not trample under foot the passions that divide, and pass united through the invisible portals of a new age to inaugurate a new life?[26]

Such faith in the power of democratic citizenship to override economic and cultural divisions appears in almost the same words in the writing of T. H. Marshall nearly a century later. Discussing the expanding social services, Marshall claims that their significance lies not primarily in equalising incomes but rather in 'a general enrichment of the concrete substance of civilized life' and a reduction of risk and insecurity. 'Equalisation is not so much between classes as between individuals within a population which is now treated for this purpose as though it were one class. Equality of status is more important than equality of income'.[27]

Toynbee discusses the significance of government intervention in social reform by distinguishing the attitudes of 'old' radicals, radical socialists, to whom he belonged, continental socialists and Tory socialists. The old radicals he bitterly attacked; proponents of justice, liberty and self-help, of suffrage and free trade, they displayed an intense dislike of state interference and complete faith in the people. Nothing shook that faith:

> not the wild cries of starving multitudes, not ignorant tumults, not violence. Nor was their stanch [*sic*] belief in the power of the people to help themselves ever weakened; nothing changed it, not even revelations of hideous suffering and degradation amongst the poorest and weakest of the labouring classes.[28]

With the Tory socialists Toynbee was more in sympathy. England had escaped revolution, he believed, by a mixture of state action and self-help. Poor law and factory legislation represented a great socialist programme carried out not by radicals but by Tory socialists and landowners. The factory acts, Toynbee thought, were in harmony with the landowners' notions about the dependence of workers and the reciprocal obligations of employers. They had stronger feelings about protecting the weak than the manufacturers and, where their own interests were not touched, tried to use their power for the common good.

In the view of the radical socialists government might do more than clear the way for combination of working men and for trade union activities, establish a national system of poor relief and regulate employment, vital though these functions were. The larger problem was not just to produce some improvement in the condition of working men but to secure their complete material independence. Toynbee followed Green in arguing that there could be no freedom of contract between men unequal in material wealth. 'When we have the labourer as an isolated individual bargaining with the employer this is unorganised competition on unequal terms'.[29] Bargaining on equal terms meant that both employer and labourer must have a 'reserve price'. The labourer needed capital if he were to be able to hold out for the wage he wanted and it was through combination that men might accumulate capital and through their trade unions that they might bargain more fairly in organised competition.

Important as co-operative effort was, however, more might be needed for 'complete material independence'. Where people were unable to provide basic necessities for themselves, the state should intervene. Government might take into its own hands, Toynbee argued, such vital businesses as railways, gas, water and perhaps the housing of labourers – a problem that had 'hitherto baffled every form of private enterprise'. A decent dwelling was of supreme importance but the great mass of the people lived in houses that were a 'danger to civilization' and with wages that were too low to pay for anything better. Progress required reform of local government, more equal local taxation and the enforcement of sanitary and building laws. The cost of dwellings should be subsidised by municipalities or the state. Toynbee pointed out that the Peabody Trust and many landowners in the country let houses at below market rents without demoralising their occupants. There was no better investment of national capital; it would bring higher standards of comfort and improved habits of living, 'a great diminution in pauperism, drunkenness and crime', and it would not represent class legislation, which radicals had always opposed, for it would be in the interests of the whole community.

> We cannot call ourselves safe until all citizens have the chance of living decent lives; the poorest class need to be raised in the interest of all classes.[30]

Proposals for more state intervention in the 1880s, as in the 1990s, had always to be defended against two charges – that they undermined independence and promoted sectional interests – and this Toynbee did with vigour. Far from diminishing self-reliance, he asserted, public help with housing was a way of putting people in a position where they would not need assistance. The radical creed did not abandon the old belief in liberty, justice and self-help; but when people could not help themselves they should be helped by the state, though on three conditions: the matter must be of primary social importance, assistance must be practicable, and it must not weaken independence. Nothing should be done, Toynbee agreed, that might interfere with the habits of individual self-reliance and voluntary association that had built up the greatness of the English people.[31]

The insistence on association and voluntary action outside the state is a further strand, after political enfranchisement and government intervention, in the development and status of citizenship. Toynbee argued that it was the value attached to such fraternal forms of organisation that distinguished radical socialists from the paternalistic Tories, and it carried with it an emphasis on duties as well as on rights. He pointed to the trade unions on the one hand – associations of working men to protect their interests and strengthen their bargaining power *vis-à-vis* their employers. On the other hand were the savings banks, friendly societies, building societies, co-operatives and even the coffee taverns that not only encouraged self-help, but also went some way to restoring the sense of community and the sociability destroyed by 'the mighty blows of the steam engine and the power loom'.

Owen's vision of self-contained communities to bring back ideas of 'brotherhood and citizenship which had been trampled under foot' was a false one in Toynbee's view. The aim should not be to encourage men to withdraw to independent communities but to make them into 'good citizens of the great community of English people'. In the past the unity of mediaeval life had come through fear of aggression, and as violence diminished independence became possible. The problem for Toynbee was to preserve independence but reconcile it with unity, without the incentive of outside threat. Political developments had raised men from the position of serfs to citizens, but industrial developments and the deadening effects of minute divisions of labour exhausted energies and dulled intelligence. The difficulties of developing citizenship were thus formidable and education of the citizen in the duties of a citizen became indispensable. Toynbee's scheme for citizen education demonstrates the intermingling of rights and duties. Its three components were political education – the history of political institutions and ideas, especially Burke and Tocqueville; industrial education, including the history of industrial institutions, of the condition of the working classes and of schemes of social reform; and sanitary education to teach the duties of citizenship in relation to the prevention and spread of disease.[32]

It was not only working men who should pursue the practice of citizenship through association, and not only they who had the duty of striving towards a better society. Toynbee wished to see Boards of Conciliation in every trade with the job of dealing with fluctuations of wages, over-production and other matters requiring regulation, not superseding but 'thrusting into the background' the trade unions and the masters' associations. This was a reasonable hope, Toynbee supposed, as 'some sentiment of mutual obligation between classes' survived in England. Capitalists, he insisted, must use their wealth as a great national trust and not shrink from reforms to secure the material independence of workers.

To a reluctant admission of the necessity for State action, we join a burning belief in duty, and a deep spiritual ideal of life . . . We do not hesitate to unite the advocacy of social reform with an appeal to the various classes who compose society to perform those duties without which all social reform must be merely delusive.[33]

In the end it was the 'deep spiritual ideal of life' rather than material advance which was, for Toynbee, the object of all efforts at social reform whether through state action, voluntary effort or co-operative association. The aspirations towards fraternal forms of government separated the radical socialists from the paternalistic Tories, Toynbee claimed. But it was the repudiation of materialism, the acceptance of private property and the rejection of confiscation and violence, that set them apart from continental socialists. It was not only a question of the redistribution of wealth but of its right use, and there was a danger that working men might not use their wages well and that increased wages might lead to increased crime.

> Higher wages are not an end in themselves. No-one wants higher wages in order that working men may indulge in mere sensual gratification. We want higher wages in order that an improved material condition, with less of anxiety and less uncertainty as to the future, may enable the working man to enter on a purer and more worthy life.[34]

The development of moral character required that people take responsibility for acting rightly. Democracy, Toynbee thought, should be praised for many things, but most of all because it made it possible, without shame, 'to preach the gospel of duty to the whole people'.[35] While capitalists must assure the material independence of workers, they in turn must reform their domestic life and put aside drunkenness and brutal violence. 'Material prosperity, without faith in God and love to our fellow men, is as little use to man as earth to the plants without the sun'.[36] Perhaps not surprisingly in the 1880s, 'love to our fellow men' had a distinctly Imperial flavour. Social progress would allow Englishmen to take part in the government of their country and also to 'rule righteously the dim multitudes of peasants who toil under the fierce light of tropical suns in the distant continent of India'.[37]

The vision of social advance to what Toynbee described as 'brotherhood in perfect citizenship' was, thus, fraught with difficulty. The greatest obstacle, he feared, was apathy and the reluctance of workmen to listen to anything which did not concern pleasure or profit. To devote scanty leisure to intellectual exertion required extraordinary effort, and there was a danger that working men would become less

eager about social and political problems as they became more prosperous – material comfort might well diminish spiritual energy. However, if political progress were not to end in spiritual degradation
the effort must be made, and it was an effort which in their various
ways all classes must share. Perhaps Toynbee's most famous words
were those he uttered in 1883 as the peroration of a lecture on
Henry George:

> We – the middle classes, I mean . . . have neglected you . . . We
> would help you workmen if we could. We are willing to give up
> something much dearer than fame and social position. We are
> willing to give up the life we care for . . . We will do this, and in
> return ask you to remember one thing . . . that we work for you in
> the hope and trust that if you get material civilization . . . if you
> have opened up to you the possibility of a better life, you will really
> lead a better life. If, that is, you get material civilization, remember
> that it is not an end in itself . . . If you will only keep to the love of
> your fellow men and to great ideals, then we shall find our happi-
> ness in helping you, but if you do not, then our reparation will be in
> vain.[38]

In Toynbee's writing the rights and duties of citizens and the
responsibilities of government, individual and collective effort in
developing them are all intermingled and all receive due acknowledgement. But as the century drew to a close the protagonists tended
to separate into opposing camps, illustrated and personalized in
McBriar's study of the Bosanquets and the Webbs.[39] On the one
side the stalwarts of the Charity Organisation Society defending
voluntary action and individual charitable effort and attacking the
advance of the machinery of the state; on the other the Fabians and
New Liberals, divided on many matters but tending to be more
favourable to government intervention in social and industrial affairs.

NOTES

1   Nettleship, 1906, p. 2.
2   *Ibid.*, p. 148.
3   Richter, 1964, p. 45 *et seq.*
4   Greengarten, 1981, pp. 32–49.

5   T. H. Green to Henry Scott Holland, December 1868, cited in Paget, 1921, p. 29.
6   T. H. Green to Henry Scott Holland, January 1869, *ibid.*, p. 31.
7   Richter, 1964, p. 19.
8   *Ibid.*, p. 122.
9   *Ibid.*, pp. 134–5.
10   Parker, J., 1989.
11   Green, 1881, p. 9.
12   *Ibid.*, p. 11.
13   *Ibid.*, p. 12.
14   Tawney, 1964 (II), p. 179.
15   Green, 1881, p. 14.
16   Greengarten, 1981, pp. 89–125.
17   Milner, 1895, p. 36.
18   Benjamin Jowett to Miss Toynbee, 1883, quoted in Mansbridge, n.d.
19   Milner, 1895, p. 55.
20   Toynbee, 'The Chief Features of the Revolution' in Toynbee 1884, p. 93.
21   Toynbee, 'Industry and Democracy' in Toynbee, 1884, p. 196.
22   Toynbee, 'The Education of Co-operators', *ibid.*, p. 226.
23   Toynbee, 'Wages and Natural Law', *ibid.*, p. 176.
24   Toynbee, 1884, p. 149.
25   Toynbee, 'Industry and Democracy', in Toynbee, 1884, p. 196.
26   Toynbee, *ibid.*, p. 201.
27   Marshall, 1949, in Marshall, 1963, p. 107.
28   Toynbee, 'Are Radicals Socialists?', in Toynbee, 1884, pp. 204–5.
29   Toynbee, 'Wages and Natural Law', *ibid.*, p. 171.
30   Toynbee, 'Are Radicals Socialists?', *ibid.*, p. 218.
31   *Ibid.*, p. 219.
32   Toynbee, 'The Education of Co-operators', in Toynbee, 1884, pp. 226–8.
33   Toynbee, 'Are Radicals Socialists?', *ibid.*, p. 220.
34   Toynbee, 'Wages and Natural Law', *ibid.*, p. 176.
35   Toynbee, 1881, *ibid.*, p. 200.
36   Toynbee, 'Are Radicals Socialists?', *ibid.*, p. 220.
37   *Ibid.*, p. 221.
38   Toynbee, 1883, p. 53.
39   McBriar, 1987.

3 Samuel Barnett 1844–1913: Friends and Neighbours

> His will is that each capacity, each taste, each quality, should be developed; that each individual should rise to the height of his being, should do his best and enjoy his most. He would have in His kingdom no lower class.
>
> *(The Service of God)*

> The best work is done by him who . . . shares (his) life with others . . . They who cannot preach or teach or give, can live and make friends among the poor.
>
> *(Worship and Work)*

The unfortunate division between Fabians and Charity Organisation Society (COS) sympathisers that found expression in the divisions of the Poor Law Commissioners of 1905–9 was reflected and to some extent reconciled in the life and thought of Samuel Barnett. Like Green and Toynbee, Barnett envisaged the good society as one where everyone would be encouraged to realise their 'best selves'. It meant mutual tolerance and respect, rich and poor living together as neighbours and joining in educational and cultural activities to foster a sense of common citizenship and civic responsibility. Barnett's understanding of citizenship was not primarily in terms of the character and opportunity of work, though he wrote and spoke about the evils of unemployment and the badly paid, hard and mono- tonous labour of the East London poor. His first concern was the nurturing of moral character, the acknowledgement of reciprocal rights and duties by rich and poor and the social institutions which would best develop the sense of mutual responsibility. This wider preoccupation with the proper responsibilities of government and charitable effort and the place of self-help in developing citizen- ship made Barnett a very significant figure in the changing debate. In his earlier years he was a supporter of and worker for the COS, subscribing to the belief that the way to social progress was through individual effort on the part of the poor encouraged by support and sympathy from the rich. Later, after first-hand experience of living and working in the East End of London, he denounced the COS for their reluctance to contemplate the state as an agent of social advance. Ultimately, however, he believed that a good society could not be created by government alone and depended crucially on the moral character of its people.

Barnett is best remembered as founder and warden of Toynbee Hall, the first university settlement, set up in 1884 and dedicated to the memory of Arnold Toynbee and to the ideals of social service and social obligation associated with his name. For Barnett, the problem confronting society at the end of the nineteenth century was much the same as that identified by Dahrendorf a hundred years later, of finding ways to extend to everyone the 'entitlements' to a common culture and a shared way of life.

> The liberal agenda is in the first instance about citizenship. This is in part a classical subject of liberal policy. Sex and gender questions are still not resolved. Civil rights are always under threat. Human rights need active defence everywhere. The new entitlement questions are however above all social. They have to do with the tendency to define people out of the social universe of the majority, with persistent unemployment, inner city blight, regional disparities and the underclass.[1]

Two aspects of Canon Barnett's personality were especially important in his approach to citizenship. First was his religion. His conception of the ideal society where men sought freedom and equality and the common good was derived from his Christianity, and it was the spreading of the Christian faith that offered the best hope of its achievement. In her biography of her husband, Henrietta Barnett remarks that he was remembered more for his efforts at social reform in Whitechapel than for his religious work but that religion 'held the main place in his heart's core'.[2] Second, Barnett was a pragmatist and a man of action who insisted that theory and doctrine, however hallowed by secular or sacred traditions of thought or faith, must adapt to changing knowledge and circumstances. Thus, the liturgy and ritual of the Anglican Church were incomprehensible to many of the people of East London and advances in the new biblical criticism and in science required a new interpretation and presentation of Christian dogma. And thus, Barnett employed some of his most powerful prose to denounce the cherished principles of the COS, especially its opposition to state poor relief, a stance he thought irrelevant and harmful in the 1890s. His words have a startling contemporary relevance in the controversies over the resurgence of political and economic liberalism in the 1990s.

> It [the council of the COS] has not said a word to lift up the heads of those who are in despair, to train the imagination of the sanguine, or to put into words unspoken hopes. Like Lot's wife, its eyes are turned back to the past, and it is every day farther in the rear of the crowd who rush wildly away from the fires of poverty . . . The council is not in sympathy with the forces which are shaping the time.[3]

The rejection of COS doctrine and the traditions of individualism and economic liberalism from which it grew was by no means total however. Barnett refused to accept that state help was necessarily demoralising but he did believe that dependency was undesirable, that co-operation in charity was necessary and that individual dealing in relief giving was essential. Equally, Barnett took from the socialists those elements of collectivism that he judged necessary to forward his objectives, but refused to allow the power and authority to government that might threaten the freedom and autonomy of individual men and women. He was a man who firmly trod the middle way and in so doing brought together some of the fundamental tenets of liberal and socialist political thought. The issues he confronted were the central questions of the responsibilities of government and people in advancing well-being and distributing the common wealth.

If Barnett was a man of action rather than of ideas this did not mean that he lacked his utopian dreams. But his brief sketch of the ideal city presented a set of values assumed to be beyond question in representing the goal of human endeavour, offering a guide to good conduct rather than an opportunity to explore the complexities of the social relationships and politics of the good society.

> In the ideal city none will be very rich and none will be very poor. Knowledge and good will join together to give to every child the best education, and to secure its use of the gift; to render every house and street as healthy as the healthiest hillside in the world; to provide the best doctor and the most comfortable hospital for everyone who is sick; and to have at hand a friend for everyone in trouble. In our ideal city art will grow out of common life, undisturbed by contrasts of wealth and poverty. The people will have pleasure in their work, and leisure to admire whatever is beautiful.[4]

Nor was the city vulnerable to criticism for, unlike that of Thomas More, the product of rational calculation of men's best interests without necessary reference to any faith, Barnett's utopia was a matter of revealed religion.

> His will is that each capacity, each taste, each quality, should be developed; that each individual should rise to the height of his being, should do his best and enjoy his most. He would have in His kingdom no lower class.[5]

The lack of a lower class did not mean that all men and women would be equal. Barnett attached more importance to good fellowship and fraternity than to equality. 'Many classes', he wrote, 'make the strength of society . . . . give charm to intercourse and stability to government . . . . by their variety make unity.' There was nothing wrong in the existence of classes but there was the greatest wrong in their antagonism.[6] The idea of fraternity as the basis for social order, may never have found its way to the centre of political debate, though A. H. Halsey insists that it takes sociological priority over both equality and liberty in that it is the principle that defines the group within which social values are to be applied.[7] The problem, then, for Barnett remains today: it was to find ways of encouraging a city of many classes to work not for one of its parts but for the whole; rich and poor to consider one another and to work for common ends; pride in the city to take the place of pride in the dominance of one class.[8]

The commitment to the common good runs through all of Barnett's writing. In 1905 he set out far-reaching proposals for dealing with the unemployed, but reforms would only reach their end, he warned, as members of a community realized their mutual responsibility to ensure that the capacities and talents of each were raised to the highest level.[9] A crucial element in the elevation of collective well-being above the interests of individuals or classes was the idea of 'service'. Men and women, Barnett declared, were sent into the world to be one another's servants.[10] In a Christian society the ideal life would lie in 'being' not 'having'. Members of society should accept no luxury which did not make them more interesting or more serviceable to their neighbours, enjoy no luxury unless it could be shared and seek to possess nothing which they could not desire that everyone should possess in a perfect state.[11] 'God said of old; "Thou shalt do no murder". God says now; "Make common what is best. Give by sharing" '.[12]

The giving by sharing did not imply equality of material possessions as much as equal opportunities for all to enjoy the best in education, in art and in religion.

> The poor need the best . . . . Not just comfortable dwellings but those architecturally most beautiful; not just open spaces but spaces made as interesting as a nobleman's park; not just broad, clean light streets, but streets as varied, as suggestive as a page of history; not just books but the best books; not just pictures to amuse, but pictures to awake sleeping imagination and kindle embers of fancy; not just churches which are weather-proof, but churches rich in colour, form and sound; not just missionaries able to tell the Gospel story but teachers cultivated in all knowledge – the most refined members of our great universities, men and women of the poet mind'.[13]

The acute destitution that Barnett found in Whitechapel had to go because it threatened civilised human relationships and individual freedom. But the less extreme social and economic differences would be readily bridged by mutual respect, a sense of service and commitment to the common good.

Freedom was the second great ideal to be enshrined in Barnett's utopia. Not the meagre freedom from want that is acknowledged by the most doctrinaire of nineteenth-century economic liberals, and accepted by Hayek as a proper objective for a welfare state[14] but the much grander concept of freedom for all to develop their abilities to the utmost, to escape 'the limits put upon the growth of men's souls'[15] by both pauperism and luxury alike. Freedom depended on the power to take advantage of its possibilities; it implied a moral claim to health, knowledge, sanitary dwellings, open spaces, schools, universities and to all the means of life making for true enjoyment.[16]

But freedom for Barnett, as for Green, also meant living under authority. The later part of the nineteenth century he saw as a time of 'masterless' men. Old forms of authority had succumbed to the increase in individualism. Many of the rich owed no duty to tenants nor to work people and suffered the 'weariness of doing as they like'.[17] A masterless class of workpeople was restless and unreliable and without the power of association, and consciousness of danger aroused a desire for strong government. Ecclesiastics offered some peace through submission to doctrine, but no place for free thought. Socialists offered an ideal society but a materialist conception that was fatal to freedom, endangered the family and enslaved the individual.[18] Freedom in Barnett's utopia rested on the authority of the Christian religion.

The England in which Barnett lived presented a stark contrast with the society he wished to see. Industrialisation and the growth of towns had separated rich and poor and broken the bonds of mutual respect and obligation which he assumed had softened the distinctions of rank and status in the past and afforded some security and dignity to the poor. The two nations were represented vividly in London where Barnett found the wretchedness and brutality of life in the streets around Toynbee Hall a continuing indictment of the 'careless luxury' further west. The gross inequalities were an affront to fairness and justice in their denial of civilised life to a large proportion of working people but they also impoverished the cultural life of the whole community and threatened civil order. This was the 'social problem' that was arousing increasing attention in the 1860s and 70s. It inspired some men and women to the reform of the nation's poor laws and to charitable effort and others to a variety of collective measures to establish a better life and wider social and economic opportunities. During his years in Toynbee Hall Canon Barnett moved from a belief in the power of organised charity to deal with social distress to a conviction that state intervention was essential for social reform.

Although it was degradation of character rather than material deprivation that most disturbed the Barnetts in their early years in Whitechapel, they gradually became more aware of the power of people's surroundings to shape their moral and spiritual lives. Gross social inequalities corrupted both rich and poor and opened a gulf between the classes that prevented the growth of a sense of fellowship and common purpose. Around Toynbee Hall, Barnett noted, one-fifth of the people suffered from lack of food, and 'hasty charity' led only to 'waywardness of mind and bitterness of spirit'.[19] While a hundred thousand East Londoners dwelt in single rooms, their childhood spent in the streets, their old age in the workhouse, the people in West London, knowing this, carelessly spent their money in profitless vanities.[20] As the rich moved further west, Barnett observed, the two classes developed different tastes and pleasures, different manners, speech, dress and ethical standards in their different habitats.[21]

Moreover, while the classes were increasingly divided in wealth, leisure and culture, the poor were beginning to receive the education to arouse both aspirations and resentment at their lack of opportunity. Reconciling social antagonisms thus assumed great importance,[22] but it was made harder by the 'insolent and degrading' use of wealth by a poorly educated propertied class. Luxury, Barnett claimed, was a greater social danger than drunkenness in fostering social divisions[23] and he denounced it in Veblenesque terms:

> The West End shops with their many objects, costly and useless . . . the fruits highly priced only because they are out of season, the dresses whose outrageous extravagance seems designed to show that their wearers cannot be workers, the barbaric show of jewels and precious stones.[24]

Not only was the conspicuous display of wealth an affront to the wretchedness of the poor, it also corroded the character of the rich. Luxury was as fatal as pauperism to freedom, understood as the power of an individual to develop to the limit of his abilities. It stifled the finer qualities in human nature, Barnett declared, and induced men and women to pursue their own ease and pleasure. It destroyed powers of judgement, for those who made their own enjoyment a law unto themselves could not be keen to secure justice for the drunkard and the vicious. Absence of moral indignation over crime was due not to charity but to the self-indulgence of those who made public opinion.[25] Luxury was also socially wasteful for it called for the employment of labour which might have been used to increase national resources, while the law of diminishing satisfactions meant a rich man gained less from the extra pounds he spent than would a poor man. And, finally, luxury exalted false values. The example of the rich was a direct cause of the poverty of the poor for if a chief good were an abundance of possessions other values were crushed.

If the excesses of the rich were damaging both to themselves and to society, so the privation of the poor both limited individual freedom and excited social unrest and discontent. Barnett distinguished a particular personality that he attributed to working people; they were strenuous, modest, unaffected, generous and with good sense, but they lacked a wide outlook, were indifferent to knowledge and beauty and their pleasures were restricted.[26] Workmen were 'scant of life', of the interests and visions and hopes that came of knowledge, and they tried to supply the lack through drink and gambling. This view of the working class led Barnett to fear that the Labour Party in power would be as narrowly committed to the pursuit of material advantage as was the propertied class to the defence of its own interests. There would be change without progress, the same carelessness of things for common joy, the same indifference to beauty and the same exaltation of rights above duties.[27]

But it was pauperism that was the fatal disease to which the working class was vulnerable. In 1911 Barnett pointed to the symptoms – listlessness, discontent, vindictiveness and servility. The pauper was not a free man, nor desirous to be; he was content to eat and not to work, to take gifts and be ungrateful. Without the capacities to take part in the government of his country, without and not wishing the privileges of citizenship, the pauper added nothing to the common wealth and had no ambition to do so. The sudden death of all paupers, Barnett continued, terrible though it might be to say, would be a great economic gain and hardly a social loss.[28] Responsibility, however, lay firmly with the state which by its laws had created pauperism. In failing to enable the poor to develop their capacities it had treated them as animals to be driven or led. It had substituted punishment for education.[29]

Such opinions led Barnett to wholesale condemnation of government housing, education and poor law policies, and of organised charity. But he also maintained a persistent optimism about the extent and growth of private benevolence and sympathy for the poor. In 1897 he wrote that some antagonism did exist between the classes but that it was often misrepresented by 'socialists and cynics'. The rich showed much kindly interest in the poor, Barnett thought, though also a sense of superiority. Relief was too often seen as a favour rather than a right and hostility developed if the poor appeared ungrateful, but the chief cause of antagonism was ignorance. 'If rich and poor could see one another as God sees each; if they could get rid of the ignorance which hides from each the real goodness of the other there would be on earth peace, and good will among men'.[30] The times were full of promise, Barnett insisted. People were more aware of the need for reform and never before was there such sympathy with suffering. Great physical improvements had occurred in Whitechapel and class barriers were falling before the 'still small voice of friendship'.[31]

Alongside this cheerful assertion of increasing benevolence, however, lay a contradictory view of a society fatally divided. East London was very inadequately paid for what it did for the West in hard, dull, unbroken toil in East End factories. 'All have received from the poor but few acknowledge the debt'.[32] By 1904 Barnett was emphasizing the conflict between the classes. The rich were chiefly concerned with defending property, the poor, represented by the Labour Party, concerned for the interests of labour. Each class struggled for its own rights. Class pulled against class: 'Each has its eye on an ideal in which its own members are dominant, not one in which all the citizens get equal benefit.'[33]

The question was how the two nations of late Victorian England might join together in a commonwealth of free men and women united by mutual respect and service and where the best things were shared. Barnett tried to find an answer to the question in his life in Whitechapel as vicar of St Jude's and warden of Toynbee Hall. It was not a simple answer, for it reflected the deep ambivalence in Barnett's analysis of social and class relationships. Were the resentments and antagonisms due to the ignorance and misunderstanding of essentially benevolent and well-intentioned people or to the unavoidable opposition of class interests?

Experience in the East End eventually convinced Barnett that neither individual good will nor organised charity alone could deal with the material and spiritual poverty of the London working class. State action was also needed. But the state had its limitations. Legislation could not make moral people. Progress towards the ideal city could only come as men and women accepted their responsibilities for one another, and this for Barnett meant accepting the teaching of the Christian church, just as for Titmuss in a more secular age it meant accepting the ethic of altruism and practising the 'gift relationship'. These three main strands in Barnett's approach to social reform appear in his work in Toynbee Hall, in his later rejection of COS principles in favour of a more interventionist state, and in his teaching as an Anglican minister, whose Christian beliefs informed all he did.

THE VOLUNTEERS

Samuel and Henrietta Barnett went to St Jude's in 1873, to a church, 'empty and unused' and a poverty-stricken parish 'inhabited mainly by a criminal population much corrupted by doles'.[34] The first task, and one that absorbed Barnett throughout his life, was to make the church more relevant to the experiences and needs of Whitechapel people, an ambition echoed in the Archbishop of Canterbury's Enquiry into Urban Priority Areas just over one hundred years later.[35] At St Jude's the services were modified and pictures and music brought into the church. But making religion 'a more vital matter for the man in the street'[36] was not the only object. The community and citizenship for which Barnett strove was founded

on faith but required cultural and social opportunities and education
to give people freedom and the chance to enjoy beauty. This led
the Barnetts into campaigning for local amenities, for libraries, play-
grounds, open space, wash houses, dispensaries and for the removal
of slaughter houses. Following Octavia Hill's example they bought
an old building to convert to model dwellings with the help of lady
rent collectors who would befriend the tenants and urge self-improvement and social harmony. It also led to service on local voluntary
and statutory bodies as poor law guardians or school managers
and the establishing of a Country Holiday Fund for Whitechapel
children. And it also meant setting up a church library, arranging
art exhibitions, lectures, discussion groups and organizing men's and
boys' clubs.

The conviction that social improvement rested on friendly intercourse was central to the work at St Jude's. Barnett counted it a
religious duty to give parties, and guests were carefully invited from
different social classes so that common talk might break down barriers built by mutual ignorance.[37] But it was not only distinguished
visitors who came to the East End. Barnett was also attracting under-
graduates to spend their vacations in Whitechapel, a movement that
received formal recognition in the establishing of Toynbee Hall in
1884.

The settlement movement exemplified Barnett's belief in the power
of knowledge and social intercourse to dispel class antagonisms and of
personal friendship to unite rich and poor in the face of huge cultural
and material inequalities. Educated, leisured, and public-spirited men
would revive the local institutions, the vestries, the poor law and
charitable bodies, all enfeebled by the lack of people to serve on
their committees. It was the duty of the rich to labour for the welfare
of those whose labour created their own wealth. These might have
been Barnett's words but they were spoken by Philip Lyttleton Gell at
a Cambridge meeting in 1884 when it was resolved to co-operate with
Oxford in settlement work. Neglect of the labouring poor, Gell continued, would lead to social chaos which might be avoided either by
'socialistic officialdom' with a band of officials maintained at public
expense or by calling back to their civic responsibilities the 'wealthy
middle-class deserters from the common wealth . . . to . . . take up
the burden of their forgotten duty to their neighbours'.[38] Meanwhile
university men were to 'fill the breach', inspired by love for their
fellow men, sorrow for suffering and sin, 'and faith in the power of
the friendship which you offer him to enrich both yourself and him.

Personal contact and personal friendship inspired by such feelings is the medicine needed for every social difficulty'.[39]

At the same Cambridge meeting Professor Michael Foster, not a friend, he said, to philanthropy, emphasised the need for education to remove obstructions to individual progress and education not only of the poor but of those who tried to help them. Work had the quality of mercy, it was twice blessed – especially among the poor. Out of the settlements enlightenment would come to aid the solution of social problems. More immediately, urged Professor Westcott, the West would be saved by destroying the East. The blessings associated with leisure, refinement and culture – the delicacy of home life – could and must be made universal, and university men in East London might help to attain that end:

> I have always believed that what is wanted . . . is not so much the power and means of happiness as a clear vision of the aim of life, a firm apprehension of the motive of action, and the ready offering of guidance. And surely that is what those who have the privilege of learning and working here ought to be able to give.[40]

These were the ideas to which Barnett attempted to give practical form at Toynbee Hall. There university men would gather to fulfil the duties of citizenship, to offer friendship, service and education to the poor, and to learn about social problems and how they might be overcome. Although in later years Barnett increasingly emphasised the importance of social enquiry and state intervention, in the earlier period philanthropy and personal service were the major activities of the settlement.

> Friendship is the channel by which the knowledge – the joys – the faith – the hope which belonged to one class may pass to all classes. It is distance that makes friendship between classes almost impossible, and, therefore, residence among the poor is suggested as a simple way in which Oxford men may serve their generation.[41]

But while friendship and personal service were indispensable in attempting to deal with the 'great social questions of the day', indiscriminate doles for the poor created, in Barnett's view, infinite damage. Influenced by Octavia Hill and Charles Loch and the doctrines of the COS, he fully accepted that charitable relief should be given only after careful enquiry into individual circumstances, and subscribed to the policies of the Local Government Board in the 1880s to cut back outdoor relief. Universal provision by either state or voluntary effort without investigation of individual cases was demoralising to the recipient and destroyed thrift and independence and family relationships. This was the conventional wisdom of the COS in the later nineteenth century. By the end of the 1890s, however, Barnett had explicitly rejected some of the society's most fundamental principles. It is his growing willingness to accept state responsibility for welfare that represents the second strand in his approach to social reform, and his interest in the rights as well as the obligations of citizenship.

Barnett's criticism of the COS doctrines that stood in the way of more collective provision for the poor was delivered at a meeting of its council in 1895.[42] 'Independence of state relief' and 'saving' had, he claimed, become idols, defended by the COS as an idol defended by its priest. The Society opposed state pensions financed from rates and taxes and objected to municipal experiments in finding work for the unemployed as 'increasing the habitual dependence of the poor'. But, said Barnett, it made no attempt to discover whether all forms of state relief did in fact induce demoralising dependence, nor whether a pension from the state was more degrading than one from a neighbour, nor did it suggest better ways of dealing with the unemployed. The COS opposed municipal control of London hospitals but without any argument to show why a man should be degraded by being cured in a poor law infirmary but not if he were treated in Guy's. 'There appears to be no evidence of enquiry as to the respective results of state or voluntary relief, and the Council seem to think the proposal for municipal control is sufficiently crushed when it is condemned as a form of state socialism'.[43]

Barnett then turned to the importance the COS placed on saving as a means to independence. It was by no means clear, he said, that a man earning less than £1 a week, of whom there were many in London, should save his money rather than spend it on the 'development of the bodies, brains and souls of his children'. The Society gave no adequate consideration to any of these things but exalted saving to the glory of a principle. 'The Council, in regard for its idol, "thrift", makes a new Beatitude – "Blessed is he who has remembered himself".'[44] It had no proposals for dealing with the old or the sick or the unemployed. It had lost touch with the problems of the times. 'Abuses increase, beggars parade the streets, indiscriminate giving demoralizes whole neighbourhoods, and the Society's voice is hardly heard. Working men can find no work, striving homes are broken by want, and the Society suggests no remedy.'[45]

THE STATE

However Barnett might differ from the COS in his view of the role of the state in social affairs, his own approach to public authorities and the machinery of government was cautious. Social advance depended on raising cultural, spiritual and moral values. Philanthropy was unhelpful and aroused resentment because the rich gave charity which offended self-respect, built orphanages where individuality was crushed and offered entertainments where 'higher aspirations for beauty' were forgotten. How, then, might progress come about? Even in 1904 Barnett's answer to this question makes no direct reference to public services. He suggested three solutions. First, rich and poor should live close together and this would arouse mutual sympathy and willingness to work for the common good. Second, there should be plainer living for the rich and higher thinking for the poor. Luxury increased social divisions and was a greater social danger than drunkenness. Workmen wanted education only for higher wages and increased comforts but needed education to enlarge their imagination, enrich their leisure and help them to respect their opponents. The best in knowledge and beauty must be within reach of all, for there could be no unity if people were prevented from admiring the same things, taking pride in their fathers' great deeds and sharing the same great literature. Third, Christian teaching must be related to contemporary social problems and experience.[46] The three solutions did not imply aversion to statutory action, but rather Barnett's conviction that benevolent legislation could only develop if men and women were tolerant and educated and Christian. When rich and poor 'thought morally' many causes of poverty would be removed. Religion would encourage laws to remove the ignorance which prevented so many citizens 'enjoying their best and doing their utmost'.[47]

Legislation, however, must be carefully scrutinized, the test being whether it would increase morality in the nation[48] and it was in this spirit that Barnett considered statutory responsibility for pensions, for the unemployed, for feeding hungry children and for poor relief generally. Pensions should be universal, a form of deferred wages relieving anxiety in old age and recognising that everyone had directly or indirectly contributed to the national wealth. In this way they would strengthen a sense of national obligation. The exclusion under the 1908 Act of those who had habitually refused work and of those possessing ten shillings a week should cease. Such provisions meant intrusive enquiries that provoked resentment. They also discouraged thrift and led to deceit – to pretences of transferring money to children and to 'dodges to keep income low'. The desire to fashion more generous social security arrangements that respect citizens' rights and privacy persists and appears in criticisms of means testing in the 1990s. By contrast, governments through the 1980s have argued that lower and more selective benefits are not only more economical, but more effective in stiffening moral character and strengthening thrift, independence and incentives to work.

Unemployment and the pauperism associated with it assumed major importance in the 1880s and 1890s, defying the attempts to deal with them of both organised charity and the poor law authorities. By 1909 Beveridge had firmly identified unemployment as a problem of industrial organisation, but the 1834 New Poor Law had been posited on the assumption that able-bodied unemployment was voluntary and best tackled by a deterrent system of statutory relief, with charity providing for the deserving. The obvious social distress through lack of work at the end of the century aroused mingled sympathy and alarm but deterrent poor law policies continued and twinges of public conscience were assuaged, at any rate in part, through voluntary doles for the poor, the diverse charitable activity ineffectually co-ordinated by the COS, and subscriptions to the inter-mittent Mansion House funds for distribution to the unemployed.

The refusal of the COS to contemplate new policies for working men who could find no work had been one of Barnett's main criti-cisms in 1895. By 1903 he had elaborated his own plan for action, a co-operative effort of statutory and voluntary bodies.[49] The unem-ployed must be distinguished from the unemployable and supported by their friends and the trade unions, whose funds should be subsid-ised by the state. But society must provide for the unemployable, otherwise the social costs of disease and delinquency would be too great. Deterrence was fashionable, but it would not make people work. So Barnett proposed a mixture of education, training and discipline. Men incapable of independent work would live in 'com-munities', updated workhouses where they might contribute some-thing to their own support. These 'labour schools' would be in the country and would require men to live apart from their families – a deterrent element necessary to prevent abuse. But unlike workhouses they should be modelled on schools not prisons and would open to everyone a 'door of hope', removing from the labour market a group who depressed wages but whose labour could now be for the common good. Moreover, the scheme would offer opportunities for befriending and visiting, vital for Barnett as it was only 'one by one' that the mass of human beings could be raised. Vagrants should be detained, though without degrading treatment, and workhouses and inebriate homes transformed into sheltered communities where people should be encouraged to be useful. For no remedy would be effective that did not strengthen the will and raise aspirations.[50]

> The community would, in fact, say to its prodigals, 'we cannot afford to let you waste yourselves and our substance; you must be restrained, but you shall not be degraded or shut out from hope. You shall have work worthy a man's doing; you shall have necessary recreation and interests; you shall be able to earn and save money; you shall have the chance which you missed of fitting yourself for citizenship. You shall have everything except liberty, and that you may win. If, however, you misuse this chance, then you must be relegated to prison and prison fare'.[51]

Barnett also insisted on the necessity for other forms of statutory intervention. Men were out of work not only because they were unfit (born of feeble parents and untrained) but because industry was badly organised. There must be adequate unemployment insurance, government schemes of public works and above all better education, with young workers under sixteen required to attend three evening classes a week.

The public feeding of school children raised more awkward dilemmas. On the one hand undernourished children were unable to learn, but communal feeding would remove one of the bonds of family life. The family meal, Barnett believed, fed the memories as well as the bodies of children. 'It stores in their minds the thought of their parents' care, it brings out their sympathy with one another's needs, it teaches manners, provokes common conversation, impresses the use of order'.[52] The best way to ensure that children were properly fed, he thought, would be to 'enlist Christian charity' to discover the reason for underfeeding and then to deal with the ignorance, carelessness, disease or poverty. It would be far better for children to eat in families than at a 'barracks mess'. But Barnett acknowledged that Christian charity had failed; children were starving and the problem was to devise ways of feeding them without damaging self-respect and weakening family responsibility. He considered it immaterial whether the money came from charity or from public funds so far as the effect on family life was concerned. What was important was to avoid any attempt to distinguish the deserving from the undeserving, any marking off of a pauper class which might 'increase in the nation habits of suspicion or of cringing'.[53] The compromise that Barnett proposed was a porridge breakfast for all, a nutritious diet but one that he thought unlikely to remove the sense of duty either of parents to provide for their children or of society to enquire into the causes of poverty.[54]

The narrowness of state welfare provision was attracting increasing criticism by the end of the nineteenth century. It was a criticism that Barnett joined and that led him to argue for the reform of poor law policy and administration as well as for the development of wider public services. He denounced the workhouse, a central feature of the poor law, as unsuitable for old people and for children, and urged that more use should be made of other resources. Barnett calculated in 1902 that boarding out ten adults and ten children could help a rural economy to the tune of £400 a year. Parish councils would supervise boarding out arrangements and be 'dignified by the trust'. Moreover there might be reciprocal services. An old man or woman could be worth two or three shillings a week in child-minding, fruit picking, sewing and so on, an insistence on the importance of old people's contribution to general well-being which has been increasingly empha- sised in the later part of the twentieth century. 'As to those boarded out', Barnett continued, 'it goes without saying they would be happier and more fit for life'.[55] The workhouse stood for the punishment of poverty and was out of place in modern society, he declared, where poverty was not the fault of individuals. The punishment of misfor- tune was unjust.[56] Children should not be under the poor law at all but removed to the education authority which should provide for each according to his needs, offering the same opportunities and attention that other children received.[57]

It was not surprising that Barnett welcomed the recommendations of the Poor Law Commission of 1905–9. The most important new principle, he thought, was that relief should involve treatment to restore the individual to his place in society, recognising that none was beyond the reach of education. A second vital principle was that prevention was better than relief. The Commissioners had pointed to the disorganization of industry and the misuse of boy labour. Barnett wanted full-time employment of young people forbidden and atten- dance at continuation classes required and he endorsed the proposals for labour exchanges and insurance protection for the unemployed.[58]

The problem of poverty for Barnett was inextricably bound up with the problem of wealth, and here too was cause for state action. Not only might wealth destroy the moral character of its possessors in leading to extravagance and luxury, it also represented the waste of resources that might have been used to help the poor. It was the duty of the nation to limit luxury and to check accumulations that were not the result of the owner's work; to prevent the loss of freedom through wealth as well as the loss of freedom through poverty.[59] Here, Barnett was supporting the version of the theory of surplus value developed by Hobhouse and Hobson and the New Liberals. No individual had the right to control 'millions of money'. He should restore to the community whatever he possessed 'beyond what he required to develop his own being, or beyond what he could personally direct for his neighbour's use'.[60] There was also room for more vigorous statutory measures to tackle drunkenness, vice and ignorance. Drink destroyed freedom and the capacity for life. The nation should control the drink traffic but also protect people against it by regulating overcrowded dwellings and unhealthy work and opening up the means to a fuller life. There should be more education and more leisure and public museums, galleries, libraries, music and gardens with which to enjoy it.

The nation cannot indeed make people sober by act of parliament, but it has power to do what no individual and no voluntary society can do; it can train the children to seek for truth and to admire beauty, and bring within everyone's reach things which are true and beautiful.[61]

By 1911 Barnett believed that although the spread of education had increased respectability and 'sober enjoyment' there remained a want of knowledge that left men and women prey to sensational newspapers, restricted individual freedom and prevented the majority exercising the judgement that would guide the nation to peace and greatness. 'Their political action is vacillating, their philosophy of life limited, and their pleasures such as are not humanizing'.[62] The dangers of ignorance required university education to be widely available and free. Elementary and secondary education were not enough. Men must be able to reason as well as accumulate information.

Barnett's advocacy of more collective responsibility was never an advocacy of a mere extension of statutory bodies and statutory power. Rights must never be divorced from duties. The test of legislation was its power to stimulate effort, to make it more difficult for 'idlers and loafers' among the poor to live on relief and also to stir 'rich idlers into some form of fruitful energy', for as a stimulus to effort 'an open way down is as important as an open way up'.[63] But stimulus to effort could only come through personal relationships.[64] The progress of social reform depended on legislation but also on voluntary service. Thus, in education the officials possessed knowledge and experience but administration could easily become mechanical and rigid. It was the lot of volunteers acting as school managers to inspire and also to control the experts. In poor relief there was need for centralised administration by officials to avoid confusion and variety of practice, and officials brought both knowledge and devotion. But, again, administration tended to become mechanical, to alienate 'public interest from public duty', and the safeguard was that officials be responsible to a body of 'ordinary citizens'.[65] The question of the balance of power and responsibility between government and people is an ancient one. For Barnett it arose in the conflict between officials and volunteers and might be resolved by the latter acting as guardians of the public interest.

The need for both official and voluntary effort is a continuing theme in Barnett's writing, and one of the justifications of his work at Toynbee Hall. Settlers, he believed, could mitigate class suspicion and increase goodwill and they could also inspire local government with a 'higher spirit'. Social improvement required organisation and officials but it was a true instinct to distrust 'machinery'. Settlements brought into poor neighbourhoods people whose training made them sensible to abuses and whose humanity made them conscious of others' needs, and they brought into local government people who could 'formulate its mission'.[66]

In the end, however, neither voluntary action nor legislation was a reliable means to the society Barnett wished to see. Social progress called for redistribution of resources, personal service and individual effort that would be painful and difficult for all classes. Only religion could give the impetus and provide the sustaining force for the legislation and the sacrifice and the endeavour that would be necessary.

THE CHURCH

The religion wanted, and 'by which most might be done', was not one 'that ranged men in sects' to discuss doctrine nor even to go to church. It was one, as Barnett put it, 'through which men became conscious of an immanent God'.[67] This meant 'moral thoughtfulness'. Social reform depended on individual reform. 'When we are changed, God through us will change the world'.[68] How, Barnett demanded, if an employer prayed could he countenance a 'law of trade' that fixed wages below subsistence, defend offices and workshops that destroyed health or permit a man who had worked for him for forty years to become a pauper in old age. If a workman prayed what would he think of the work he scamped and the minutes he idled. The employer might not at once raise wages, Barnett conceded, but he would not be a hard master and the more thoughtful workman would recognise the employer's goodwill.[69]

The power of religion to bring about social harmony however was not at all the same thing as the power of the Anglican Church. On the contrary, church leaders had failed to deal with current issues, to relate Christianity to the economic and scientific movements and thought of the last fifty years, or to find ways of resolving the antagonism between rich and poor.

> They go on using a phraseology which is not understood, preaching sermons about dead controversies and condemning controversies long forgotten. They teach, but the people, tried and troubled by the thoughts of duty to the rich or duty to the poor, find no help in their teaching. Their sermons have become almost a byword for dullness and inaptness.[70]

So Barnett set out to revive the service at St Jude's and shake off the 'dull weight' of the past. The church was not his, he wrote, but the parishioners'. They could hope for more adequate forms of service in the future but in the meantime that of the Church of England seemed to Barnett the best available, though it needed widening and enriching with history and literature, music and art.

> It is by knowing grand lives . . . that men now living will themselves strive to live holy lives . . . It is . . . by the sight of grand pictures . . . that men are able to understand what lies behind the life of every day . . . Lastly, it is in grand music that men find the truest expression for thoughts and prayers which voices cannot utter.[71]

Music and art, Barnett saw as evidence of a religious effort to spread goodwill and good fellowship that should be universally available – even on Sundays. He had to defend such views to the Bishop of London who had written in disapproval of Sunday exhibitions. Barnett maintained that his duty as a minister of the Church was to bring people to the knowledge of God; the preaching of a puritan

Sunday would only convince people that the clergy were interfering with innocent pleasures, and the Church had a higher aim and Christianity a wider basis than the sanctity of a day. 'I cannot think that you would say it is better, for the value of old Sunday associations, to keep the people amid the paralysing and degrading sights of our streets than to bring them within view of the good and perfect gifts of God'.[72]

More generally, Barnett believed that religious teachers could contribute to the solution of economic and social problems in arousing 'moral thoughtfulness' and offering a modern conception of a Christian society. As it was there was little regard for the misfortunes of the weak. Competitive trade required a supply of ready labour but when their labour was no longer needed men and women were thrown aside as 'old machines on a scrap heap'. Sanitary laws were enforced but these were as necessary for cattle as for men and women and there was little care that workers should have pleasant homes and inspiring recreations. New laws and new methods of relief would be vain without a greater sense of Duty and a greater devotion to Right; it was this that the Church must teach.[73] It is ironical that during the 1980s and 90s relations between organised religion and government have grown increasingly acrimonious as church leaders have become increasingly outspoken in their criticism of widening social inequalities.

Thus, in his approach to citizenship Barnett's priorities were moral and religious rather than economic and political. The machinery of government he distrusted; administration was only as good as those who carried it out, officials were prone to rigidity and should be answerable to volunteers who would keep them in touch with the wishes of the people. Social improvement must come 'by growth from within, and not be accretions from without'. During his visit to America in 1867 Barnett noted the difference between himself and a radical American lawyer, the American believing that every man had a right to vote, Barnett believing that it was first every man's duty to make himself fit to vote.[74]

In his relations with the Church, as in his attitudes to the state, Barnett belongs to the Christian Socialists, a group of men more or less Christian and more or less socialist, among whom Dr Norman includes Ruskin, not a churchman, beset by religious doubts, seeking extensive social change but without belief in the political apparatus required to bring it about.[75] For all the Christian Socialists the response to social evils was religious rather than political; they were shocked not so much by the low wages and insanitary dwellings as by the debased leisure and alienation of the poor. While Chartism was a social and religious movement with a political programme, Norman suggests, Christian Socialism was a religious and moral movement intended to make political activity unnecessary.[76]

Barnett stood aside from the socialist reformers whom he saw as wishing to rebuild society, and also from those whom he called individualists who wished to develop a system of rewards and punishments for the deserving and undeserving poor. As a Christian he emphasised neither unfairness, as did the socialists, nor suffering, as did the individualists, but rather 'the limits put upon the growth of men's souls'.[77] Tawney put it slightly differently when he wrote that one wing of social reformers had gone astray, being preoccupied with relieving distress and patching up failures. This was good and necessary but it was not tackling the social problem, nor a policy that would ever commend itself to the working classes. What they wanted was security and opportunity; not assistance in exceptional misfortunes but a chance of leading an independent and fairly prosperous life.[78] But for Tawney as for Barnett and for William Morris material progress was fraught with moral danger in so far as it brought an increasing demand for discreditable pleasures. The hopes of social advance therefore rested on education and the spreading of Christian values so that new opportunities might be rightly used. Education was the first and greatest need of the industrial classes, then shorter hours of labour and then the free provision of the best forms of pleasure.[79]

It was the priority that Barnett gave to attending to men's minds and souls rather than their material circumstances that led him to refuse an invitation to serve on the Royal Commission on the Poor Laws in 1905, preferring to devote himself to 'the direct teaching of his faith'.[80] Earlier, before leaving the East End for Bristol in 1892, he had written that if everyone were Christian there would be no need for socialism and that until everyone was Christian, socialism was impossible. The practical thing therefore was for everyone to cultivate personal friendship with his neighbours.[81]

The cultivation of personal friendship with neighbours was one of the primary aims of Toynbee Hall but it was an aspect of the settlement's activities to which Barnett attached less importance in later years; not that he ceased to think attention to individual relationships necessary, only that it was not sufficient to ensure reform. Under his guidance the emphasis of work at Toynbee Hall shifted from local philanthropy to more far-reaching research.

The early ideal of a settlement as a foundation of citizenship where rich and poor could meet in friendship, sharing common interests and a common culture so that working men might experience the best in art and music and literature, a means to life rather than to a livelihood, was perhaps doomed from the beginning. One of the early settlers, A. P. Laurie, suggests Toynbee Hall was in the wrong place. Whitechapel's population was a mixture of immigrant Jews and semi-criminals and the settlement was irrelevant to both. It would have been better further east among the artisans and labourers who had no public institutions, no education facilities, no public opinion and incompetent and corrupt local government. Laurie and several others moved out of Toynbee Hall, wanting closer contact with the people of east London, especially with the Labour leaders. Slumming had become a fashionable amusement and Toynbee Hall was very much in the limelight. 'After a good dinner a crowd of men and women in evening dress would be personally conducted through the worst slums known, prying into people's homes and behaving in an intolerable manner. We wanted to get away from all this.'[82] Barnett himself was well aware of such dangers. After ten years at St Jude's he wrote of the increasing public interest in the poor and of the temptation to seek out the painful as a stimulant to effort. 'It is a fearful thing to find a half pleasurable interest in the sight of human degradation.'[83]

It may well have been true that Toynbee Hall was in the wrong place. Few of the Whitechapel poor attended the lectures, classes and entertainments intended to spread 'the best' and open wider opportunities among them. Audiences were drawn from the middle classes, from board school teachers and from better off working men, many of whom came from other parts of London. It was the classes in commercial subjects directly linked to job opportunities that were the more popular among East Enders.[84] Abel claims that many settlement activities, like the travellers' club that tended to exclude working men because it was too expensive, had little impact on the mass of the poor; they drew out of society only those already deviant, Matthew Arnold's aliens.[85]

There is little doubt, however, that the more modest ventures into practical philanthropy had some effect on the local community. Settlers ran clubs for children and for working men as well as for board school teachers; they served on school boards, poor law boards and sanitary aid committees; later they organised a poor man's lawyer service and tenants' protection societies and later still they served on the care committees set up to administer the 1906 Education Act and the juvenile advisory committees attached to the Stepney Labour Exchange after 1909. Moreover, the Barnetts' social entertainments, art exhibitions and musical evenings can have done little harm and may have given some pleasure, as one settler remarked. Above all, perhaps, Whitechapel children were sent for two weeks holiday into the country. The first nine left St Jude's in 1877 but in 1913 45 000 went for a fortnight into the surrounding countryside. In all, a million children had spent two weeks away from the East End by 1916.

After 1900 Toynbee Hall grew increasingly important as a centre for social investigation and a training place for public service. In 1903 Beveridge became sub-warden and wrote to his father that he for one did not believe that colossal evils could be remedied by small doses of culture and charity and amiability. The use he wished to make of Toynbee and similar institutions was as centres for the development of authoritative opinion on the problems of city life.[86] And many others, A. P. Laurie, R. H. Tawney, C. R. Ashbee, T. E. Harvey and indeed Barnett himself, shifted the emphasis of settlement work away from practical benevolence to social investigation, recognising that the problems of the East End would never be solved in Whitechapel. Some saw Toynbee Hall under Canon Barnett as a place radiating influences that touched the universities, the press, and politics for more than a generation and drawing great men from near and far.[87] Harold Spender, recalling that he went to live in East London led by a 'prophet', Barnett, remarked with some dismay that the newer settlers who came after him tended to join the ranks of Labour and became more socialist than the British working man. 'That was not our idea of our task. We were there . . . to bridge the gulf between Disraeli's "two nations": not merely to cross the gulf and pitch our tents on the other side.'[88]

Perhaps one of those most anxious to cross the gulf was Tawney, who went to Toynbee in 1903, seeing settlements as centres for gathering information that might lead to collective action, places where rich and poor could meet to discuss matters of common concern to every citizen. But Tawney was uneasy with that aspect of the work of Toynbee Hall that involved imposing one culture and set of values on another – in spreading 'the best' among a deprived and degraded population.[89] After three years he left, with Barnett's encouragement, to devote himself to teaching and particularly to the Workers Educational Association (WEA).

Barnett's refusal to commit himself to particular political or religious doctrines or dogma offended some who went to join him in

Whitechapel. Ashbee parodies him in the Rev. Simeon Flux, conduct-ing a latitudinarian mission, trying to square a vague theory of Christianity with modern scientific knowledge in an earnest if empir-ical attempt to solve economic difficulties. But he 'could not take the cold plunge of the twentieth-century Socialism, the ripple of which he touched with a shivering toe'.[90]

Most of those who knew him, however, were more impressed by the liberality and tolerance of Barnett's vision of citizenship. In Laurie's view he was too sound a thinker to adopt cut and dried ideas about what the future commonwealth should be or how it might be attained. He abjured party politics and left the organisation of Toynbee Hall 'very elastic', Laurie remarked, avoiding the trap of narrow doctri-naire socialism. 'I doubt if he ever expected it to have much influence on East London. He regarded it rather as a post-graduate university for young men from Oxford and Cambridge who might ultimately become members of parliament or civil servants.'[91] Beveridge saw Barnett as infinitely wise with a strong temper controlled and directed by love of God and love of man, the strength of the house he founded lying in its ability to use many different sorts of people.[92] This judge-ment is echoed by Albert Mansfield, who attributed some of the most successful achievements of the WEA to Barnett's advice and help. Toynbee Hall was his most obvious creative effort, but 'his power to create ideas in the minds of others and to inspire their hearts was his outstanding characteristic'.[93]

For Spender, Barnett was a prophet. 'He stimulated without eclips-ing. He guided without crushing . . . he conveyed a spirit.'[94] And Beatrice Webb describes him as a man of 'fathomless sympathy' and a 'nineteenth-century saint', his prophetic vision of a state built on social justice where the interests of each individual were fused with the well-being of the whole community. Perhaps, as Mrs Webb suggests, Barnett was too intent on the end or purpose of human life, and 'a noble state of mind in each individual and in the community as a whole', to concentrate on the means by which it might be reached.[95] If so this only attaches him all the more firmly to the Christian and ethical socialist tradition described by Dennis and Halsey;[96] to men and women who believe with Tawney that 'happiness and content-ment are to be found not in the power of man to satisfy wants, but in the power of man to regard his position in society and that of his fellows with moral approval or satisfaction'.[97]

NOTES

1 Dahrendorf, 1988, pp. 175–6.
2 Barnett, H. O., 1918, p. 24.
3 Barnett, 'Charity Reform' in Barnett, 1897, p. 341.
4 Barnett, 1913, p. 149.
5 Barnett, 1897, pp. 54–5.
6 Barnett, 'Rich and Poor', *ibid.*, p. 99.
7 Halsey, 1986, p. 17.
8 Barnett, 'Class Divisions in Great Cities' in Barnett and Barnett, 1909, p. 29.
9 Barnett, 'The Unemployed', *ibid.* p. 86.
10 Barnett, 1897, p. 10.
11 Barnett, 1913, p. 172.
12 *Ibid.*, p. 84.
13 Barnett, 1897, pp. 281–2.
14 Hayek, 1960, p. 29.
15 Barnett, 'Pauperism' in Barnett, 1911, p. 41.
16 Barnett, 1913, p. 141.
17 Barnett, 1897, p. 272.
18 *Ibid.*, pp. 275–6.
19 *Ibid.*, p. 80.
20 *Ibid.*, p. 102.
21 Barnett, 'Class Divisions in Great Cities', in Barnett and Barnett, 1909, pp. 26–7.
22 Barnett, 1897, p. 309; 'Class Divisions in Great Cities' in Barnett and Barnett, 1909, p. 28.
23 Barnett, 'Class Division in Great Cities' in Barnett and Barnett, 1909, p. 29.
24 Barnett, 'Luxury', in Barnett, 1911.
25 *Ibid.*, p. 60.
26 Barnett and Barnett, 1909, p. 16.
27 Barnett, 'Labour and Culture', in Barnett and Barnett, 1909, p. 216.
28 Barnett, 'Pauperism' in Barnett, 1911.
29 *Ibid.*, p. 42.
30 Barnett, 1897, p. 103.
31 *Ibid.*, p. 253.
32 *Ibid.*, p. 255.
33 Barnett, 'Class Divisions in Great Cities', in Barnett and Barnett, 1909, p. 28.
34 Letter from the Bishop of London to Samuel Barnett on his move to St Jude's, in Barnett, H. O., 1918, p. 68.
35 The Archbishop of Canterbury's Commission, 1985.
36 Barnett, H. O., 1918, p. 110.
37 *Ibid.*, p. 153.
38 Gell, 1884, pp. 8–9.
39 *Ibid.*, p. 11.
40 *Ibid.*, p. 21.

41   Barnett, 1888.
42   Barnett, 'Charity Reform' in Barnett, 1897, p. 337.
43   *Ibid.*, p. 339.
44   *Ibid.*, p. 340.
45   *Ibid.*, p. 343.
46   'Barnett, 'Class Divisions in Great Cities' in Barnett and Barnett, 1909, pp. 27–9.
47   Barnett, 'Ignorance' in Barnett, 1911, p. 140.
48   Barnett, 'Pensions and Morality' in Barnett and Barnett, 1909, p. 174.
49   Barnett, 'Poverty', *ibid.*, p. 67.
50   Barnett, 'The Unemployed', *ibid.*, p. 76.
51   Barnett, 'The Unemployed Workman's Act 1905', *ibid.*, p. 95.
52   Barnett, 'Public Feeding of School Children', *ibid.*, p. 108.
53   *Ibid.*, p. 114.
54   *Ibid.*, p. 116.
55   Barnett, 'Pauperism', *ibid.*, p. 122.
56   Barnett, 'The Workhouse', *ibid.*, p. 154.
57   Barnett, 'Children', in Barnett 1913, p. 36.
58   Barnett, 'Pauperism', in Barnett, 1911, p. 51.
59   Barnett, 'Luxury', *ibid.*, p. 72.
60   Barnett, 'Millionaires', in Barnett, 1913, p. 108.
61   Barnett, 'Drunkenness', in Barnett, 1911, p. 95.
62   Barnett, 'Ignorance', *ibid.*, p. 122.
63   Barnett, 1907, p. 29.
64   Barnett, 'The Unemployed', in Barnett and Barnett, 1909, p. 86.
65   Barnett, 'Unemployed Goodwill', *ibid.*, pp 58–9.
66   Barnett, 'A Retrospect of Toynbee Hall', *ibid.*, pp. 265–9.
67   Barnett, 'Rich and Poor' in Barnett, 1897, p. 105.
68   Barnett, 'Godliness and Social Justice', *ibid.*, p. 261.
69   Barnett, 'Employers and Employed', *ibid.*, pp. 129–33.
70   Barnett, 'Sunday Reform', *ibid.*, p. 320.
71   Barnett, 1913, pp. 92–3.
72   S. A. Barnett to Bishop Temple, quoted in Barnett, H. O., 1918, p.   545.
73   Barnett, 1913, pp. 176, 186.
74   Abel, 1969, p. 11.
75   Norman, 1987, pp. 121–5.
76   *Ibid.*, pp. 6–10.
77   Barnett, 1911, p. 41.
78   Tawney's Commonplace Book, *Economic History Review*, 1972, p.   13.
79   Barnett, 1913, p. 28.
80   Barnett, H. O., 1918, p. 677.
81   *Ibid.*, p. 664.
82   Laurie, 1934, p. 74.
83   Quoted in Aitken, 1902, p. 106.
84   Abel, 1969, pp. 204–35.
85   *Ibid.*, p. 240.
86   Beveridge, 1953, p. 17.
87   Rogers, 1913, p. 321; Mansbridge, 1948, p. 62.
88   Spender, 1926, p. 71.

89   Meacham, 1987, p. 158.
90   Ashbee, 1910, p. 175.
91   Laurie, 1934, p. 72.
92   Beveridge, 1953, p. 38.
93   Mansbridge, 1948, p. 60.
94   Spender, 1926, p. 70.
95   Webb, B., 1926, p. 181.
96   Dennis and Halsey, 1988.
97   Tawney's Commonplace Book, *op. cit.*, p. 19.

II Citizenship and Work

(i) Moralising the People

4 Robert Owen 1771–1858

No people or population can be good, intelligent, or happy, except by a rational and natural education and useful employment or occupation.

(*The Life of Robert Owen*)

If citizenship is about the freedom and ability to join in social activities in ways that preserve dignity and self-respect then the opportunity for work that is socially valued is fundamentally important. It is through their labour that most people provide for themselves and their families and contribute to the national economy, so it is a source of both individual satisfaction and collective prosperity. For the fortunate it is also intrinsically interesting and enjoyable. The overwhelming significance of work for individual welfare and for society and, hence, its central place in discussions about citizenship are evident in the long tradition of political, economic and philanthropic literature to do with employment and unemployment. In the early nineteenth century the social consequences of a rapidly growing and largely unregulated industrial economy attracted the attention of a multitude of writers shocked by the working and living conditions associated with the use of increasingly elaborate industrial machines which turned factory labour into a monotonous routine, and by the acute poverty and demoralisation of the men whom they displaced.

Among those who inveighed against the misery and injustice of early industrial society was Robert Owen, wealthy cotton manufacturer and trader but celebrated less for his commercial enterprise than for his vision of a New Moral World to replace the iniquities of the old one. Owen was born in 1771 in Newtown in Montgomeryshire in the Welsh borders, where his father was a saddler and ironmonger. He remained only a short time in his home town. Leaving school at nine years old, he departed for London when he was ten to join the household of his elder brother and thence to apprenticeships with shopkeepers in London and Stamford. He appears to have been diligent and successful, accumulating much knowledge of the textile trade and being highly regarded by his employers. He also read widely, on his own account, having a keen interest in Christianity and all other religions. The interest was not entirely theoretical: when he was 12 or 13 years old, he records, he wrote to the prime minister to urge the government to take steps to 'enforce a better observance of the sabbath'. Nevertheless, he later found himself obliged to reject all religions as all, he asserted, were based 'on the same absurd imagination' that people formed their own qualities, thoughts and actions and were responsible for them to God and to their fellow men. Owen's reflections led him to different conclusions; that Nature gave the qualities and Society directed them – and he thereupon abandoned all belief in 'every religion which had been taught to man'. His religious feelings were immediately replaced, he claimed, by 'the spirit of universal charity, – not for a sect or a party, or for a country or a colour, but for the human race, and with a real and ardent desire to do them good'.[1]

By the time he was nineteen, Owen had established his own spinning factory with three machines in a shed in Manchester. Moving on to become manager and then partner of a mill with 500 workers, he speedily became an innovative and highly successful trader in the rapidly developing cotton industry. But his fame rests not on his enterprising commercial activity but on his vision of the New Moral World, and his endeavours to turn the vision into reality. To begin with this meant industrial and social and educational reforms at New Lanark and later various experiments in communal living and tireless propaganda, not only in his own country but in America, Europe and Russia, to try to persuade statesmen and governments to adopt the social arrangements that Owen believed would unfailingly produce rational, charitable and benevolent human beings.

It would be hardly surprising if Owen's achievement failed to match his Messianic aims. But his voice was continually raised in opposition to the liberal individualistic and *laissez-faire* political economy of his time to proclaim the rights of all to a decent standard of living, to education, training and work, and the duty of society – of government and employers or co-operative associations – to provide those things. Perhaps most importantly he was able to demonstrate that kindly treatment of the men and women and children at New Lanark, with education, regular wages and decent houses, was compatible with a profitable enterprise as well as vastly improving the health and contentment of the mill workers.

THE NEW MORAL WORLD

What, then, did the idea of citizenship mean to Owen? What rights and duties attached to the notion? How did he define the social problems that he saw around him at the close of the eighteenth and the beginning of the nineteenth centuries in a country in the early stages of industrial development? And how did he suppose those problems might be overcome? Owen rarely used the term 'citizenship' but his dream of a New Moral Order was founded upon assumptions about social behaviour – about the rights and obligations of individuals and the power and responsibilities of public authorities which together composed the status that citizenship entails.

The nature of Owen's utopia reflected his two most deeply held beliefs. Like Bentham and Mill, he assumed that the end of government was the greatest happiness of the greatest number.[2] And he also believed that 'any general character, from the best to the worst...may be given to any community...by the application of the proper means'. The road to the utilitarian paradise was clear. Public authorities or benevolent individuals or workers, banding together into communities, must so arrange the environment as to produce amiable, charitable, peaceful and happy men and women.

The details of Owen's vision of the New Moral World and the measures he believed would bring it about, his own experiments in that direction and his endeavours to persuade governments to follow his example, will be discussed later. All his proposals, however, may be understood as an effort to attack and vanquish what he conceived as the two great evils of his time: the bigotry, superstition and false teaching of all religions, and the mechanisation of industrial work combined with the all-too-common remorseless entrepreneurial pursuit of profit. Of the two religion was the worse, for although the uncontrolled use of machinery threatened unemployment and appalling conditions of labour, it also opened up possibilities of hitherto unimagined prosperity. Owen believed that superfluity of wealth at all times for all and a good character were the two preconditions for achieving happiness.[3]

The crime that Owen imputed to all religions was the doctrine professed by all that men be held responsible and accountable for their actions. This directly contradicted his own fundamental belief that men were formed by their circumstances, that free will did not exist, and that praise or condemnation of human behaviour was therefore inappropriate and irrelevant. The insistence on moral responsibility was, Owen maintained, the 'strongest cause of repulsive feeling' between individuals, driving out charity and love and preventing peace, knowledge and happiness.[4] 'It generates and perpetuates ignorance, hatred and revenge, where, without such error, only intelligence, confidence, and kindness, would exist'.[5] Owen maintained that people were made by circumstances; though writing at the end of his life in his autobiography he recognised the power of circumstances *before* as well as after birth,[6] thus acknowledging the increasing interest in evolution and heredity which was developing through the nineteenth century.

In a series of public meetings during 1817 setting out his plans for the human race, Owen denounced the pernicious effects of religious dogma and insisted on the need for toleration and freedom. According to one of his biographers, this resulted in the loss of powerful friends, Owen discrediting himself as much by his inability to answer criticisms about the implications of his plans for expenditure and for population increase, as by his arrogance.[7] It is clear from his own record of his life, however, that Owen took considerable pleasure in his performance. When he went to the second meeting he was, he declared, the most popular individual in the civilised world, and possessed the most influence with leading members of the British cabinet and government. He went to the meeting to destroy that popularity but in so doing 'to lay the axe to the root of all false religions and thus to prepare the populations of the world for the reign of charity in accordance with the actual laws of humanity'.[8] Owen believed that he achieved his objective and that bigotry, superstition and all false religion received their death blow on that day. He claimed that in subsequent travels in foreign countries the 1817 meetings had prepared for him 'a kind and reverential reception among the highest and most advanced minds with whom I came into communication'.[9] However, he was obliged to notice some opposition from politicians and religious sects in Britain. His addresses in 1817 were considered, he admitted, to be several hundred – some said several thousand – years in advance of their time. Owen himself was more modest in suggesting they might be 50 years early.

Religious dogma was one of the great evils denying the spread of knowledge and destroying any chance of developing a benevolent, charitable, prosperous and happy society; the other was uncontrolled industrial growth. As the nineteenth century wore on it became commonplace to point to the huge social and economic inequalities, to the existence, sometimes side by side though later tending to be geographically separated, of great wealth and desperate poverty, represented in Disraeli's *Two Nations* and Mrs Gaskell's *North and South* among the many 'social' novels and political and religious tracts of the time. At the end of the century came attempts at precise definition and measurement of poverty and at explanations of its causes which provided useful evidence for those wishing to argue for change. But in the early 1800s social attitudes to the poor and popular ideas about the plight of the labouring classes lacked the discipline of systematic empirical enquiry and were therefore, perhaps, the more readily coloured by a complex set of values and beliefs.[10] For some, the trials of this world faded into insignificance, especially if borne by other people, compared with the promise and expectations of the next; for others, they might represent the wages of sin; and for yet others the unavoidable price of controlling population growth or of securing a healthy political economy.

Owen was among the dreamers of dreams, the movers and shakers of the world, who desired a New Moral Order of tranquility and kindness where citizenship would bring education, employment, decent living arrangements and support for those who could not work. Nor was the appeal of the New Moral Order only to benevolence and philanthropy; it was also in the interests of the privileged classes, Owen believed, to co-operate with those trying to promote general happiness in order to dispel social discontent and destroy 'those irritable feelings that have so long afflicted society'.[11] The poor and the working classes numbered over 15 million people, nearly three-quarters of the population of Great Britain in 1813, Owen claimed, and they lived in circumstances leading to vice and misery – the worst and most dangerous subjects in the Empire. He considered the conditions of British and Irish operatives more miserable than those of slaves in the West Indies. Slave proprietors were becoming more humane, he thought, and it was in their own interests to be so; slaves were better dressed, more independent in manner and more free from anxiety than a large proportion of the working class in Great Britain.[12] While denouncing the condition of young children in the British cotton mills, oppressed by machines and worse off than Jamaican house slaves, Owen also pointed to the further threat from machinery in the displacement of human labour. If the use of machines were not curtailed millions must starve to death; machinery must be made subservient to labour, not allowed to supersede it.

One result of widespread unemployment after the French wars was the appointment of a committee of investigation under the Archbishop of Canterbury. Invited to give evidence, Owen took the opportunity to attack what he called the new school of political economists among whom he counted Malthus, Mill, Ricardo, Hume, Place and Bentham, attempting to persuade the committee that education and employment were the solutions to social distress. Mr Malthus was

correct, he conceded, in arguing that populations adapted themselves
to the available food supplies, but had not considered how much more
food an intelligent and industrious people would produce from the
same soil than ignorant and ill-governed workers.[13] The political
economists were right when they accepted the case for education but
wrong when they argued for competition and individual responsibility
and rejected the public provision of work.[14]

This was the heart of the quarrel. Owen disdained insistence on
competition and individual responsibility. In his *Essays on the Formation of Character* he denounced the glaring injustice that left generation after generation to be taught crime from their infancy and then
hunted 'like beasts of the forest until they are entangled beyond
escape in the toils and nets of the law.' Had the circumstances of the
'poor unpitied sufferers' been reversed with those surrounded with the
pomp and dignity of justice, the latter would have been at the bar of
the culprit and the former in the judgement seat.[15]

Owen's attack extended beyond the political economists to the new
manufacturing class who embraced their doctrines. He preferred the
older style conservatives who governed with more ignorance, but with
more humanity. 'The old aristocracy of birth ... were in many respects
superior to the money-making and money-seeking aristocracy of
modern times'.[16] Owen gave full rein to his views about the industrial
system and prevailing standards of industrial behaviour and their
social consequences in describing his separation from his early partners in the New Lanark venture who grew alarmed by his educational
schemes and opposed better pay for the workers, having been 'merely
trained to buy cheap and to sell dear':

> This occupation deteriorates, and often destroys, the finest and best
> faculties of our nature ... I am thoroughly convinced that there can
> be no superior character formed under this thoroughly selfish
> system ... It is a low, vulgar, ignorant and inferior way of conduct-
> ing the affairs of society; and no permanent, general, and substan-
> tial improvement can arise until it shall be superseded by a superior
> mode of forming character and creating wealth.[17]

Here is Owen's wholesale condemnation of what he saw as the essential nature of early industrial Britain, as he looked back in 1857. What
did he wish to be put in its place? And how might his ideal society be
brought about?

Believing, as he did, that men and women were moulded by their
circumstances, Owen's hopes for a society governed by kindness and

mutual goodwill rested on comprehensive arrangements for education, the provision of employment, and support for those who could
not work. It involved close, if benevolent, supervision of behaviour in
domestic and industrial life 'from the cradle to the grave', to use the
phrase that Beveridge coined nearly 150 years later to describe his own
far more restricted social security scheme.

Unlike Beveridge, however, who in 1942 was writing prescriptions
for government, propounding the principles of legislation, the administrative organisation and the minutiae of regulations, Owen
was formulating his beliefs about the rights and responsibilities of
citizens at a time when no government machinery existed to put
them into effect and when the extension of state power which would
have been required to give them reality would have been regarded
with incredulity. In that sense, Owen's utopia lay outside politics.
And in another sense too: he never had much sympathy with the
wider political movements for reform – for Chartism or for the repeal
of the corn laws – and his biographer suggests that he thought it a
waste of time to tinker with obsolete constitutional machinery which
the New Moral Order would soon sweep away. Owen's idea of reform
meant change imposed from above rather than through the people's
struggles for social betterment.[18] Moreover, anticipating Ruskin
and the unease of the many reluctant democrats amongst the Fabians,
Owen considered that the Charter, if gained, would be but a pyrrhic
victory as the leaders of the movement were too ignorant to find
the right remedy for national ills. Chartists, he thought, were
only united over means; almost every one of them had different
ideas about ends.[19]

Nevertheless, although the coming of Owen's new society depended
on a universal change in moral values and rejection of the false and
harmful doctrines of religion and political economy, the moral transformation might be assisted through argument. Persuasion and propaganda among statesmen, princes and churchmen of all nations,
among political economists and manufacturers could encourage
experiment in educational and social reform. Owen believed that
government had an important part to play in regulating factory
labour, devising a national education system and providing employment. He was active and enthusiastic in the agitation for factory
legislation and the reform of the poor laws, but parliament was slow
to act on his proposals to ameliorate social distress.

Notwithstanding the failure of government to adopt his sugges-
tions, Owen remained confident that the power of the truth and

goodness of his vision would eventually overcome falsehood and evil. At the end of his life he acknowledged that he had met much opposition, but was encouraged by recalling one 'important seance' where all attending affirmed their aim 'to reform the world and to unite the population as one family or one man'.[20]

NEW LANARK

The practical demonstration of the way to reform the world was Owen's experiment in social and educational reform at New Lanark. He bought his first share in the mills in 1797 when he was 28 years old and three years later took on the management and supervision of living and working conditions of the employees. His object, he explained, was to discover whether character was better formed or society better constructed by falsehood, fraud and force or by truth, charity and love, and he claimed that his plan was the first practical attempt to change the principles of social organisation.[21]

It was a large aim, but Owen appears to have been markedly successful in improving the conditions of the mill workers – if not in changing the principles of social organisation. He found New Lanark a settlement of 1300 with an additional 500 pauper children. On his own account it was a daunting place: theft, idleness, drunkenness and falsehood were rife; civil and religious dissension a daily commonplace; and the people, suspicious of strangers and particularly of an Englishman, united only in 'a zealous systematic opposition to their employers'.[22] But Owen was not deterred. Working on his essential belief that men were formed by society, he set out to transform the conditions in which the workers lived and to create a social environment that inhibited vice and encouraged virtue. Punishment of crime and misdemeanours had no part in Owen's scheme, for men were not responsible for their behaviour; the object was rather to prevent wrong doing by removing the circumstances that caused it. This kind of intervention, he believed until the end of his life, was both practicable and efficacious.

Theft was all-pervasive at New Lanark but Owen avoided penalties and arranged that the benefits of honesty be explained to offenders who were instructed in legal and useful occupations that would be more profitable. The harmful effects of drink were pointed out by their more prudent comrades to habitual drunkards at the 'proper moment' when they were 'soberly suffering from the effects of previous excess', and pot and public houses were moved away from dwellings. It seems that such gentle remedies were not always sufficient; Owen's biographer notes further sanctions used to control drunkenness – streets were patrolled and offenders were first fined and then dismissed on their third apprehension.[23] Owen's description, however, emphasises persuasion and rationality. Falsehood and deception were condemned and their evil consequences explained. Dissension and quarrelling were reported to the manager, who would urge reconciliation and tell disputants that if they would devote as much time to making one another happy and comfortable as they had to making one another miserable, they would 'soon render that place a paradise, which, from the most mistaken principles of action, they now made the abode of misery'.[24]

In regard to religion, Owen insisted that no sect should receive any preference, that it was impossible to say what doctrines might be right or wrong and that all men and women should attend to the 'essence of religion' rather than ignoring it and devoting their talents to making money. Nor did Owen hesitate to intervene in relations between the sexes. Any 'irregular intercourse' was held in disgrace and incurred fines which were paid into a community fund used to support the sick and the old and workers suffering accident or injury.

A notorious evil of the early nineteenth century was the employment of young children in the cotton mills. When he arrived at New Lanark Owen found pauper children relatively well housed and clothed and receiving some education, but too tired to profit from it after working from six in the morning until seven at night. So he ended the practice of taking apprentices from the poor law authorities and encouraged permanent settlers with large families, building comfortable dwellings to house them. He excluded young children from the mills, advising parents to keep them in education and other healthy activities until they were ten years old. Even ten was too young for children to be working 13 hours a day, Owen recognised, preferring that they should not start until they were 12, but such a change would have to wait until parents had been 'trained' to afford the loss of earnings. In the meantime, children were taught reading, writing and arithmetic in the village school between the ages of five and ten without any payment from their parents and care was taken to make school work a pleasure so that progress might be rapid. There was no sectarian religious teaching; pupils were instructed only in those precepts of Christianity that were common to all denominations.

While endeavouring to mould individual character in these ways, Owen was also attending to other matters. Houses were improved, streets cleaned, a public store established which sold good quality cheap provisions, saving workers 25 per cent of their bills Owen estimated, but still making a profit that was used to support the school. In addition, a savings bank was set up, a sick fund organized through workers contributing one-sixtieth of their wages, and medical attendance provided for all.

The community at New Lanark won widespread renown. The Grand Duke Nicholas, later Tsar, invited Owen to go to Russia (and to take two million of the surplus population of Britain with him).[25] Visitors from nearer home, a deputation sent to inspect New Lanark by the Leeds Guardians of the poor, found much to commend and moral habits exemplary: intoxication seemed unknown; the people were well clothed and fed and their dwellings inviting; there were no quarrelsome men nor brawling women; the religious character of the settlement was praiseworthy; and illegitimate births had almost disappeared, those that had occurred being mainly the result of the activities of 'non-resident interlopers'. These effects were attributed to the 'moral culture' of the place, the absence of public houses and seclusion from the world. They were not the outcome of high wages, which were in fact relatively low.[26] This appraisal, though more cautious, was consistent with Owen's view that New Lanark employees and proprietors both gained incalculable benefits from his system. Workers had been taught to be rational, he said, and they acted rationally. They became 'industrious, temperate, healthy, faithful to their employers and kind to one another', and the employers received loyal and willing work almost without supervision.[27]

Although Owen appears to have had considerable success in moulding the behaviour of his adult workers by these various means, it was, perhaps, his educational experiments for children and infants that best reflected his conception of the New Moral Order and of how its citizens might be prepared to enter it. If people were formed by circumstances their experiences when young might be supposed to be particularly important. 'No people or population can be good, intelligent, or happy', Owen declared, 'except by a rational and natural education and useful employment or occupation'.[28] His educational system was based on Owen's belief that children would learn best if they were happy and amused and treated with unfailing kindness. He disapproved of the repetitive rote learning in the Anglican and Quaker schools founded by Bell and Lancaster and condemned the dogmatic nature of their religious instruction, while sympathising with the pioneering efforts of Pestalozzi and Father Oberlin and de Fellenberg, all of whom he visited, in developing more relaxed and informal schools for the poor.

Owen thought that children should start school, under the super-intendence of suitable people, as soon as they could leave their parents, at six months or a year old. Instruction was to be rooted in moral training. The most important lessons they should learn were that they must never injure others but do everything possible to make them happy.[29] At New Lanark, the youngest were taught through dancing and singing, outdoor play and military drill. Children used no books until they were five or six, but were encouraged in practical activities and to examine and talk about all manner of natural objects. Nor did they have 'useless' toys, for Owen believed that children were well able to amuse each other. After six years old they proceeded to the more conventional learning of reading, writing and arithmetic and using books, on the assumption that they had by then acquired a solid foundation of good manners and habits, and a friendly disposition and conduct towards others. No marks of merit or demerit were awarded and no praise nor blame, but more attention was given to less able children. There were no rewards or punishments because children could not be held responsible for their performance. 'Punish-ment...will never be required, and should be avoided as much as giving poison in their food'.[30] Thousands of people came to see the school, and galleries were built in the school rooms for the benefit of visitors. According to Owen, his Institution for the Formation of Character was considered by the 'more advanced minds of the world' to be 'one of the greatest of modern wonders'.[31]

The New Lanark experiment was Owen's great achievement. It was one of the earliest and perhaps the most famous example of the philanthropic activities of nineteenth century industrialists who were anxious to take immediate steps to improve the living and work-ing conditions of their employees. But Owen was unusual in that he aimed not only to build better dwellings and cut working hours for the people in his factory, but also to inculcate a new social morality. He believed that the community at New Lanark, with its schools, its clean streets and houses and its temperate, honest, industrious and contented inhabitants, was not merely a local curios-ity but proof of the possibility of transforming social and economic relations; the precursor of a New Moral Order which would spread to all mankind.

POLITICAL AGITATION

Owen's ambition to change the world led him beyond New Lanark and Scotland and Great Britain to Europe and America. It involved him in many different strategies: in pressing governments to intervene in welfare matters; in efforts to persuade statesmen, intellectuals and ordinary people that they must adopt new moral attitudes and behaviour; and in further attempts to set up co-operative communities. His ideal society required strong government, not only to regulate factory work but also to develop a national education system, to provide employment, to promote health and to control social behaviour. In 1815 he was urging statutory action to exclude children under 12 years old from the cotton mills, to impose a 10-hour day, to make employment conditional on an educational test, and to require factories to be kept clean. He gave evidence before a House of Commons committee, but considered Sir Robert Peel's bill to have been 'mutilated' by other manufacturers in its passage through the House.[32] His biographer describes Owen as a pioneer of factory legislation who forced the state to attend to the new duties that changing circumstances were thrusting upon it.[33]

During the next few years, Owen turned his attention to the poor laws and unemployment. Believing that people could only be made good, intelligent and happy through rational education and useful work, and that it was of first importance to prevent bad behaviour rather than encourage and then punish it, Owen insisted that government must provide not only education but 'perpetual employment of national utility' in building roads, canals, harbours, docks and ships.[34] The idle poor existed, he asserted, because a large part of the population was allowed to grow up in ignorance and without work. They should be regenerated through education, training and occupation and so placed in circumstances that would remove temptation and unite interest and duty. Such sentiments are echoed by governments in Britain in the 1980s and 1990s in their efforts to deal with unemployment and dependency and particularly by Frank Field, Minister of Social Security, in *Making Welfare Work*. Owen thought that communities of 500 to 1500 people should be established to be as self-sufficient as possible, with a superintendent, schoolmasters, clergymen and surgeons, for those who would otherwise be supported by the poor law. And, finally, the state should collect statistics about available work and the price of labour and maintain labour bureaux to offer information about employment opportunities and wage rates.[35]

The grand plan for social regeneration should be financed, Owen proposed, by voluntary subscription, by the local poor law authorities or by central government. Aimed initially to rescue the unemployed, it developed into the idea of community villages which he hoped would gradually replace other forms of social organisation.[36] Such ideas were not, of course, new. Several English parishes had tried to settle paupers in small farm colonies and organise 'workhouses' that actually provided work.[37] And there were also examples of apparently successful religious communities in Europe and in America where Owen was later to set up his New Harmony.

Over and above its fundamental responsibilities for education, training and work, government had other duties in pursuit of the greatest happiness of the greatest number. It must disclaim the pernicious doctrine that men form their own characters, Owen declared, withdraw laws emanating from that belief and suppress the false tenets of the national church. Drinking of spirits should be restrained by prohibitive taxes and the state lottery, which robbed the ignorant and trapped the unwary, should be abolished. Owen dismissed likely protests about the resulting loss of revenue, declaring that the only legitimate source of revenue was labour; the job of government was to train the population for effective work and thus increase the power of Britain.

Although his attempts to persuade parliament to initiate legislation had little immediate effect, Owen was important in the movement for factory reform that began to have some success in the 1830s. There was little substantial progress, however, in the earlier years. The 1816 Committee on the Poor Laws, to which Owen submitted evidence, declined to call him for examination, and in 1820 parliament refused a petition to consider his *New Views of Society*. A year earlier he had stood for parliament but was not elected. In 1823 he appeared before a select committee examining the condition of the poor in Ireland, but his proposals for getting rid of 'idleness and profligacy' were dismissed as impracticable and visionary, though it was agreed that good education and early moral training were desirable.

Disappointed in his efforts to influence the British government, Owen shifted his energies to more general propaganda through writing and public speaking and, under the patronage of the Duke of Kent, through meetings and discussions with European scientists, intellectuals and politicians. In 1818 he presented two memorials to the leaders of the allied powers, assembled at Aix-la-Chapelle, recapitulating his plan for redeeming mankind. Elected an honorary member of the Swiss National Society of Natural History, he was received by the Duke of Orleans, later Louis Philippe, and also by the French prime minister who, according to Owen, was exceptionally polite and attentive, expressing great interest in New Lanark and telling Owen that his views on religion were true but too advanced and profound to be widely accepted at that time.[38]

Perhaps his rejection of conventional religion in his public addresses of 1817 appealed to French intellectuals of the eighteenth-century rationalist tradition; and Owen continued to denounce the Church for spreading values that destroyed social harmony. In Cincinatti in public debate in 1829, he declared that all the religions of the world were founded on ignorance, that they opposed the laws of human nature and were the causes of dissension and misery, and that they were the only bar to the development of virtue, intelligence and charity. Dispute and discussion continued for eight days, attracting an audience of 1000 or so, and was transcribed and published in London in 1839.[39]

From the 1820s onwards, Owen devoted much effort to arousing popular interest in his plans for social reform, not only through education and employment but through the development of co-operative enterprises to replace market exchanges and the competitive organisation of work. The first Co-operative Congress was held in 1831, and the following year Owen started to publish his newspaper, *Crisis* , which continued after 1834 until 1845 as *New Moral World*. Becoming known as socialists, he and his followers advocated settlements for the unemployed organised on co-operative rather than competitive principles. The ideals and aspirations of the early co-operators were described by another early socialist, William Thompson:

> They were small associations of artisans and others, met together in the common hope of ultimately founding a Community in which they could live together in fellowship, enjoying in common the whole fruits of their labour, islanded from the poverty and degradation around them, and leaving to their children an inheritance more precious even than this material well-being, in minds and characters moulded by a rational system of education to the full stature of a man. To these early co-operators the word co-operation was synonymous with brotherly love; the petty trading profits were an earnest of liberty for themselves and their children; and the grocery store appeared as an ante-chamber to the millennium.[40]

Over the years Owen became more ambitious in proclaiming the New Moral Order world-wide. This took him to Munich and an audience with King Ludwig and to Vienna to be received by Metternich. But for the most part it meant public meetings and discussions in Britain, with regular Sunday morning lectures in London. In 1835 the Association of all Classes of all Nations was formed to bring about 'an entire change in the character and condition of the human race'. Four years later it had 53 branches and was renamed the Universal Community Society of Rational Religionists. Ten paid missionaries were appointed and the organization was registered as a statutory friendly society. By 1840 there were nine more branches and Owen's paper, *New Moral World*, estimated that some 50 000 people were attending the Sunday lectures and services held in the main towns throughout the country. These meetings involved hymns, readings and sermons, the latter objectionable to many churchmen. But where local authorities refused to lend their town halls or public rooms the Society built 'halls of science' to house its followers.

Owen was a deist rather than an atheist, but denying that men were able to comprehend the nature of God. His biographer suggests that his theology, like other of his opinions, was borrowed from pre-revolutionary France.[41] He was, nevertheless, presented to the queen by Lord Melbourne in 1839, carrying with him an address soliciting the government to investigate the measures through which he proposed to regenerate society. As was to be expected, however, Owen's socialist doctrines and his refusal to acknowledge moral responsibility increasingly incurred the wrath of the church. He was attacked in the House of Lords by the Bishop of Exeter as the leader of a powerful and dangerous sect, publishing a weekly newspaper and subversive tracts, holding regular meetings and building assembly halls, supported by mayors who lent their public rooms; an arch heretic who had also been presented to the sovereign. The bishop called for an enquiry into the activities of Owen and his followers, in spite of the opposition of Lord Melbourne, but no record of its proceedings survived.[42]

After 1840 opposition to Owen's brand of socialism intensified. He was more frequently denied the use of meeting places, and violent disturbances began to occur at socialist gatherings. In some cases socialist workmen were sacked and there were a number of prosecutions for blasphemy, at least three of which were successful. Nevertheless, Owen seems to have maintained his faith in the coming of a better world as a result of his teaching:

When he published his *New View of Society*, he looked for the regeneration of the world to begin on the morrow: throughout his long life that high vision, ever receding as he advanced, was still before his eyes: and he died at the age of 87 happy in the belief that the millennium was even then knocking at the door.[43]

He displayed a distaste for argument, however, and a preference for asserting the truths he wished to reveal. In one public debate in which Owen was worsted by a vehement opponent and which ended with a virtually unanimous resolution condemning socialism, he defended his performance with unshaken confidence. 'It would have been the loss of most precious moments for me to have attended to anything Mr Brindley might say, instead of using them to tell the world what I wished it to hear from myself'.[44]

CO-OPERATIVE COMMUNITIES

The final strand in Owen's endeavour to realise the New Moral World was his attempt to give practical form to his ideas in setting up a variety of co-operative communities. After New Lanark, the first of these was in 1824 in Indiana. Here Owen bought a village covering some 20 000 acres and including a number of industries which had earlier been inhabited by disciples of George Rapp, who had moved from Wurtemberg in 1804 to form the Harmony Society near Pittsburgh. Rapp had established 600 'pious, sober, thrifty and industrious German peasants' who flourished and multiplied and moved to Indiana in 1815, where they called their settlement Harmony. Owen named the village New Harmony and within a year, after public meetings in Washington, some 900 people had arrived. In 1826 a constitution was drawn up. The title of the group was to be the New Harmony Community of Equality. All members were to be considered as one family, and none to be regarded as higher or lower on account of his occupation. All were to have similar food, clothing and education and to live in similar houses. All were to give their best service for the good of all. Each was to work according to his ability, and to receive the necessary food, clothing and shelter. There was to be no discrimination between the value of different kinds of work, nor any buying or selling among the settlers.

After two or three years, however, the community collapsed and Owen suffered substantial financial losses, though New Harmony survived as a scientific and educational centre, guided by his sons. The failure in the original purpose seems to have stemmed from the character of the settlers – previously dissatisfied with their lives, but not selected by Owen nor necessarily sharing his vision and his values. The colony offered no rewards for industry and no penalties for idleness, and the hoped for community of equality and co-operation failed to develop.[45]

Subsequently a number of co-operative settlements were established in Britain but most of them were short lived. One of the most ambitious was the Queenswood community, set up at East Tytherly in Hampshire in 1839. The Universal Society of Rational Religionists provided the capital to buy 533 acres of land and Owen nominated John Finch as governor of the settlement. According to Heaton Aldam, the 'practical director', things got off to a good start.

> Our days are spent in united industry, our evenings in mutual improvement... Our simple meals have the relish of good appetites and the charm of good conversation, and a generous strife pervades us as to who shall most promote the general happiness, and be most obliging and useful. Who that could see us early in the morning, washed and shaved, seated at our books reading or writing, then taking our wholesome meal of the nutritious products of the dairy; waiting after this till the grey mists of morning are dispelled to commence our united labours for the advancement of our delightful colony – who could see all this and say that we lived in a stye?[46]

The reference to 'stye' followed a derogatory newspaper account of the community, but the spirited rebuttal seems to have been over-optimistic. Troubles developed after only a few months. There was opposition from the Church, but more serious was internal dissension among the settlers, who lacked agricultural experience and lived in poor, overcrowded and unhealthy accommodation. The governor resigned, and shortly afterwards so too did the person who replaced him, both finding the job too difficult. Aldam also resigned, and his replacement died. By 1840 quarrels had become acute. Owen was brought in as governor and promptly named the settlement Harmony, and the Co-operative Congress gave money for new buildings, including a Harmony Hall.

In 1843 there were 800 acres under cultivation and 43 residents, though Owen had advised that 260 to 300 were needed if the community were to flourish. The following year there were 94 children in the school, though two-thirds of them were paying fees. But residents were beginning to complain that they had no share in the government of their community and that they had only bread and water for supper. Subscriptions were invited from the public but Queenswood continued to eat up Congress resources, to the growing discontent of local branches. At the Congress of 1844 Owen failed to win election and resigned both as president of the Rational Society and as the governor of Harmony. This led to the appointment of a new board of directors who found the Queenswood finances to be in such a bad way that they were obliged to sell the estate, and the enterprise ended in 1845.

Owen's life and work were a sustained indictment of the social, moral and economic consequences of uncontrolled industrial development. His vision of a finer society whose citizens would live peaceably together in modest material comfort and spiritual and physical well-being, all striving to promote the general happiness, was for him no utopian dream but an achievable future state which would be realised if only men and women would adopt the values he preached and the forms of social organisation he enjoined. As in Barnett's ideal city, there were to be no status distinctions between citizens in Owen's New Moral World; none was to be higher or lower by virtue of occupation, and co-operative labour was to replace competition. All this was to be brought about through education and the provision of useful employment. Like Ruskin after him, Owen refused to measure social progress by economic growth and rejected the doctrines and priorities of the political economists, absorbed with the quantity of the goods that were produced rather than the quality of the goods that were consumed. But, unlike Ruskin, he saw the way to a better society not so much through a kind of work that would allow the development and expression of individual personality but through education which would transform the moral character of mankind and thus all social and personal relationships.

To this end Owen employed a variety of means. Government should be responsible for providing education and useful employment, but the New Moral Order would also emerge through voluntary association in co-operative, self-sufficient communities which would demonstrate the possibility and desirability of a new form of social organisation which would spread throughout the world.Throughout his life he attracted considerable fame and some notoriety, but the experiments in community living were largely unsuccessful, though his insistence on the importance of co-operation and his efforts to turn the idea into a national movement remained a significant influence in later discussion and practice of industrial organisation.

Owen's great success lay in the model village and the schools at New Lanark. The community drew visitors from many nations during his lifetime, and the schools were still flourishing, with children singing and dancing between 7.15 and 8.00 in the mornings, when the local school board was set up in 1872. His interest and experiments in nursery education, moreover, spread to other parts of the country and he was among the most vociferous of the early opponents of uncontrolled factory work for young children.

For some, however, success was too dearly bought – at the price of excessively authoritarian assumptions and practices. At New Lanark Owen introduced a system for daily monitoring of the behaviour of the mill workers on a four-point scale, the results being displayed for public inspection and noted in a book of conduct. 'The act of setting down the numbers in the book of character... might be likened to the supposed recording angel marking the good and bad deeds of poor human nature', he observed. Again like Ruskin, Owen was no democrat and took for granted that men and women needed firm government for their own proper development. Thus he aroused the ire of Cobbett and Jonathon Wooler writing in *Black Dwarf* and castigating Owen's villages as 'pauper barracks', where men, women and children were reduced to automata – fed, clothed and occupied but with no liberty nor hope of anything beyond.[47] A motion to bring Owen's plan to transform society before the Commons in 1821 was lost when it was opposed on religious and economic grounds but also attacked by Lord Londonderry and ridiculed by Hume for its paternal system of government with discipline fit for the poor house but not for a free nation.[48]

In the end, Owen's achievements were limited. He had no practicable programme to bring about his aims other than small-scale experiments in community living which represented withdrawal from national politics and which were in any case largely unsuccessful. Nevertheless, his insistence that government be responsible for providing universal education, decent living conditions and useful occupation for all was the herald of a more generous and egalitarian conception of the rights of citizens and the duties of the state; a high ideal towards which the rich industrial nations have advanced a little way, but which still needs its prophets and its evangelists, as it always will.

There was a fatal weakness in Owen's scheme for the regeneration of mankind; his unshakable belief that a proper ordering of human experience, according to his own plan, would create a perfect race of human beings to people his New Moral World:

> Let the authorities of this age now turn their attention to this subject and they will discover that they have now attained the knowledge of a moral lever by which they can with ease remove ignorance, poverty, disunion, vice, crime, evil passions, and misery from mankind. Place the human race from birth within superior spiritual and moral surroundings, and the evils and sufferings of humanity will be no longer experienced, and will be retained on record only to enhance the pleasure of this new existence for man.[49]

Owen looked for a heaven on earth of his own making, but he dismissed original sin and he ignored the persistent conflict between good and evil through which men and women fashion and re-fashion their lives as their circumstances change, and learn and forget and learn again their responsibilities to one another. That he was not able to transform the world can hardly be matter for surprise. Such huge aspirations are doomed to remain unrealised. Owen's great achievement was to offer to all who would look and listen an example of benevolence, generosity and charity in his own person, and a vision of a society founded on kindness and justice to challenge the economic orthodoxy of his time, towards which men might strive even though they might never reach it.

> He found his contemporaries obsessed by a nightmare; and if he sought to replace it by a dream, the dream was at least generous and humane. There are some who advance step by step, who build by laying stone to stone. There are others who guide their feet by the stars, and dwell in houses not made with hands... a place will be found for Robert Owen amongst those whose dreams have helped to reshape the world.[50]

NOTES

1   Owen, 1857, pp. 16–18.
2   Owen, 1813, 'Fourth Essay on the Formation of Character' in Owen, 1857, Appendix B, p. 56.

3   Owen, 1857, p. 104.
4   *Ibid.*, p. 101.
5   Owen, 1813, 'Third Essay on the Formation of Character' in Owen, 1857, Appendix B, p. 40.
6   Owen, 1857, p. 30.
7   Podmore, 1906, p. 247.
8   Owen, 1857, p. 161.
9   *Ibid.*, p. 163.
10   Himmelfarb, 1984, p. 11.
11   Owen, 1813, 'First Essay on the Formation of Character' in Owen, 1857, Appendix B, p. 18.
12   Podmore, 1906, p. 340.
13   Owen, 1813, 'Fourth Essay on the Formation of Character' in Owen, 1857, Appendix B, p. 76.
14   Owen, 1857, p. 130.
15   Owen, 1813, 'Second Essay on the Formation of Character' in Owen, 1857, Appendix B, p. 22.
16   Owen, 1857, p. 130.
17   *Ibid.*, p. 89.
18   Podmore, 1906, pp. 424–7.
19   *Ibid.*, pp. 453–8.
20   Owen, 1857, p. 200.
21   *Ibid.*, p. 61.
22   Owen, 1813, 'Second Essay on the Formation of Character' in Owen, 1857, Appendix B, p. 27.
23   Podmore, 1906, p. 168.
24   Owen, 1813, 'Second Essay on the Formation of Character' in Owen, 1857, Appendix B, p. 28.
25   Podmore, 1906, p. 170.
26   Baines, Oastler and Cawood, 1918, pp. 7, 8.
27   Owen, 1813, 'Second Essay on the Formation of Character' in Owen, 1857, Appendix B, p. 30.
28   Owen, 1857, p. 130.
29   Owen, 1813, 'Third Essay on the Formation of Character' in Owen, 1857, Appendix B.
30   Owen, 1857, p. 175.
31   *Ibid.*, p. 145.
32   *Ibid.*, p. 106.
33   Podmore, 1906, p. 208.
34   *Ibid.*, p. 77.
35   *Ibid.*, pp. 116–17; Owen, 1813, 'Fourth Essay on the Formation of Character' in Owen, 1857, Appendix B, pp. 73–4.
36   Podmore, 1906, p. 227.
37   Webb and Webb, 1963, Part II.
38   Owen, 1857, p. 168.
39   Podmore, 1906, p. 342.
40   Thompson, W., 1830. Quoted in Podmore, 1906, p. 398.
41   Podmore, 1906, p. 497.
42   *Ibid.*, p. 504.

43   Podmore, 1906, p. 124.
44   *New Moral World*, Vol. IX, p. 87, cited in Podmore, 1906, p. 516.
45   Podmore, 1906, p. 285 *et seq.*
46   *New Moral World*, Vol. VI, p. 943, cited in Podmore, 1906, p. 534.
47   Cited in Podmore, 1906, p. 238.
48   Podmore, 1906, p. 276.
49   Owen, 1857, p. 231.
50   Podmore, 1906, pp. 653, 654.

5 John Ruskin 1819–1900

The essential thing for all creatures is to be made to do right.
(*Essays on Political Economy*)

It is not, truly speaking, the labour that is divided; but the men.
('*The Nature of Gothic*')

Ruskin was born in 1819 and survived until the end of the century, so the years of his teaching and writing encompassed the far briefer lives of T. H Green and Arnold Toynbee. He was half a century younger than Owen, and most of his important work was published well before Samuel Barnett went to Whitechapel. Ruskin was neither philosopher nor social reformer – not, at least, if social reform implies reconstruction of political institutions or of the machinery of government. He was a prophet and a preacher. 'Of all men now alive Ruskin has the best talent for preaching' was Carlyle's judgement, and George Eliot venerated him as one of the greatest teachers of the age who spoke with the inspiration of a Hebrew prophet.[1] 'The works of Ruskin', Collingwood believed, 'have found their way among all classes, and his thoughts, more or less understood, and often unacknowledged, have become a part of the national mind'.[2]

The only child of a prosperous wine merchant, Ruskin's early education fell to his mother, a strict and evangelical puritan with whom he read the Bible daily and who accompanied him when he went to Oxford, taking lodgings where her husband joined her at the weekends. Ruskin's father combined his business enterprise with a love of literature and art, and Turner and Samuel Prout were among the many writers and painters who were regular household guests. The family travelled extensively during the summer, collecting orders for wine but also in search of paintings and drawings and architecture, and the journeys always included visits to romantic scenery in Scotland or the English Lakes or Wales. As the *Dictionary of National Biography* entry points out, Ruskin grew up in an atmosphere that was both puritanical and artistic, influences that shaped all his later life and writing. His early work and interests were in painting and architecture, finding expression in *Modern Painters* and *The Stones of Venice*. Later he turned his moral and aesthetic sensibilities to political economy and 'the condition of the people' question, winning fame with his impassioned writing and eloquent public lectures delivered throughout the country.

Ruskin inherited a substantial fortune from his father, which he used for charitable and philanthropic purposes. He supported many social experiments including Octavia Hill's purchase and management of decent dwellings for the poor, work schemes for the unemployed, and the establishing of the Guild of St George – a trust to develop agricultural, industrial and artistic cooperatives and settlements. He revived and encouraged crafts and handwork in Cumberland, in Langdale and around his house in Coniston, which survive and flourish to the present day.

In 1870 he went to Oxford as Slade Professor of Fine Arts, founding a School of Drawing that was named after him and where he stayed until obliged to resign through ill health. It was also at Oxford that Ruskin persuaded a group of young men, including Arnold Toynbee, to take part in a road mending scheme at Hinksey. The venture, dismissed by Milner as 'Ruskin's road mending craze' seems not to have produced very effective repairs. But for Ruskin it was an attempt to demonstrate the dignity of labour, to insist that manual and intellectual work should complement and enrich one another, and to enlist the rich in the service of the poor. One of the greatest evils that he denounced was the brutalising character of industrial labour and the widespread indifference to it displayed by the wealthy.

The development of a civilised society where men and women might live in dignity and happiness meant, above all, the spreading of right values or, as he repeatedly insisted, the putting into practice of Christian doctrine: 'The essential thing for all creatures is to be made to do right.'[3] But this true felicity of the human race must come through individual, not public effort.[4] In this sense Ruskin was a foremost exponent of the nineteenth century moral tradition exemplified by Green and Toynbee and Barnett. The entitlements and responsibilities of citizenship turned largely on the relationships between individual people – between men and women, rich and poor, master and man, the learned and the ignorant, manual and intellectual workers – and less on the relations of people to government, though Ruskin did reserve important duties for the public authorities. For the most part, however, he left it to others to decide the arrangements needed to realise his vision of the good society. Although his proposals on education and on the regulation of marriage implied intervention by both church and state, Ruskin was generally critical of the willingness or ability of the church to play any part in moral or social enlightenment, and was

equally gloomy and sceptical about the efficacy of secular government. Here, as P. D. Anthony remarks, lies a fundamental difference
between Marx and Ruskin, two of the most powerful voices raised
against the evils of nineteenth century capitalism. For Marx those
evils would eventually be resolved through socialism, but Ruskin
could not look forward to any such happy future. Socialism, on the
contrary, was a disaster: 'Simply chaos – a chaos towards which the
believers in modern political economy are fast tending and from which
I am trying to save them'.[5]

What, then, were the social and economic circumstances that denied
the possibility of decent civilised life? What did the idea and practice
of citizenship mean, for Ruskin? What kind of society would foster it,
and how might it be brought about? One of the greatest evils of
nineteenth century Britain was the degrading character of industrial
labour, the outcome of increasingly mechanised production and the
overriding desire for profit of the merchant class who, in their eager
search for gain, were 'betrayed by the plausible impiety of the modern
economists, telling us that "To do the best for ourselves is finally to
do the best for others".'[6] The first principle of government had thus
become a policy of Let Alone, and the practical religion the worship
of the Goddess of Getting-on. The upper classes, Ruskin declared,
heedless of the misery of the poor on whom their wealth depended,
devoted themselves to accumulating material possessions. Such a
path, he warned, would lead to catastrophe.[7]

The significance of work is fundamental in Ruskin's social philosophy. Rightly ordered it allowed the production of necessary or
useful goods, enabled the workman to develop his skill and ability
and was a source of satisfaction and enjoyment. Moreover it was the
only legitimate basis of wealth. Nor was Ruskin thinking of the workman as belonging to a particular social class as commonly assumed.
'There is a working class – strong and happy, – among both rich and
poor; there is an idle class – weak, wicked, and miserable, – among
both rich and poor'.[8]

The distinction between the industrious and the idle was matched
by the distinction between work and play, the first 'a thing done
because it ought to be done, and with a determined end', the second
'an exertion of body or mind, made to please ourselves, and with no
determined end'.[9] The games the playing class in England played were
making money, hunting and shooting, dressing – the ladies' game –,
literature, art and war. But these games were paid for in deadly work
somewhere: 'The jewel-cutter, whose sight fails over the diamonds; the

weaver whose arm fails over the web; the iron-forger, whose breath fails before the furnace . . . . who have all the work, and none of the play'. This state of affairs represented a distinction which was unnecessary and must in time, and by all honest men's consent, be abolished:

> Men will be taught that an existence of play, sustained by the blood of other creatures, is a good existence for gnats and jelly-fish; but not for men: that neither days, nor lives, can be made holy or noble by doing nothing in them: that the best prayer at the beginning of a day is that we may not lose its moments; and the best grace before meat, the consciousness that we have justly earned our dinner.[10]

It was the 'degradation of the operative into a machine' with no pleasure in his work, rather than hunger or 'mortified pride', which led the mass of the nations everywhere into a destructive, revolutionary struggle for freedom, Ruskin claimed. And he went on to castigate the 'great civilised invention of the division of labour':

> Only we give it a false name. It is not, truly speaking, the labour that is divided; but the men: – divided into mere segments of men – broken into small fragments and crumbs of life; so that all the little piece of intelligence that is left in a man is not enough to make a pin, or a nail, but exhausts itself in making the point of a pin or the head of a nail. Now it is a good and desirable thing, truly, to make many pins in a day; but if we could only see with what crystal sand their points were polished, – sand of human soul, much to be magnified before it can be discerned for what it is – we should think there might be some loss in it also. And the great cry that rises from all our manufacturing cities, louder than their furnace blast, is all in very deed for this, – that we manufacture everything there except men; we blanch cotton, and strengthen steel, and refine sugar, and shape pottery; but to brighten, to strengthen, to refine, or to form a single living spirit, never enters into our estimate of advantages. And all the evil to which that cry is urging our myriads can be met only in one way: not by teaching nor preaching, for to teach them is but to show them their misery, and to preach to them, if we do nothing more than preach, is to mock at it. It can be met only by a right understanding, on the part of all classes, of what kinds of labour are good for men, raising them, and making them happy; by a determined sacrifice of such convenience, or beauty, or cheapness as is to be got only by the degradation of the workman;

and by equally determined demand for the products and results of healthy and ennobling labour.[11]

Thus, it was not the geographical separation of the classes, nor the huge social and economic inequalities, that represented for Ruskin the greatest evil. It was that men should feel their souls 'withering within them . . . their whole being sunk into an unrecognised abyss, to be counted off into a heap of mechanism numbered with its wheels, and weighed with its hammer strokes: this, nature bade not, – this, God blesses not, – this, humanity for no long time is able to endure'.[12]

Here was a concept of alienation echoing Marx. The brutalising character of much manual labour was the outcome of uncontrolled industrial development, exacerbated by popular doctrines which emphasised competition and the profit motive as the driving force for individual gain and the accumulation of national wealth. Ruskin was scathing in his denunciation of the 'modern soi-disant science of political economy' that did not acknowledge the importance of moral behaviour and that assumed that the wealth of nations was properly measured by what they produced, rather than by what they consumed. All right relations between masters and operatives and all their best interests, Ruskin maintained, ultimately depended on affection,[13] illustrating his point by referring to domestic work. The laws of competition would suggest that a wise master would extract from his servant the maximum work for the least wages that would keep him in his job. But, in fact, if the master had regard to the well-being of his servant, tried to make his work beneficial to him and to advance his interests, then 'the real amount of work ultimately done, or the good rendered, by the person so cared for, will indeed be the greatest possible'.[14]

The pernicious influence of a political economy that refused to recognise the moral dimension in commercial activity was enshrined in the direction, attacked also by Owen, to 'Buy in the cheapest market and sell in the Dearest'. Not only were traders degraded, Ruskin declared, by continually thinking about their profits;[15] more importantly, the wider human costs of buying and selling were ignored. 'What made your market cheap?', he demanded, and 'What made it dear?'. Wealth might be indicative of 'faithful industries, progressive energies, and productive ingenuities', or of 'mortal luxury, merciless tyranny, ruinous chicane'.[16]

Such criticisms form the elements of Ruskin's more general assault on what he considered to be the prevailing views of the political economists – that national wealth could be satisfactorily measured by the quantity and market value of goods produced. This was a false assumption for two reasons. First, the quality of goods mattered as much as the quantity and, second, the object of all production was consumption and the important questions were about the purposes production served and how goods were used. Twenty people, Ruskin asserted, could gain money for one who could use it, and the vital question for individual and nation was not 'how much do they make?' but 'to what purpose do they spend?'[17] In posing this question, Ruskin was insisting that wealth would not be calculated by economists' sums, only by counting the well-being of people. 'There is no wealth but Life', he proclaimed:

> That country is the richest which nourishes the greatest number of noble and happy human beings; that man is the richest who, having perfected the functions of his own life to the utmost, has also the widest helpful influence, both personal, and by means of his possessions, over the lives of others'.[18]

The desire for a society of noble and happy human beings would lead Ruskin into strange paths. But the power of his writing lies less in his practical proposals for a better world than in the denunciation of poverty and degradation and of prevailing ways of thought that produced, or at any rate tolerated, them. Some of the worst consequences of policies of Let Alone were apparent, Ruskin maintained, in America, whose people set their trust in liberty and equality, 'of which I detest the one and deny the possibility of the other'. It was the fashion, he said, to talk of the failure of republican institutions in America. But there had never been in that country any such thing as an institution, nor as a *res publica* – only a multitudinous *res privata* – every man for himself.

> There you may see competition, and the 'law of demand and supply' in beautiful and unhindered operation. Lust of wealth, and trust in it; vulgar faith in magnitude and multitude, instead of nobleness; besides . . . perpetual self-contemplation, issuing in passionate vanity; total ignorance of the finer and higher arts . . . and the discontent of energetic minds unoccupied, frantic with hope of uncomprehended change, and progress they know not whither; these are the things that have failed America.[19]

The insidious doctrines of political economy played a large part in what Ruskin saw as the demoralisation of the rich, offering a justification for the consuming preoccupation with profit. The upper classes of Europe, insensible, he claimed, to suffering, uncleanness and crime, were responsible for sin and dishonoured by the foulness rotting at their thresholds. The crimes and pains of London were a disgrace to the whole body politic. The substitution of 'money power' for the power of the aristocracy brought imminent danger of war and mob violence in England, and the danger was heightened by the very products of industrial advance, 'by the monstrous forms of vice and selfishness which the appliances of recent wealth, and of vulgar mechanical art, make possible to millions'.[20]

Not only did the deceiving arguments of political economy encourage an absorption in material wealth that offended against justice and humanity, they also taught 'systematic disobedience to the first principles of its [the nation's] professed religion'.

> The writings which we (verbally) esteem as divine, not only denounce the love of money as the source of all evil, and as an idolatory abhorred of the Deity, but declare mammon service to be the accurate and irreconcilable opposite of God's service: and, whenever they speak of riches absolute, and poverty absolute, declare woe to the rich, and blessing to the poor. Whereupon we forthwith investigate a science of becoming rich, as the shortest road to national prosperity.[21]

The neglect of the precepts of religion among women was especially damaging, for on their shoulders, Ruskin averred, lay responsibility both for unjustifiable war and for unnoticed poverty. He for one, he claimed, would fain have joined 'the cadence of hammer-strokes that should beat swords into ploughshares', but that could not be because women were too thoughtless of matters beyond their immediate circle. If war, instead of unroofing peasants' houses and ravaging their fields, merely broke the china on drawing room tables; or if the upper class women of civilised Europe vowed to wear black during the course of any cruel war, with no jewel nor ornament and no excuse for prettiness, then no war would last a week.[22] 'The Bible tells you to dress plainly, – and you are mad for finery; the Bible tells you to have pity on the poor, – and you crush them under your carriage-wheels.'[23]

Ruskin's censure of women extended to a more general attack on the widespread failure to apply ethical and religious principles to commercial life. He deplored the indifference to dishonesty and cruelty in the pursuit of wealth. The Bible denounced the oppression of the poor but oppressed they were, and the likeliest form of oppression was the careless ignorance of the rich. Nothing was more ludicrous or more melancholy, Ruskin observed, than the way people talked about the morals of labourers:

> Be assured, my good man, – you say to him, – that if you work steadily for ten hours a day all your life long, and if you drink nothing but water, or the very mildest beer, and live on very plain food, and never lose your temper, and go to church every Sunday, and always remain content in the position in which Providence has placed you, and never grumble, nor swear; and always keep your clothes decent, and rise early, and use every opportunity of improving yourself, you will get on very well, and never come to the parish.[24]

The oppression of the poor was especially marked in the treatment of the supposedly undeserving, in the ruin spread by speculation by those intent on getting rich without work, and in the insistence on cheap goods whose price was less than the labour needed to produce them. 'Whenever we buy such goods, remember we are stealing somebody's labour'.[25] Whenever men endeavoured to make money hastily and permitted themselves to spend it luxuriously without regard to how far they were misguiding the labour of others, they were causing human deaths for their own benefit or pleasure. The alternatives were stark; 'the choice given to every man born into this world is, simply, whether he will be a labourer or an assassin'.[26]

Here, then, is some indication of Ruskin's conception of the society in which he lived and his understanding of its problems. We can now turn to his ideal state; the political and social institutions and the relationships between its people – rich and poor, men and women, master and servant, hand worker and brain worker – where the responsibilities and rights of all citizens would be properly observed. Although Ruskin's powerful prose and resounding rhetoric is most compelling when he attacks the reprehensible behaviour of the privileged classes and the misery of the poor of late nineteenth century England, yet there emerges a fairly clear picture of the kind of society he wished to see. It was a society founded on justice, reverence and compassion: justice in arrangements where the natural differences between men found their expression in appropriate divisions of labour and of political responsibility; reverence in the admiration and respect for 'whatever was most worthy in human deeds and human passion'; and compassion in the protection and succour of the weak and the spurning of shameful, cruel or cowardly things. The

French revolutionary vision did not appeal to Ruskin. Freedom he thought dangerous and equality impossible; only fraternity survived, albeit within a hierarchical and authoritarian, if benevolent, state.

Fundamental to Ruskin's conception of the good society and of the practice of citizenship is his understanding of the meaning of work.[27] Although man's labour had a utilitarian aim, it was an essentially moral activity. Its value rested on the nature and quality of the goods produced, which must be neither harmful nor shoddy, and on the actual experience of work which should afford satisfaction and enjoyment, as well as a fair wage.

The wage, however, was secondary. It mattered little ultimately, Ruskin claimed, how much the labourer was paid but it mattered greatly what he was compelled to make.[28] The object of political economy was to produce those material things that sustained and comforted the body, exercised rightly the affections and formed the intelligence; and that meant land, houses, furniture, food and medicine, books and works of art. Land carefully tended, with unsightliness removed and living creatures protected, was the most precious property human beings possessed, Ruskin insisted.[29] In the good society government would recognise the overwhelming importance of consumption and would foster those forms of work that would produce things 'good for life'. So far as the labourer's immediate profit was concerned, Ruskin pointed out, it mattered little whether he was employed to grow peaches or to forge bombshells, but the likely use of those products mattered a great deal: 'the difference, to him, is final, whether when his child is ill, I walk into his cottage and give it the peach, or drop the shell down his chimney, and blow his roof off.'[30]

Elsewhere Ruskin pays more attention to the level of wages. The workman should have enough to allow him gradually to enrich his home 'with more delicate and substantial comforts'; to save for his old age so that he might be independent of superannuation and sick pay that employers should provide; and to start his children 'in a rank of life equal to his own'. If wages could not meet these demands they were too low.[31] But at the other end of the social scale rewards for work might also be inappropriate. One of the most important conditions of a healthy economy, Ruskin believed, was that the property and incomes of the upper classes should be restrained to remove the temptation to devote too much time to the pursuit of wealth. Large fortunes could not in any case be honestly made by the work of any one man's head or hand. They depended on command over the labour of other men, which was then used for personal profit; or on 'treasure trove' or inheritance; or on speculation which Ruskin dismissed as a disreputable form of commercial gambling.[32] A limit on incomes for the idle classes would be no hardship: 'Let there be honorary titles, if people like them, but let there be no honorary incomes'.[33]

Those who reached the defined limit, Ruskin suggested, should withdraw from commercial activity and devote themselves to public service. They might form the legislative body of the Commons, and could receive honours to replace the unworthy satisfaction of being supposed richer than others 'which to many men is the principal charm of their wealth'.[34] And law should govern not only the amount of wealth and property that could be held, but also its use: land should not be wantonly allowed to run to waste, streams should not be poisoned by persons through whose properties they passed nor air rendered unwholesome.[35] Here Ruskin emerges as an early sympathiser with the Friends of the Earth whose ideas only gained popular respectability and political credence 100 years later.

While rewards for work were to be controlled, labour receiving a sufficiency and the profits of the rich restrained, Ruskin also believed, following Locke, that it was the experience and product of work that established the lawful basis of wealth and the proper divisions between rich and poor. Those who worked – by hand or brain – should receive the fair price for their labour, and the first necessity of social life was to enforce the law 'that he should keep who has JUSTLY EARNED'.[36] Nevertheless, the object was not the reward but the task. It was 'physically impossible', Ruskin declared, for a well-educated, intellectual or brave man to make money his chief object. Everybody, quite properly, liked to make money. A good soldier was glad of his pay, but mainly wished to do his fighting well. A good clergyman welcomed his pew rents and his baptismal fees, but his first interest was to preach and to baptise. A doctor was pleased to have his earnings but on the whole desired to cure the sick and, if a good doctor, would rather cure his patient and lose his fee than kill his patient and get it. But, Ruskin proclaimed, whenever money was the principal object with either man or nation it was both got ill and spent ill, and when it was not the principal object it and all other things were well got and well spent.[37]

The importance of work lay not only in the production of useful things at a fair price. (Ruskin assumed that dishonest manufacture, the making and selling of bad goods, was a form of theft and should be duly punished by law). It was fundamental for well-being in another sense – in providing enjoyment in developing talents and exercising skill. There were three tests of wise work: it should be honest, useful and cheerful.[38] And the task should be fitted to the character of the worker; rough work was to be done by rough men and gentle work by gentle men.[39] What justice required was that different kinds of work be appropriately allocated so that all men were in their right place. Ruskin was well aware that the existing state of affairs was very far removed from any such arrangement. The occupations that men followed were largely a matter of chance, though only too readily regarded by the comfortably off as a matter of providence.

> You well-to-do people . . . will go to Divine Service . . . and your little children will have their tight little Sunday boots on, and lovely little Sunday feathers in their hats; and you'll think, complacently and piously, how lovely they look . . . Then you will come to the poor little crossing sweeper, got up also – in its Sunday dress, – the dirtiest rags it has, – that it may beg the better: you will give it a penny, and think how good you are, and how good God is to prefer *your* child to the crossing sweeper, and to bestow on it a divine hat, feather, and boots, and the pleasure of giving pence, instead of begging for them.[40]

Christian justice, Ruskin declared, continuing his savage parody, was strangely mute or spoke only in a whisper which few heard, asking why the little crossing sweeper should not have a hat with a feather and go to church on Sundays. And the reply from the rich was that everybody should remain content in the position in which God had placed them. But that, Ruskin insisted, was the heart of the question: 'Did Providence put them in that position, or did you? You knock a man into a ditch and then you tell him to remain content in the "position in which Providence has placed him". That's modern Christianity.'[41]

Sceptical about the responsibility of Providence for existing social hierarchies, Ruskin had considerable faith in the power of a properly organised education system to sort people into their appropriate places. But he also recognised that even if justice were to prevail there would remain rough work to be done. So the question was how those who did it should be 'comforted, redeemed and rewarded'. First, there must be suitable arrangements for selection. Men only worked well and with satisfaction, Ruskin asserted, if they believed they were doing what they should and that they were 'in their place',

so labourers, who did the 'hard' work should be as carefully recruited
as anyone else. Men were enlisted for the labour that kills, Ruskin
declared, the labour of war; they were trained, fed, dressed and
praised for that. Let them also be trained, fed, dressed and praised
for the labour that feeds.[42]

Second, wholly manual occupations were nevertheless degrading.
Rough work 'takes the life out of us', so there should be ample
opportunity for rest and for play – though the play must be wholesome:

> not in theatrical gardens, with tin flowers and gas sunshine, and
> girls dancing because of their misery; but in true gardens, with real
> flowers, and real sunshine, and children dancing because of their
> gladness.[43]

Working men should have as comfortable firesides to sit at – when
they had time to sit – as anybody else, and as good books to read –
when they had time to read – for it was dangerous to separate labour
and thought; 'it is only by labour that thought can be made healthy,
and only by thought that labour can be made happy, and the two
cannot be separated with impunity'[44]

However, although it might be possible to lighten the burden of
manual labour in these various ways, some 'foul and mechanical'
work would necessarily remain. It was the mark of a noble race that
such work be reduced to a minimum. Persons in 'higher stations of life'
should diminish their demand for such work by every means in their
power, the first principle of political economy being to live with as few
wants as possible in so far as wants involve the degradation of others:

> See that you take the plainest you can furnish yourself with – that
> you waste or wear nothing vainly; – and that you employ no man
> in furnishing you with any useless luxury.[45]

Even with mechanical work reduced to a minimum, however, there
still remained the problem of its distribution. If it could not be given
to slaves, such work should take the form of punishment or proba-
tion, the dangerous and painful jobs being allotted to criminals. At the
same time, much labouring and agricultural work – rough but pre-
sumably wholesome in Ruskin's view – should fall to the lot of the
upper classes because it was necessary for 'repose and mental func-
tioning', and any remaining inferior labour should be done by those
who were fit for nothing better.[46]

Such an organisation of work represented Ruskin's endeavour to match occupation and character. A hierarchy there must be, for however perfect the education system infinite differences would remain between men. Some natures tended to the 'lordly' and some to the 'servile' and it was essential to separate the two, 'since the lordly part is only in a state of profitableness while ruling, and the servile only in a state of redeemableness while serving'.[47] Thus, while the right organisation of work was fundamental to Ruskin's conception of a good society, the organising principles themselves reflected his particular convictions about the significance of equality and the nature of freedom.

In his famous discussion of citizenship, T. H. Marshall gives a prominent place to the growth of political rights to vote and to serve on national and local government bodies, developing in Britain through the nineteenth century and paving the way for the growth of social rights through the following 50 years. But in Ruskin's view contemporary agitation for political reform was misguided and dangerous. It threatened his ideal of a tranquil and stable society in which all men and women had their ordained place by challenging the rather special definition of freedom and the thoroughgoing denial of equality on which it was based.

Misgivings about the consequences of more democracy were, of course, endemic in the nineteenth century, part of the long struggle for a wider franchise. Toynbee welcomed the extension of the suffrage in 1867[48] but feared that the political developments that raised men 'from serfs to citizens' were threatened by the industrial developments and division of labour that 'exhausted energy and dulled intelligence'. To devote scanty leisure to intellectual exertion required extraordinary effort, and there was a danger that as working men became more prosperous they might become 'less eager about political and social questions'. This made the education of the citizen in his duties as a citizen indispensable.[49] In similar vein, Barnett was apprehensive that the Labour Party, though taking politics seriously as a matter that concerned 'the daily bread of the people' yet represented workmen who were 'scant of life', lacking the interests and visions and hopes that came from knowledge, and prone to drink and gambling. Like William Morris he believed education essential; otherwise labour in power would be set on its own material advance and careless of the common good, exalting rights over duties just as did the propertied class. 'In its ignorance of the principles of progress . . . it would probably drive the Ship of the State on the rocks. The Labour Party . . . must have knowledge.'[50]

While Barnett put his faith in knowledge, Ruskin asserted that the essential thing for all creatures was to be made to do right.[51] His was a Platonic conception of freedom, a condition in the individual – or in the state – where the 'higher' or rational faculties controlled the disorderly appetites and emotions. The exercise of compulsion by one person over another was not in itself wrong – a principle that would no doubt win agreement today though some of Ruskin's interpretations might be controversial. He maintained, for example, that it was better and kinder to flog a man to his work than to leave him idle until he robbed and then flog him afterwards. The preference for prevention rather than cure has become a familiar platitude of present day social policy, though twentieth century British opinion might be less ready to accept flogging.

Ruskin's understanding of the nature of freedom, however, seems to open the way to the most oppressive of republics. A man's right or claim upon his fellows had two aspects, he declared: a claim not to be hindered from doing what he should; and a claim to be hindered from doing what he should not.[52] Thus, 'common insolences' and 'talk of equality' among the people would pass away as they were 'raised and purified', and evidence of such elevation would lie in added power of discerning and patience in submitting to their 'true counsellors and governors'.[53] In considering the virtues of different forms of government Ruskin distinguished between monarchy, oligarchy and democracy or republicanism, the latter often confused with anarchy, he claimed – thinking perhaps of his own predispositions. None was to be praised or condemned as such, but all were good in so far as they attained the one vital necessity of policy; 'that the wise and kind, few or many, shall govern the unwise and unkind'.[54]

So Ruskin was no democrat, and regarded the extension of the franchise with the deepest distaste. In particular, it would be impossible to elect a good government on the principle of one man one vote. At the very least, discrimination was needed so that more votes could be allotted to age and wisdom (one at 20, ten at 50) and to wealth (one at £100 a year, ten at £1000 – provided wealth were the reward, as it should be, for industry and sagacity), more for masters than for men, more for holders of national office, and so on.[55] In the then state of education and knowledge among labourers, however, any further parliamentary rights would be useless. In one of his letters to the working men of Sunderland, Ruskin made short shrift of their political ambitions:

You are all agape, my friends, for this mighty privilege of having your opinions represented in Parliament. The concession might be desirable, – at all events courteous, – if only it were quite certain that you had any opinions to represent. But have you? Are you agreed on any single thing that you systematically want? . . . You know well enough that there is not one of these questions, I do not say which you can answer, but which you have ever *thought* of answering . . . your voices are not worth a rat's squeak, either in Parliament or out of it, till you have some ideas to utter with them.[56]

Thus, political representation, Ruskin believed, would be futile. What mattered was debate and co-operative effort among the workmen themselves. 'You have perfect liberty and power', he told them, 'to talk over and establish for yourselves whatever laws you please'.[57] And when they had decided what they wished to be done, they would find that not only could they do it themselves without the intervention of Parliament, but that 'nobody *but* yourselves can do it'.[58]

This readiness to dispense with the parliamentary process stems from Ruskin's fundamental conviction that individual and social well-being is in the end far more heavily dependent on individual attitudes and behaviour than on the activities of government. The state must provide and indeed compel education, and must guarantee work and a decent maintenance in old age. But once education and training arrangements had enabled people to move into jobs appropriate for them, the qualities of citizenship would be best expressed in striving to perfect the life chosen, or which circumstances had decreed. 'Thus, I think the object of a workman's ambition should not be to become a master; but to attain daily more subtle and exemplary skill in his own craft'.[59] If laws were 'inconsistent with present circumstances', workmen should not 'make a noise' about them nor 'call meetings in parks' about them, but keep them in mind and sight as 'objects of patient purpose and future achievement by peaceful strength.' Change would come if workmen were steadfastly true to themselves and to all men, but 'No political constitution ennobles knaves'.[60]

Quite apart from the limited efficacy of government action in advancing well-being, the natural superiority of the upper classes, Ruskin maintained, made it fitting that they should rule, keep order among and teach their inferiors, endeavouring, however, to 'raise them always to the nearest level with themselves'.[61] Corruption might occur, Ruskin conceded, if those who ought to be rulers and guides sought only their own pleasure and advantage. But the best hope of breaking the tyranny of a corrupt aristocracy was 'patience and strength of private conduct'. For corrupt as aristocratic institutions might be, they were infinitely preferable to those of the Americans who set their trust in liberty and equality, the one detestable and the other impossible; who as a nation were wholly undesirous of rest and incapable of it, discontented with what they were, yet having no ideal of anything which they desired to become, 'as the tide of the troubled sea, when it *cannot* rest'.[62]

Ruskin's denial to working men of the freedom to govern themselves is entwined with his insistence that inequality is part of the natural and proper ordering of human existence. Provided that wages were sufficient, workers should not be enticed into the hope of changing their condition, so becoming discontented with their existing circumstances. Even if a rise in social rank were possible for all well-conducted persons, it would not make them happier. Education should be valued for itself alone, not as a means of 'getting on in the world but a means of staying pleasantly in your place there'.[63] For some, indeed, greater freedom or greater equality would be seriously damaging. The nature of slavery, Ruskin alleged, was commonly misunderstood. It was not a political institution, but rather 'an inherent, natural and eternal inheritance of a large portion of the human race – to whom the more you give of their own will, the more slaves they will make themselves'.[64]

Nevertheless a duty rested with the upper classes to set a good example to the lower orders, outside as well as inside Parliament. Ruskin refers to a letter he had received from the wife of a village rector who was troubled because it was the men with the highest wages in summer who came to his door destitute in winter having spent their money in the tavern parlour 'ladling port wine not out of bowls but out of buckets'. But who taught them, Ruskin demanded, and went on to recall his own first college supper as a freshman, where the diners helped themselves with ladles not from buckets but from bowls as large as buckets, and where he, having poured ladles of punch into his waistcoat rather than down his throat, helped to carry four of his fellow students head first down the stairs and home: 'we find fault with our peasantry for having been too docile, and profited too shrewdly by our tuition'.[65]

In particular, merchants and employers would behave with total honour and rectitude in Ruskin's ideal state. The obligations of citizenship would require them to produce perfect goods at the cheapest price using methods of production most beneficial to employees. The master must become a father to the youths working under him, whom he should treat as he would his own sons. Merchants tended to lack respect, Ruskin said, because they were assumed to act selfishly. But the true merchant could be just as honourable as any member of the other four great intellectual professions who might on occasion be called upon to die for his country. The soldier would die rather than leave his post in battle, the pastor rather than teach falsehood, the physician rather than leave his post in plague, the lawyer rather than countenance injustice. So the manufacturer in any commercial crisis or distress would 'take the suffering of it with his men', and even take more for himself – 'as a father would in a famine, shipwreck, or battle, sacrifice himself for his son'.[66]

It should never be assumed by the well-to-do that the condition of the poor was just, or their own lives beyond reproach, Ruskin warned. Someday perhaps, he suggested approvingly, we might pay our ploughman a little more and our lawyer a little less. While there must always be 'captains of work', there was a wide difference between being captains, or governors, and taking all the 'treasure'.[67] 'It is the merest insolence of selfishness to preach contentment to a labourer who gets thirty shillings a week, while we suppose an active and plotting covetousness to be meritorious in a man who has three thousand a year'.[68] Thus substantial inequalities were an unavoidable feature of Ruskin's good society, but they were inequalities which carried with them inescapable responsibilities which bound all citizens together. It is a conception of citizenship where personal duty and social obligation are the forces that shape social relationships and preserve social order and where the resulting harmony owes little to the state. Ruskin summed up his creed in an address to the Royal Academy in 1869:

All land that is waste and ugly, you must redeem into ordered fruitfulness; all ruin, desolateness, imperfectness of hut or habitation, you must do away with; and throughout every village and city of your English dominion, there must not be a hand that cannot find a helper, nor a heart that cannot find a comforter.[69]

The church, however, had a very important part to play in regulating social behaviour as well as in spreading the faith. One of Ruskin's more aberrant proposals was that a Christian state should have bishops or overseers for every hundred or so families to watch over both their interests and their conduct so that neither 'unknown want' nor 'unrecognised crime' could occur. Help and observation should not be officious and intervention should be limited by law. The overseers were to be not only pastors but biographers preparing public records to indicate which families might receive public honours. Ruskin hoped that such chronicles of worthy and unworthy events would discourage crime and stimulate good conduct, though nothing should be recorded against the wish of the family head unless the law were broken. Thus the everyday activities of citizens would be governed by a highly developed sense of moral responsibility to work honestly and honourably, to show kindness, compassion and respect to others, well-doing encouraged and wrong-doing discouraged by the benevolent inquisition of the bishops. For Ruskin, effectual advancement towards the 'true felicity of the human race' must be by individual not public effort. Certain laws might guide such advancement but the measure and law first to be determined were those of every man's home.[70]

There did remain, however, a fundamental role for the state in determining the laws which would establish the circumstances which would allow such social behaviour to thrive. The secular government must provide education and training, it must prevent or punish all forms of theft, it must protect property and ensure its proper use, it must safeguard and develop happy and healthy family life through the regulation of marriage and it must support its citizens in old age.

Education and health came first: 'I hold it for indispensable', Ruskin declared, 'that the final duty of a state is to see that every child born therein shall be well housed, clothed, fed and educated, till it attain years of discretion'.[71] Such a huge commitment would require, he acknowledged, a degree of governmental authority over the people undreamt in England when he was writing. There was a 'curious feeling', Ruskin noted, against educational law; an assumption that government should not interfere with liberty until people had done wrong. But this was misguided: 'Make your educational laws strict and your criminal ones may be gentle; but leave youth its liberty and you will have to dig dungeons for age'.[72] And he continued with an eloquent call for early state action:

> for the yoke of youth, if you know how to hold it, may be of silken thread; and there is sweet chime of silver bells at the bridle rein; but for the captivity of age, you must forge the iron fetter, and cast the passing bell.[73]

True education, for Ruskin, lay in the development of sensibility – in the perception of beauty, fitness and rightness – and of the will. Science was not education; 'you do not educate a man by telling him what he knew not, but by making him what he was not'.[74] Education was an experience which moulded the inmost emotions and values of men's souls, its aim to make people not merely do but enjoy the right things.[75] This transformation might be achieved, Ruskin thought, by teaching the laws of health and the mental graces. Schools would have an Owenite character; they would be in the country in the fresh air, giving instruction in riding and running, exercises in offence and defence and lessons in music. Reverence, the first of the graces, would be taught by masters whom children could not but love and respect and from whom they would learn about the most noble human deeds and achievements. The second of the graces, compassion, would be learned by the equal weight placed on the shame of cruel as of cowardly actions. And thirdly, children would be shown the virtue of truth – of spirit, word, thought and sight.[76]

The other principal subjects of education should be history, natural science and mathematics, and then every child should learn 'the calling by which it is to live'. Every child, too, should learn to work finely with his hands so that among the middle class much house furniture would be made by the master and his sons, 'with much furtherance of their general health and peace of mind, and increase of innocent domestic pride and pleasure, and to the extinction of a great deal of vulgar upholstery and other mean handicraft'.[77]

What education was powerless to do, in Ruskin's view, was create more equality or turn every man into a gentleman. On the contrary, just as Michael Young a hundred years later satirised the perils of meritocracy, Ruskin gave dire warning of the destructive divisions that would mark a meritocratic society. The lower orders, he said, desired education because they thought it would make them upper orders and do away with social distinctions. Nothing of the kind:

> They will be mightily astonished, when they really get it, to find that it is on the contrary, the fatallest of all discerners and enforcers of distinctions; piercing, even to the division of the joints and marrow, to find out wherein your body and soul are less, or greater, than other bodies and souls, and to sign deed of separation with unequivocal seal.[78]

But if education were not to enable men to move into higher positions, would it not make those obliged to remain in unpleasant

jobs all the more wretched? Ruskin was very clear that such arguments could never justify withholding educational opportunities: 'it is
a very profound state of slavery, to be kept, myself, low in the fore-
head, that I may not dislike low work'.[79] Education was to develop
men's faculties and sensibilities and prepare them for employment,
but Ruskin had little fear that the process would lead to a dearth of
recruits for the more disagreeable mechanical jobs. He believed pro-
foundly in natural inequalities among men which would ensure sufficient labour for whatever rough and dangerous work was
unavoidable. It must, of course, be properly organised. Mechanical
labour must be made more palatable by mixing it with brain work,
limiting the hours spent on it, guaranteeing fair wages and reducing
the demand for its products. Criminals, and those who were fit for
nothing better should be selected for the very worst jobs.

Government responsibilities were not limited to education and
training for work; they extended to the provision of jobs and the
maintenance of employment. Workshops should be set up 'for the
production and sale of every necessary of life, and for the exercise of
every useful art'[80] which would compete though not interfere with
private enterprise and where the unemployed would be occupied. If
incapable through ignorance they would be taught, if through sickness
they would be tended, if found objecting to work they would be
compelled to do the more painful and degrading forms of necessary
toil, in mines and other dangerous places.[81]

After education and work, it was the duty of the state to regulate
marriage. This Ruskin saw as the foundation of all moral law. There
was no licentiousness so mortal as licentiousness in marriage. Young
men and women should be allowed to marry only when they could
show they had lived a modest and virtuous life and possessed the skill
in their proper handicraft and in household economy which would
enable them to teach and maintain their children honourably. Girls
should not receive permission before they were 17 nor youths before
they were 21, and public festivals with dancing and music should
mark the giving of consent. Every couple should be able to claim
income from the state, if needed, for the first seven years of marriage
but those well endowed through inheritance should receive a lesser
sum so that in the beginning of the 'war of life' rich and poor would
not be separated too sharply.[82]

Finally, the state had a part to play at the end of life, providing
'comfort and home' for the old and destitute. There would be no
stigma in Ruskin's poor relief in old age – no withholding of state

help to induce individuals or families to provide for themselves – no shameful incarceration in the workhouse. A labourer served his country with his spade, Ruskin asserted, just as a man in the middle ranks of life served it with sword or pen. If service were less and therefore wages in health less, then the reward when health were broken might be less – but not less honourable:

> and it ought to be quite as natural and straightforward a matter for a labourer to take his pension from his parish, because he has deserved well of his parish, as for a man in higher rank to take his pension from his country, because he has deserved well of his country.[83]

In a prescient attempt to forestall and disarm his critics, Ruskin ends his 1862 preface to *Unto This Last* by reminding the reader that in a science dealing with human nature it is only possible to answer for the final truth of principles, not for the direct success of plans; and that in the best of plans what can be accomplished at once is always questionable and what can be finally accomplished impossible to conceive. But in so far as his plans lay in the 'moralization of the employing and ruling classes' and the rejection of democracy, Ruskin could not escape the criticism of those who placed more faith in government. As Hobson put it, individual moral action could not remedy the social situation; it would remain ineffectual unless it led to public action.[84] Moral individualism was common, however, Hobson conceded. What was not common was Ruskin's searching analysis of social and economic relations between the classes in industrial society, and his insistence on the importance of non-commercial as well as commercial values.[85] It is, perhaps, the sustained and fervent protest against the tendency to see advances in welfare in the multiplication of commodities, and the preoccupation with measures of production rather than consumption or the quality of life, that makes Ruskin's writing particularly relevant at the present time.

NOTES

1   Quoted in Middlemiss, 1896, p. 3.
2   Collingwood, 1893, p. 254.
3   Ruskin, *Essays on Political Economy*, p. 142.

102   *Citizenship and Work*

4   Ruskin, 1960, p. 169.
5   Ruskin, quoted in Anthony, 1983, p. 179.
6   Ruskin, 1895, p. 110.
7   *Ibid.*, p. 113.
8   *Ibid.*, p. 28.
9   *Ibid.*, p. 31
10   . *Ibid.*, p. 37.
11   Ruskin, 'The Nature of Gothic' in Wilmer 1985, p. 87.
12   *Ibid.*
13   Ruskin, 1960, p. 8.
14   *Ibid.*, pp. 11–12.
15   Ruskin, 1867, p. 135.
16   Ruskin, 1960, p. 58.
17   *Ibid.*, pp. 144–53.
18   *Ibid.*, p. 156. Note the United Nations' *Human Development Report* series dedicated since its inception in 1990 to 'ending the mismeasure of human progress by economic growth alone'.
19   Ruskin, *Essays on Political Economy*, p. 134.
20   Ruskin, 1867, p. 79.
21   Ruskin, 1960, p. 104.
22   Ruskin, 1895, p. 169.
23   *Ibid.*, p. 170.
24   Ruskin, 'The Two Paths' in Wilmer 1985, p. 132.
25   *Ibid.*, p. 133.
26   *Ibid.*, p. 136.
27   See Anthony, 1983, for an excellent analysis.
28   Ruskin, 1895, p. 10.
29   Ruskin, *Essays on Political Economy*, p. 14.
30   Ruskin, 1960, p. 153.
31   Ruskin, 1867, p. 9.
32   Ruskin, *Essays on Political Economy*, p. 87.
33   Ruskin, 1895, p. 193.
34   Ruskin, *Essays on Political Economy*, p. 11.
35   *Ibid.*, pp. 124–5.
36   Ruskin, 1895, p. 40.
37   *Ibid.*, p. 46.
38   *Ibid.*, pp 60–63.
39   *Ibid.*, p. 49.
40   *Ibid.*, p. 54–5.
41   *Ibid.*, p. 56.
42   *Ibid.*, p. 51–2.
43   *Ibid.*, p. 42.
44   Ruskin, 'The Nature of Gothic' in Wilmer, 1985, p. 90.
45   Ruskin, 1867, p. 132.
46   Ruskin, *Essays on Political Economy*, p. 120.
47   *Ibid.*, p. 121.
48   Toynbee, 'Industry and Democracy' in Toynbee, 1884, p. 196.
49   Toynbee, 'The Education of Co-operators', *ibid.*, pp. 227, 229.
50   Barnett, 'Labour and Culture' in Barnett and Barnett, 1909, p. 217.

51 Ruskin, *Essays on Political Economy*, p. 142.
52 *Ibid.*, p. 12.
53 *Ibid.*, p. 129.
54 *Ibid.*, p. 135.
55 *Ibid.*, p. 140.
56 Ruskin, 1867, p. 14.
57 *Ibid.*
58 *Ibid.*, p. viii.
59 *Ibid.*, p. 8.
60 *Ibid.*, pp. 15–16.
61 *Ibid.*, p. 139.
62 *Ibid.*, p. 140.
63 *Ibid.*, p. 97.
64 Ruskin, *Essays on Political Economy*, p. 143.
65 Ruskin, 1895, p. 191.
66 Ruskin, 1960, p. 36.
67 *Ibid.*, p. 107.
68 Ruskin, 1867, p. 10.
69 Ruskin, 1895, p. 202.
70 Ruskin, 1960, p. 169.
71 Ruskin, 1867, p. 74.
72 Ruskin, *Essays on Political Economy*, p. 71.
73 *Ibid.*
74 *Ibid.*, p. 116.
75 Ruskin, 1895, p. 95.
76 Ruskin, 1867, p. 97.
77 *Ibid.*, p. 135.
78 *Ibid.*, p. 170.
79 *Ibid.*, p. 105.
80 Ruskin, 1960, p. xvii.
81 *Ibid.*, p. xviii.
82 Ruskin, 1867, pp. 122–8.
83 *Ibid.*, p. xx.
84 Hobson, 1898, p. 202.
85 *Ibid.*, p. 195

6 William Morris 1834–1896

> If I were to work 10 hours a day at work I despised and hated, I should spend my leisure, I hope, in political agitation, but I fear in drinking.

The Poor Law Amendment Act which enshrined in legislation the liberal economic theory of the day, requiring that public relief for the able bodied be less attractive than the standard of living of the lowest paid independent worker, reached the statute book in 1834, the year when William Morris was born. This administrative application of Bentham's pleasure–pain principle was intended to make sure that men would choose the worst paid jobs rather than risk the degradation of the workhouse; to reduce the poor rate and perfect the free market by removing any form of parish assistance that might diminish incentives to work. But the poor law authorities were not asked to enquire into the availability of employment nor to investigate conditions of labour in the meanest jobs.

It was the detachment of government from the economy, the unwillingness to contemplate – let alone attempt to ameliorate – the working and domestic circumstances of the industrial classes, that aroused protest and hostility to the doctrines of the *laissez-faire* economists from men as different as Owen and Ruskin, Carlyle and the Romantic poets, Arnold Toynbee and Samuel Barnett. The social reform movements of the nineteenth century were as diverse in their origins as in their aims. They drew their inspiration from revolutionary hopes of liberty, equality and fraternity, as well as from the Christian Socialists and from Tory traditions of social obligation and the responsibility of the wealthy for the dispossessed. And the reforming paths led in many directions; some to co-operation and self-help, some to Chartism and the vote and trade unions, some to more government intervention in domestic matters and some to the restoration of the vanished trust and benevolence between rich and poor thought to have been lost in the advance of industrialisation.

For Morris, as for Owen and Ruskin, it was the advent of production based on increasingly elaborate machines that brought fearful dangers for the labouring classes, albeit offering also the prospect of previously unimagined wealth. The character and consequences of industrial work – the division of labour, the displacement of men by

104

machines and the substitution of unskilled for skilled work – all threatened to remove any satisfaction the labourer might find in his employment. The polemics and exhortations of men like Morris and Ruskin and Owen were rooted in their recognition that factory work robbed the operatives of any chance to develop into Ruskin's 'noble and happy human beings'. And the blatant inequality in the distribution of wealth, with large profits going to the owners and a meagre subsistence to the workers, further emphasised their impoverishment. Poverty in a civilised society, Morris observed, was far more painful than the poverty of barbarism.

The insistence on the need for work which provided a decent livelihood – which was enjoyable, which allowed the exercise and development of skill, and which resulted in goods that were useful or beautiful – as the essential basis of citizenship was a natural reaction to early industrial development. The factories and increasingly sophisticated machinery that spread after the close of the eighteenth century were a novel experience that affected both working and domestic life. Poverty and unemployment were intensified by the ending of the French wars, poor harvests and a rapidly growing population. But protest encompassed not only the conditions and outcome of industrial work; it also decried the political economy of the time that was pre-occupied with maximising wealth but careless of the personal and social costs involved, the quality or utility of the product, and the equity of its distribution.

Work that was enjoyable and useful was a precondition of citizenship. Owen looked to education in benevolence, the creation of jobs for the unemployed and the substitution of co-operation for competition to reform human nature and establish the New Moral World. Ruskin saw division of labour as an affront to the dignity and integrity of the workman – it was not the labour that was divided but the men – and scorned the shoddy goods that swelled the measures of GNP as 'illth' not wealth. Morris, too, insisted that satisfying work was the foundation of well-being. But unlike Owen, who believed that the necessary transformation of society and reorganisation of working life could come about through education and benevolence, or Ruskin, who was more concerned with denouncing injustice and the pernicious doctrines of Mill and Ricardo than in constructing a better world, Morris came to believe that only socialism could improve the condition of the working classes. E. P. Thompson claims that Morris added a revolutionary content to the social criticism of industrial capitalism, and that the work of Ruskin and Carlyle and the 'Romantic Revolt' assumed a new importance and interest in the light of his transformation of the tradition.[1] Certainly Morris emphasised the inevitability of conflict between social classes under capitalism and the need to dispossess the capitalists if the lives of the workers were to be substantially improved. But the character of the revolutionary change that he anticipated is unclear from his writing, and the society he expected to emerge to display the equality, freedom and fellowship of which he dreamed, remains as elusive as Owen's New Moral World.

Morris' dream, recounted in *News from Nowhere*, is of a country freed from the corruption, oppression and violence which disfigured his own society. Born into a prosperous family that became wealthy, moving to Woodford Hall, a substantial Georgian house with 50 acres of parkland, when he was six years old, he received a private income of £900 a year on coming of age. At Oxford he belonged to a group including Burne-Jones and Swinburne who read Carlyle and Ruskin, the Romantic poets and the Christian Socialists in addition to the classical writers, and who devoted themselves to denouncing what they considered to be the false values and hypocrisy of the age; the degraded tastes and blunted sensibilities of the middle classes and their callous exploitation of the poor.

Early thoughts of forming an Anglican brotherhood faded, and Morris and Burne-Jones abandoned their intention of taking orders and turned instead to architecture and art. Falling under the influence of Rossetti, Morris soon relinquished architecture for painting but eventually established himself as a designer, illustrator and successful manufacturer as well as a writer of prose and verse. For more than 20 years he lived the life of a poet and craftsman; a capitalist shocked by the ugly conditions and attitudes of industrial society and intent on bringing the civilising power of art and beauty into the daily lives of the people. Only in the 1880s did Morris become politically active as a writer and speaker and member of the Democratic Federation.

The rejection of contemporary conventions and institutions and the hope for a finer future were evident enough, however, during the earlier years of relative political quiescence. 'I can't enter into political-social subjects with any interest', he wrote in 1856, 'for on the whole I see that things are in a muddle . . . My work is the embodiment of dreams in one form or another'.[2] But not everyone's work permitted dreams, and it was this that lay at the heart of Morris' social criticism and stirred deep guilt: 'I have been ashamed when I have thought of the contrast between my happy working hours and the unpraised, unrewarded, monotonous drudgery which most men are condemned to. Nothing shall convince me that such labour as this is good or necessary to civilization.'[3]

The monotonous drudgery was the product of the division of labour or, as Ruskin had insisted, the division of men. For Morris, the division of men also appeared in the separation of the 'cultivated' and the 'degraded' classes bred by competitive commerce. It was evident in the denial to the workman of pleasure or spontaneity in his work. In a properly ordered society the artist, the technical designer and the weaver should all be familiar with one another's craft and the same man should be able to do all tasks.[4] The hand-worker should be able to express his own intelligence and enthusiasm in the goods he produced, striving always to make things better and refusing to turn out poor work, whatever the public might want or think they wanted. Work that could not be done with enjoyment was not worth doing, Morris declared, and it endangered the development of civilised social relationships. 'If I were to work 10 hours a day at work I despised and hated, I should spend my leisure, I hope in political agitation, but I fear in drinking'.[5]

During his earlier years, and still in the 1880s, Morris put his faith in the power of art to transform the drudgery of industrial work. The way to a decent society – to save men from savagery, poverty, brutality and drunkenness – was through employment that fostered self-respect, dwellings that were pleasant and surroundings that would 'soothe and elevate'. Only art could provide those satisfactions.[6] In his first public lecture in 1878 he hailed 'On The Nature of Gothic' as the truest and most eloquent words that could ever be uttered, adding that it was useful to re-iterate the truth lest it be forgotten. It was not labour that was cursed but the stupidity and injustice that surrounded it. No one would wish to do nothing – 'to live like a gentleman as fools call it'. The spread of the decorative arts could end dull work; they were the 'sweeteners' of human labour for those who worked in them and for those influenced by the sight of them.[7] The degradation of much of the art and architecture of the nineteenth century was both cause and effect of the degradation of human life. 'Have nothing in your houses that you do not know to be useful or believe to be beautiful', he adjured his countrymen.[8]

Through the 1880s the focus of Morris' attention shifted from the nature of work, its conditions and rewards, to the economic and social environment that shaped its character. By this time his reading included Marx and Engels and Henry George as well as the Christian

Socialists and Ruskin and the English Romantics, and it was during
these years that his attack on social inequality sharpened. Work, he
asserted, was unfairly divided between the classes; between those who
did none, those who did a fair amount but had 'abundant easements
and holidays', and those who worked so hard they did nothing else
and were accordingly called 'the working classes'. The rich, Morris
declared, consumed a great deal and produced nothing and were kept,
like paupers, by those who did work. The middle class consumed out
of all proportion to their share. And the working class supported both
itself and the other classes but was relegated to an inferior position
'involving a degradation both of mind and body'.

The degradation took different forms. Some of the working
class were not producers but soldiers or shop assistants or such
like, all equally engaged in the service of 'the private war for wealth'.
The majority, however, were employed in making articles of 'folly'
or 'luxury' for the rich which people leading a 'manly and uncorrupted life' would neither ask for nor desire. Such things, Morris
claimed, were not wealth but waste. Finally, there were those
who were obliged to produce shoddy goods which were all that
the poor could afford. The great mass of civilised men, Morris maintained, were poor but – entering the long and still contested debate
about the nature of poverty – their experience could not be compared
with that of the 'resourceless savage' who knows nothing other
than his poverty. Civilisation bred desires which then 'she forbids us
to satisfy'.[9]

It was robbery by the minority that kept the majority poor, Morris
asserted in 1885 in his discussion of useful work and useless
toil, a theme to which he returned in 1896, choosing May Day as a
fitting time for the protest of the disinherited against the system of
'robbery and waste' that shut them out from a decent life.
The 'artificial' poverty of civilisation was far bitterer, he claimed,
than the 'natural' poverty of the rudest barbarism. 'For it is undoubtedly true that full-blown capitalism makes the richest country in
the world . . . poorer than the poorest, for the life of by far the greater
part of its people'.[10] Nor was there any hope that increasingly cheap
and easy production would mean that the possessing classes would
be able to spare more of the 'great heap of wealth' for the producing
classes. Not all the discoveries of science, nor all the tremendous
organisation of the factory and the market would produce true wealth
as long as the aim of it all was profit for the privileged. The only
outcome would be more waste of material and of labour, for few

wage-earners were engaged in producing utilities: 'Waste, in one word, of LIFE'.[11]

Disenchantment with the middle classes was, of course, nothing new. Quite apart from Marxist and socialist writing, there was the native tradition of social and political criticism represented by Carlyle and Owen and Ruskin. In the 1860s Matthew Arnold published *Culture and Anarchy*, castigating the worship of freedom and the blind faith in machinery that failed to consider the ends for which the freedom and the machinery might be used. The common notion of the importance of a man being able to do as he liked threatened a drift to anarchy, Arnold warned. Englishmen, he feared, unlike the classical Greeks or some contemporary Europeans, had little sense of the State as representing the nation in its collective character and controlling individual wills in pursuit of the common good. The middle class, representative of trade and Dissent, with its maxims of every man for himself in business and religion, dreaded interference. These were Arnold's Philistines, though he extended his censure to the aristocracy – the Barbarians – and to the working class – the Populace.[12] But in denouncing enormous social inequalities as a danger to civilisation, Arnold reserved his severest strictures for the middle classes who knew neither men nor the world; they had no 'light' – or culture in the sense that Arnold understood it as a searching after truth – and could give none.

The refusal to admit that Victorian commerce had brought 'real' wealth was as persistent a theme in Morris' speaking and writing, as it was with Ruskin. It was not wealth that civilization had created, but riches. Wealth was what Nature gave and what reasonable men could make from Nature's gifts for their reasonable use. It was sunlight, fresh air, food, raiment, decent and necessary housing, the storing and dissemination of knowledge, and works of art and beauty which man created when he was most aspiring and thoughtful – all things, in short, that gave pleasure to free, manly and uncorrupted people.[13] Riches, by contrast, could not exist without poverty. The mass of the people, Morris claimed, were the victims; condemned at best to a life without education or refinement, leisure, pleasure or renown, and at worst to an existence lower than that of the most brutal savage.[14] The time would come, he asserted, when people would find it hard to believe that so rich a community 'could have submitted to live such a mean, shabby, dirty life as we do'. It was the hunt of profit, Morris declared, that drew men into huge, unmanageable towns; that crowded them into dwellings without gardens or open spaces; that wrapped whole districts in sulphurous smoke; that turned beautiful rivers into filthy sewers; and that condemned all but the rich to houses at best cramped and confined, and at worst for whose wretchedness there was no name.[15] 'What have you done with Lancashire?', he demanded, 'Were not the brown moors and the meadows, the clear streams and the sunny skies, wealth?'.[16]

The society of Morris' dreams was one that he termed Socialist:

> a condition of society in which there should be neither rich nor poor, neither master nor master's man, neither idle nor over-worked, neither brain-sick brain workers nor heart-sick hand workers, in a word, in which all men would be living in equality of condition, and would manage their affairs unwastefully, and with the full consciousness that harm to one would mean harm to all – the realization at last of the meaning of the word COMMON-WEALTH.[17]

The aim of such a society was to provide for all its citizens a free and full life, with pleasurable and useful work, a decent standard of living, and leisure for art and recreation. 'Mere work' would no longer be the end of life but 'happiness for each and all'.[18] Every-one, under socialism, would be able to satisfy his needs by using his powers for the benefit of the race. Thus, economic well-being would be combined with recognition by each of his responsibility for his fellows. 'Socialism aims, therefore, at realizing equality of condition as its economical goal, and the habitual love of humanity as its rule of ethics'.[19]

This was a large aim comparable with Owen's New Moral World. It meant transforming the nature of work, transforming educational arrangements, transforming social relationships and fostering a sense of community to encourage individual fulfilment and mutual bene-volence. It was work, however, that should be the central pleasure of life and the way to other satisfactions. The labourer should receive

> Money enough to keep him from fear of want or degradation; leisure enough . . . to give him time to read and think, and connect his own life with the life of the great world; work enough . . . and praise of it, and encouragement enough to make him feel good friends with his fellows; and lastly . . . his own due share of art, the chief part of which would be a dwelling that does not lack the beauty which Nature would freely allow.[20]

But the 'due share of art' would only emerge through the aspirations of the people towards beauty and the 'true pleasures of life', aspirations that could only be born if there were 'practical equality of economic condition among the whole population'.[21]

It was a revolutionary reorganisation of work that would enable labourers to live as citizens in Morris' utopia. Human needs included good health, education and abundant leisure. Wages must be high enough to avoid anxiety about gaining a livelihood, and the task must not be too onerous, dull or mechanical. Machines should not be used to cheapen labour but to make sure that the minimum time was spent on disagreeable jobs, and rough or distasteful work should be largely voluntary, with short hours. The working environment would be pleasant; labour might be dispersed to small towns, but where large factories were necessary they would be centres of 'full and eager social life' and of intellectual activity.[22] Finally, work would be 'reasonable' – such as a good citizen could see the necessity for – not killing people nor making 'trifling toys' for fools.[23]

Morris also recognized that a liberal education was needed to prepare people for satisfying work. The lamentable rote learning of the Board schools must go, so that all might share in 'whatever knowledge there was in the world' according to their capacity and interest, and also in 'skills of hand' and the fine arts – painting, sculpture, music, drama and so on. Such a system would benefit both individuals and community; it would draw out talent, discover what different people were fit for and help them along the road that they were inclined to take, so making daily work more satisfying and interesting. The whole community would benefit from the development of intelligence, and from the public galleries and libraries that should be established – necessary helps to a decent and civilised life but which not even the rich could provide for themselves.

Abundant leisure was an essential feature of Morris' ideal state, and critically dependent on the new ordering of work and education. If work were redistributed to make everyone producers everyone could have adequate wealth and rest, for if all were engaged in useful work the share of each would be small and would leave ample opportunity for relaxation. 'When class robbery is abolished, every man will reap the fruits of his labour, every man will have due rest – leisure that is.'[24] But proper use of leisure, just as enjoyment of work, depended on education that nurtured talents and skills and interests which could be pursued in free time as well as in working life. Handicrafts encouraged and practised in childhood, Morris supposed, would be largely a leisure time occupation, though the sharp division between working and not working would be blurred in the Socialist society. Morris described in *A Factory as it Might Be* a centre of 'work, light in duration and not oppressive in kind, education in childhood and youth, serious occupation, amusing relaxation . . . leisure', and offering 'beauty of surroundings'.[25] Education which was no longer a preparation merely for commercial success or irresponsible labour but an endeavour to make the best of an individual's powers would require leisure through life, for it would never be ended.[26] As men developed their skills and interests they would increasingly demand the leisure to practise them.

The new arrangements for work and education and leisure in Morris' visionary society were linked to further changes in modes of living and political organisation. His hatred of the squalid and polluted industrial cities, his view of London as a 'sordid, loathsome place' led him to an alternative fantasy of rural peace and simplicity:

> Suppose people lived in little communities among gardens and green fields so that you could be in the country in five minutes' walk, and had few wants, almost no furniture for instance, and no servants and studied the (difficult) arts of enjoying life, and finding out what they really wanted: then I think one might hope that civilization had really begun.[27]

This was Morris writing in the early 1870s. Twenty years later he had grown increasingly suspicious of bureaucracy; the multiplication of boards and offices and the 'paraphernalia of official authority' which was a burden even when that authority was delegated by the people and was exercised in accordance with their wishes.[28] With communism, he supposed, following the Marxist prediction, the central machinery of the state would disappear and all citizens would share the responsibilities of government:

> To my mind in the New Society, we should form bodies like municipalities, county-boards and parishes, and almost all the practical work would be done by these bodies, the members of whom would be working at a living by their ordinary work, and . . . everybody who had any capacity for such work would have to do his share of it.[29]

Larger units of government would be needed but their functions would be limited to protecting the values of the new commonwealth and spreading information as to the wants of the population and the means of supplying them. Morris' vision was of a settled, decentralised way of life with minimal government. Nations as political entities would cease to exist and civilisation would mean a loose federation of communities administered by direct assembly. Beyond the self-governing townships a central council of the Socialist world would make sure the smaller units observed the fundamental principles of socialism.[30]

How was all this to come about? However vivid and appealing in its rejection and scorn of the political economy of the late nineteeth century, the way to Morris' new society was, understandably, uncertain. About one thing he was quite clear; that change would only come through concerted pressure and action from the working classes themselves. But whether the pressure and action should be on and through parliament or whether it would involve some kind of popular movement outside parliament, how long the transformation of society might take and what might be the most effective ways of helping it along, were matters on which his views altered. The faith of men such as T. H. Green, Arnold Toynbee and Samuel Barnett in the 'active citizenship' of the middle classes – a profound sense of social obligation which would take friendship and knowledge and cultivation to the poor in the east end of London and other industrial towns – as a way to a fairer and better society was never shared by Morris. The whole basis of society with its contrasts of rich and poor was 'incurably vicious', he wrote in 1883, and would not be redeemed by 'careful attention to duties of good citizenship'. The isolated acts of a few persons of the middle and upper classes were powerless against it. Feeling this, Morris said, he was bound to act for the destruction of the system which would only come about 'by the united discontent of numbers'. The antagonism of the classes which the system had bred was the natural and necessary instrument of its destruction. Whether the change would be peaceful or violent would depend on whether or not the middle classes recognised the urgent need for fairness and redistribution and displayed 'the proper type of a useful citizen, into which all classes should eventually melt'.[31]

In 1884 the Democratic Federation became the Social Democratic Federation (SDF) intent on socialising the means of production, distribution and exchange under a democratic state, emancipating labour from the domination of capitalism and landlordism, and establishing social and economic equality between the sexes. The SDF, however, was soon beset by internal dissension, not least the disagreement between those, including Hyndman, who were prepared to work through existing political parties and those who dismissed the parliamentary process as a charade. Through much of the 1880s Morris belonged to the latter. He likened parliamentary legislation to a doctor dealing with symptoms and leaving the cause of the disease alone; such palliatives were a bourgeois device for checking the advance of socialism. The mental degradation, hypocrisy, cowardice and joylessness of the middle classes, he declared, precluded any chance of reform through parliament – 'their beloved instrument of amelioration'.[32]

Rejecting parliamentary reform, Morris left the SDF at the end of 1884 after much squabbling. A few months later he founded the Socialist League, a body devoted to propaganda and the education of the working classes in the meaning of socialism, an education which was essential if the revolution were to be managed effectively without violence and without degenerating into anarchy. Improvements in the condition of the working class could make for a constructive revolutionary movement, for 'starvelings can only riot', he wrote to his daughter in 1884.[33] By the later 1880s, however, Morris' belief in the likelihood of any kind of revolutionary movement was fading. Diary entries for early 1887 reveal dismay at the 'frightful ignorance and want of impressibility of the average English workman' and at the apathy among an audience of 'better trade workmen and small tradesmen' who listened respectfully to socialism but were 'perfectly supine and not inclined to move'.[34]

The Trafalgar Square riots of 1886 and 1887 added to Morris' sense of defeat in the face of events moved by forces beyond his control. The uncompromising suppression of demonstrations in favour of free speech underlined the strength of capitalism and his revolutionary hopes receded further into the future. *News From Nowhere*, written in 1890, describes a utopia set in the 1950s. In 1889 Morris was still insisting, as against those Fabians who believed in working through existing political parties to promote socialism, that revolution without the class struggle was an absurdity and an impossibility. Socialism would only come when the working class demanded it,[35] but the demand could be through parliament:

> I cannot fail to see that it is necessary somehow to get hold of the machine which has at its back the executive power of the country . . . and that the organisations and labour which will be necessary to effect that by means of the ballot-box will . . . be little indeed compared with what would be necessary to effect it by open revolt.[36]

A year later, Morris wrote in *Commonweal* with mingled uncertainty, disappointment and hope. It was seven years, he observed, since socialism had revived in England. There had been quarrels and mistakes, but also some progress. Modern society was changing and the way to reach socialist ends must be reconsidered, for people were not only discontented but more hopeful of improvement, though unsure how best to act. Morris dismissed palliative action through trade unions, and also riots, for neither trade unions nor rioters knew what socialism was about. Nor did he have much faith in state socialism, though it might be a step towards the new order. The way forward was through education:

> Our business, I repeat, is the making of Socialists, i.e., convincing people that Socialism is good for them and is possible. When we have enough people of that way of thinking, *they* will find out what action is necessary for putting their principles in practice. Until we have that mass of opinion, action for general change that will benefit the whole people is *impossible* . . . all but a very small minority are not prepared *to do without masters*. They do not believe in their own capacity to undertake the management of affairs . . . When they are so prepared, then Socialism will be realized; but nothing can push it on a day in advance of that time.
>
> Therefore, I say, make Socialists. We Socialists can do nothing else that is useful, and preaching and teaching is not out of date for that purpose; but for those who, like myself, do not believe in state socialism, it is the only rational means of attaining the New Order of Things.[37]

The Socialist League collapsed in 1890 and after this date, Mackail remarks, the 'weary work of militant socialism' was over for him. Nevertheless, he went on to form the Hammersmith Socialist Society, aiming to spread the principles of socialism through lectures, street meetings and publications. Its manifesto, written by Morris, advocated passive resistance as the proper mode of opposition to the existing order and spoke of the combination of labour as the hope for the future that would slowly drive out capitalism.[38] A firmer acceptance of the importance of both theoretical and practical efforts for reform appeared in a Fabian lecture, 'Communism', in 1893 and in 'Socialism: Its Growth and Outcome', a collection of earlier *Commonweal* articles published in the same year. Also in 1893, Morris joined Shaw and Hyndman in producing the Manifesto of English Socialists, a document expressing the welcome of the Fabians, the SDF and the Hammersmith Socialist Society for remedial measures, thus embracing the strategy that Popper later dubbed 'piecemeal social engineering'.[39] The more comfort, education and leisure the working class enjoyed, the more, it was supposed, they would be able to work towards a new social order based on equality of condition. Socialists could form a distinct party with definite, if initially limited, aims; for an eight-hour day, an adequate minimum wage, the suppression of sub-contracting and sweating, and universal suffrage.[40]

What, then, is Morris' particular contribution to the continuing debate over the rights and duties of citizenship, the significance of work, the entitlements of individuals and the responsibilities of government? His ideal society was fashioned out of his rejection of the industrial civilisation of his time conditioned, as he saw it, by the pitiless pursuit of profit and leading to long hours of dull, hard, mechanical labour. The commercial system compelled men to live in squalid and hideous places where none could keep his sanity without losing all sense of beauty and enjoyment of life. 'Men living amid such ugliness cannot conceive of beauty and, therefore, cannot express it'.

The appreciation and creation of beauty was of profound importance in Morris' new order of things. But these were experiences that must be part of the lives of all citizens. Like Tawney after him, Morris insisted on equality of condition rather than the more niggardly, and liberal, equality of opportunity, a commitment expressing mingled compassion and guilt. In thinking about men's circumstances, he wrote to C. E. Maurice, he had but one rule; to ask himself how he would bear it if he were poor. And the answer made him more and more ashamed of his own position.[41] His commitment to the decorative arts was fiercely democratic. 'What business have we with art at all', he demanded, 'unless all can share it?'.[42]

Morris was an idealistic visionary. He assumed that once capitalism, with its remorseless search for profit that drove the mass of the population to the borders of destitution, was abolished, civilised and benevolent social relationships would emerge. Common ownership of the means of production would permit an organisation of education and of work that would encourage everyone to develop their talents, take part in government according to their abilities and live in harmonious accord. Morris recognised that the new society would require a transformation in the values, habits and outlook bred by exploitation and commercial competition but, like Owen, he had no doubt that a carefully arranged environment could effect the change. It is a faith apparently shared by E. P. Thompson who, commenting on Morris' emphasis on communal life, remarks that this was something he could safely deduce from the common ownership of the means of production and the consequent change in social ethics.[43]

For Thompson, Morris' great achievement – one of the great achievements of the nineteenth century, indeed – was in bringing together the moral protest of Carlyle and Ruskin with the 'historical genius' of Marx.[44] Those more doubtful of the universal validity of Marx' historical writing prefer to emphasise the power of the moral protest; the denunciation of the miserable and stunted lives of the industrial workers and of the economic and political system that produced them, and the insistence that the proper aim of society was to maximise chances of individual development for everybody. Nor was it only a matter of developing aesthetic qualities or intellectual talents: 'I demand the utter extinction of all asceticism. If we feel the least degradation in being amorous or merry or hungry or sleepy, we are so far bad animals, and therefore miserable men'.[45]

At the same time, Morris refused to define progress in terms of more wealth or 'gadgets' or leisure. The object should be varied, pleasant and creative work for all even if this meant a simpler way of living. Paul Thompson sees Morris' importance in his insistence on the potential, and the right, of all human beings to develop their intelligence and responsibility. 'He was confident that with a lighter burden of work, a higher standard of food and housing and a general opportunity for education, all human beings were capable of a far higher development . . . of a responsibility, creative imagination and sensitivity sufficient for full democracy and equality. This is why Morris is still relevant today'.[46]

However, Morris' contribution to ideas about citizenship was more as an activist than as a thinker. Believing all men were redeemable, he devoted himself to spreading the gospel of socialism, not only during the 1880s in his more explicitly political speaking and writing as a leading member of various socialist organisations, but also in his poetry and prose romances – *The Earthly Paradise*, *The Pilgrims of Hope*, *The Dream of John Ball*, for example, and later, *News from Nowhere*. Discussing his influence, Paul Thompson points to the symbolic value of a celebrated poet and great designer marching with working men, preaching at street corners and lecturing in dingy halls.[47]

Nor were Morris' ideals confined to his writing and speaking; his beliefs governed his daily living. He was an ethical and aesthetic socialist by example. He sold the greater part of his library to devote the proceeds to socialism, and his principles on the organisation of work informed his own business enterprise. Nothing was done in his workshops that Morris himself did not know how to do, and he worked as weaver and designer alongside the craftsmen and artists whom he employed. This personal expression of a more benign form of capitalism emphasising the worth and dignity of labour was an important part of Morris' contribution to ideas about the entitlements of citizens. But in the end his most powerful influence was in asserting a moral position which has enduring relevance. Asa Briggs points out that Morris' writing provides as telling a critique of twentieth century socialism as of nineteenth century capitalism, in insisting that society be judged by its success in creating equality of condition and the means to individual fulfilment.

The more theoretical aspects of Morris' work, the belief – albeit rather wavering – in the inevitability and desirability of violent revolution as a necessary and perhaps sufficient condition for a fairer society, has stood the test of time less well. Nor did he ever attempt to spell out the details of the political and social arrangements that might maintain his new social order. This task was left to the Webbs and others of the Fabians who had more faith in the power of the state and the machinery of government to advance individual and collective well-being. None of this should detract from the grandeur of Morris' vision. As his earliest biographer observes, 'The dreams which the present may have of an elusive or dimly conjectured future . . . must be no rational human forecast, but a tale told, like the vision of Er in Plato's 'Republic', by one neither alive or dead'.[48]

NOTES

1   Thompson, E. P., 1955, p. 842. See also Williams, 1958.
2   Morris to Cornwell Price, quoted in Thompson, E. P., 1955, p. 71 and in Mackail, 1907, vol. 1, p. 107.
3   Morris, 1883, quoted in Mackail, 1907, vol. 2, p. 100.
4   Morris, Evidence to the Royal Commission on Technical Instruction, 1882, quoted in Mackail, 1907, vol. 2, p. 50.
5   Morris, quoted in Mackail, 1907, vol. 2, p. 65.
6   Address to the Wedgwood Institute School of Science and Art, 1881, quoted in Mackail, 1907, vol. 2, p. 21.
7   Morris, 'The Decorative Arts' in Briggs, 1986, p. 88.
8   Mackail, 1907, vol. 2, p. 63.
9   Morris, 'Useful Work versus Useless Toil' in Briggs 1986, pp. 119–23.
10 Morris in *Justice*, 1 May 1896, in Briggs, 1986, p. 305.
11 *Ibid.*, p. 306.

12   Arnold, 1869.
13   Morris, 'Useful Work versus Useless Toil', in Briggs, 1986, p. 121.
14   Morris, quoted in Mackail, 1907, vol. 2, p. 84.
15   Morris, 'How We Live and How We Might Live' in Briggs, 1986, p. 175.
16   Morris, quoted in Thompson, P., 1967, p. 234.
17   Morris, 'How I Became a Socialist' in Briggs, 1986, p. 33.
18   Bax and Morris, 'Manifesto of the Socialist League', 1885, in Thompson, E. P., 1955, p. 852.
19   Morris, 'Four Letters on Socialism' in Briggs, 1986, p. 151.
20   Morris, quoted in Mackail, 1907, vol. 2, p. 63.
21   *Ibid.*, p. 206.
22   Morris, 'Useful Work versus Useless Toil' in Briggs, 1986, p. 132.
23   Morris, 'How We Live and How We Might Live', *ibid.*, p. 174.
24   Morris, 'Useful Work versus Useless Toil', *ibid.*, p. 125.
25   Morris, quoted in Thompson, E. P., 1955, p. 756.
26   Morris, 'Socialism: Its Growth and Outcome', *ibid.*, p. 800.
27   Morris, letter to Mrs Alfred Baldwin, March 1874, *ibid.*, p. 232.
28   Morris, 'True and False Society', *ibid.*, p. 798.
29   Morris, 'What Socialists Want', *ibid.*, p. 799.
30   Thompson, P., 1967, p. 253.
31   Morris to C. E. Maurice, Mackail, 1907, vol. 2, pp. 105–8.
32   Morris, 'Socialism and Politics', *Commonweal*, July supplement 1885, in Thompson E. P., 1955, pp. 449–50.
33   Morris to May Morris, *ibid.*, p. 393; see also Morris to T. C. Horsfall in Briggs, 1986, p. 150.
34   Morris, diary, in Thompson, E. P., 1955, p. 34.
35   Morris, *Commonweal*, 28 September 1889, in Thompson, P. 1967, p. 214.
36   Morris, *ibid.*, p. 212.
37   Morris, *Commonweal*, 15 November 1890, quoted in Thompson, E. P., 1955, p. 666.
38   Mackail, 1907, vol. 2, pp. 240–1.
39   Popper, 1962.
40   *Ibid.*, p. 290.
41   Morris to C. E. Maurice, in Briggs, 1986, p. 136.
42   Morris, *Manchester Examiner*, March 1883, *ibid.*, p. 139.
43   Thompson, E. P., 1955, p. 797.
44   *Ibid.*, p. 630.
45   Thompson, P., 1967, p. 245.
46   *Ibid.*, p. 254.
47   *Ibid.*, p. 216.
48   Mackail, 1907, vol. 2, p. 295.

II Citizenship and Work

(ii) Elevating the State

7 Fabians, New Liberals and Tawney

> The workman who is unemployed or underpaid through economic malorganisation will remain a reproach not to the charity but to the justice of society as long as he is to be seen in the land.
>
> (Hobhouse, *Liberalism*)

As the nineteenth century faded into the twentieth the debate about the significance of work, for individuals and for society, began to take on a different character. New political circumstances brought a more powerful and democratic central government, with an electorate of whom two-thirds were working men. This meant that it was easier to imagine national policies to deal with unemployment and other social ills. It also meant that it was more likely that the distress of people out of work would become a national concern. The Webbs, for example, deplored the futility of local efforts to provide for the unemployed through a mixture of the poor law, private charity, distress committees and municipal relief works that had developed through the nineteenth and into the twentieth century.[1] Writing in 1929, and recalling the minority report of the Poor Law Commissioners twenty years earlier, they urged a national effort to prevent unemployment by anticipating economic fluctuations and increasing or reducing public works accordingly.

Government remedies for unemployment remain elusive, but interest in national policies has grown over the past century. Rather than devising ideal societies without clear strategies for realizing them, writers seeking a New Moral World have increasingly attended to means as well as ends, proposing to use the more elaborate government machinery to make their policies effective. The Webbs were prominent among those who showed almost limitless faith in the power of the state to create a new social order. But such views were fiercely challenged by the New Liberals and by those among the Fabians who supported more active government but, with Barnett, Morris and Tawney, also believed that a good society could be built only with the consent of free and moral men and women. 'Therefore', proclaimed Morris, 'make Socialists'; this was the only way of attaining the New Order of Things.[2]

While discussion of unemployment moved from the local to the national stage and from utopian dreams to practical politics, it also changed its character in that the meaning of work gradually came to be redefined. It came to be seen not only as a matter of paid employment but also as including the services offered and exchanged within families and communities and voluntary associations for no financial reward. Such activity, it was claimed, was as important a contribution to the general well-being as any paid work. People involved in it should be recognised as full citizens and accorded the consequent rights and status – some kind of 'participatory' income and security in old age and sickness. Along with greater appreciation of unpaid work some scepticism has developed about the value of work that is paid. This is in the old tradition of nineteenth century criticism. It echoes Ruskin's insistence that what matters is consumption – the nature and quality of the things that people buy and use. And it also echoes the attack on the concentration of wealth in Victorian England; the huge share of the rich was unjust because it resulted less from individual enterprise and achievement than from the economic, social and cultural endowments that society had bestowed.

The Fabians were an eclectic body, recognising no single leader and accepting no single doctrine. However, they mostly believed in democracy and gradualism, rejecting revolutionary movements for social change and relying on parliamentary measures that had the support of the people. They also believed that the root of social problems lay in economic organisation; the outcome of democracy should be control by the people not only of political institutions but also, through them, of wealth and of production. Thus, in *Fabian Essays*, Sydney Webb looked to 'the gradual substitution of organised co-operation for the anarchy of the competitive struggle' and to the recovery for the people of the enormous share which the owners of the means of production had hitherto taken from the produce.[3] The municipalities, Webb suggested, had done most to socialise industrial life; their activities reflected an unconscious repudiation of individualism and the 'anarchic competition of private greed'.[4] He continued to point to the wider but 'immediately practicable' demands of most socialists for further legislation set out in the radical programme of 1888. This included the revision of taxation to shift the burden away from workers to the receivers of rent and interest; education reform to give the poorest children the best; and reorganisation of the poor laws to provide generously and without stigma for the old and the sick. It also included extending factory legislation to establish a minimum wage

and a maximum working day, and making the municipalities responsible for organising labour for all public purposes, so eliminating
private capitalists and middlemen.

However, in tackling the persistent problem of how to reconcile the
individual and collective good, Webb leaned heavily on the idealist
tradition of Hegel and Green, elevating the state and compromising
democracy, and anticipating his later admiration for Soviet communism by insisting on the importance of the 'social organism'. The
proper end for an individual was not necessarily the highest development of individual personality, but 'the filling in the best possible way,
of his humble function in the great social machine'. Such ideas, Webb
acknowledged, put individualism to rout. But the development of
sociology, he declared, required a re-evaluation of the importance of
liberty and equality.

Others among the Fabians, while seeking public action, were more
careful of individual freedoms. Annie Besant, like Webb, dismissed
utopias as useful guides to the better organisation of industrial
life, preferring small but practicable advances to win what was possible rather than what was best. But plans must be devised by the
people, not imposed upon them. Services should be run by local
or national authorities, and the main job of the county councils
would be to deal with unemployment. Mrs Besant favoured the local
arrangements that later received short shrift from the Webbs
and, having denied the value of utopian fantasies, proceeded to out-
line her own highly utopian schemes. Councils should organise productive industry, not relief works. There should be county farms, self-
supporting settlements in the manner of Robert Owen, that would
need craftsmen, schools and entertainments as well as agricultural
workers and where communal living would be encouraged, with public 'meals rooms' to save housewives time and trouble. The aim should
be to employ everyone in what they did best and in their own trades in
municipal factories or municipal service wherever their work was
needed. Unpleasant work would have shorter hours and would rely
more heavily on machinery.

In such ways Mrs Besant believed the unemployed would be turned
into communal workers and private enterprise would gradually die
out. Ignoring the universal and persistent struggle to establish and
preserve differentials, she wanted equal pay for all work as she
thought it was impossible to assess the relative worth of different
jobs; and the sick and the old and children should have an equal
share with the workers. Those refusing to work would have no relief,

but the idle would be disciplined, she supposed, by other employees. Thus, municipal dealings with the unemployed would open up 'avenues to the higher life':

> The desire to excel, the joy in creative work, the longing to improve, the eagerness to win social approval, the instinct of benevolence: all these will start into full life, and will serve at once as the stimulus to labour and the reward of excellence.[5]

For Shaw, the desirability and justice of socialism was beyond dispute albeit widely unrecognised. The economic aim was to collect all rents and pass them over to the national treasury. The state was not an abstraction, but a machine to do certain kinds of work. Local democratic government, however, was also required. Councils would run municipal industries, offering decent wages and driving out sweaters. There was nothing new, Shaw declared, about the programme for socialism; it only involved the application of principles already admitted. Reform was sure to come, but the 'sordid, slow, reluctant, cowardly path to justice' excited Shavian rage:

> I venture to claim your respect for those enthusiasts who still refuse to believe that millions of their fellow creatures must be left to sweat and suffer in hopeless toil and degradation, while Parliament and vestries grudgingly muddle and grope towards petty instalments of betterment. The right is so clear, the wrong so intolerable, the gospel so convincing, that it seems to them that it must be possible to enlist the whole body of workers – soldiers, policemen and all – under the banner of brotherhood and equality . . . Unfortunately, such an army of light is no more to be gathered from the human product of nineteenth century civilisation than grapes are to be gathered from thistles. But if we feel glad of that impossibility; if we feel relieved that change is to be slow enough to avert personal risk to ourselves then I submit to you that our institutions have corrupted us to the most dastardly degree of selfishness.[6]

In more measured insistence that progress must be based on informed consent, Hubert Bland warned that state control was not socialism though socialism might increase state control. Socialism meant the common holding of the means of production and exchange, and the holding of them for the equal benefit of all.[7]

Faith in the state as a moralising power, as a wise dispenser of appropriate services, combined with mistrust of those receiving its benevolence, sometimes lay uneasily with the Fabian commitment to democracy. Beatrice Webb was one who leaned more to the state, an inclination that became more marked in later years in her appprobation of the U.S.S.R. but was evident in her earlier dislike of Lloyd George's insurance plans (widely relished as 'dishing the Webbs' and the bureaucratic socialism they represented) because they contemplated unsupervised doles. Relief ought to be conditional on good conduct; public policy must force self-improvement.

Members of the Poor Law Commission of 1905–9 who, led by Mrs Webb, produced the minority report called for compulsory registration of the unemployed and penal labour colonies for those refusing jobs as well as for the retraining and maintenance of surplus workers. They opposed the National Insurance Bill of 1911, arguing that insurance did nothing to prevent unemployment; distress should be dealt with by public funds suitably controlled, not by insurance. The insistence that government should be responsible for preventing rather than simply relieving distress was the hallmark of the minority report and of the campaigning body – the National Committee for the Prevention of Destitution – set up to try to win support for its proposals. Relief was wasteful when the need for it might be avoided. It was also unreliable, likely to be stigmatising and robbed people of their civil and political rights. Meanwhile, however, the Labour Party and the trade unions supported the insurance bill, and the campaign for wider state responsibilities for preventive action had little immediate effect.

While the denial of citizenship was clearest under the poor law, which was based on the principles of deterrence and less eligibility, it was also evident in the labour market where the employee was at the mercy of the employer and subject to dismissal when an enterprise ceased to be profitable. Workers should have a voice, some began to argue, in the organisation of the industries that controlled their lives. Although syndicalist and guild socialist proposals for workers' control found little support among the older Fabians, questions about the position and autonomy of industrial workers were central in J. A. Hobson's writing on poverty and unemployment through the 1890s and early 1900s. Following in the tradition of Owen and Ruskin, he pointed to the damaging effects of machinery and factory employment on the working class; the geographical separation of employers and workmen, the destruction of personal relationships, the displacement of labour and the changing character of work.[8]

Parting from the older tradition, however, Hobson divided reformers between those wishing to place responsibility on employers and those wishing to establish a larger independence among the employed. Ruskin and Carlyle had led the 'clamour' for more responsible employers who 'reviving a dead feudalism should assume unasked the protectorate of their employees'.[9] Hobson did not believe that decent conditions of industrial work could be guaranteed by benevolent employers, nor could the refusal to buy cheap goods solve the problems of sweated labour; diminishing purchases would not bring decent wages for producers. Rather, the hope for a better industrial system lay in a mixture of state intervention and co-operative effort. The factory acts should be extended to cover all forms of employment and there should be co-operative production and organisation of labour. Hobson thought trade unionism a more hopeful development in regulating work than the co-operative movement, but unions did not cover unskilled workers who were excluded by skilled men anxious to protect their own wages. There should be an eight-hour day, which would go some way to absorb excess labour. If, in reducing unemployment and improving conditions for the low skilled, it also interfered with economic growth and raised the price of goods, this was a cost the community could well afford to pay.[10]

The surplus of unskilled labour remained a problem that seemed to defeat solution and one that has emerged again at the end of the twentieth century. Checks on population were hardly practicable, Hobson thought, and in any case restraint was least likely where it was most needed; emigration either removed men the country could not afford to lose or those whom the colonies did not want; and Booth's scheme to establish industrial settlements would do less to reform and improve the poor than to remove excess labour whose products, if placed on the open market, would only serve to depress wages and increase unemployment, thus exacerbating the problems it was intended to resolve.

Hobson regarded women as a special and particularly awkward group of unskilled workers who threatened to undercut men's wages. Outwork was hard to control, it was difficult for women to combine, and many were prepared to work for low pay as they tended to be second earners. Hobson sought to resolve the problem by discouraging the industrial employment of married women either inside or outside their homes. This might help to deal with immediate economic difficulties and it would also be advantageous in freeing women for the vital business of bearing and rearing children. If women neglected to prepare for and perform the responsibilities of domestic life and maternity by engaging in laborious and unhealthy industrial occupations, 'so long shall we pay the penalty in that physical and moral deterioration of the race which we have traced in low city life'.[11] The first duty of society, Hobson maintained, should be to secure healthy conditions for the lives of the young, a home life that provided for sound physical, intellectual and moral growth 'at whatever cost of interference with so called liberty of action'.[12] Later writers have been more tender towards individual liberty and women's rights and have preferred to suggest that child rearing should be supported through family allowances or some form of citizen's income or public arrangements for child care.

If Hobson was ready to insist on women's distinctive responsibilities for the 'progress of the race' he was also ready to exact a contribution from the wealthy. Poor people, he maintained, had neither time, energy nor desire to be clean, thrifty, industrious, steady, moral, intellectual or religious. They would only become so when they had the necessary conditions for healthy physical life; better food, warmer clothes, surer shelter and secure employment at decent wages:

> It is the bitterest portion of the lot of the poor that they are deprived of the opportunity of learning to work well. To taunt them with their incapacity, and to regard it as a cause of poverty, is nothing else than a piece of bland insolence.[13]

The protection of the poor justified limiting the freedom and property rights of the rich. It required not only factory legislation but also state and municipal undertakings, and the control of public utilities which might become monopolies under private enterprise. Moreover, society had a just claim on all forms of capital, for its accumulation depended as much on cultural, economic and social conditions as on individual effort.

As well as women and the unskilled, old people were especially vulnerable in relation to citizenship and work, Hobson observed – recognising a problem that has become more evident as the population has aged and the labour market changed dramatically. The skill and experience of the old counted for less compared with the strength and speed of the young, and unemployment or compulsory retirement led not to comfortable leisure but to a degrading struggle for bare subsistence. This, Hobson declared, was one of the most terrible aspects of the problem of unemployment.[14]

Solutions in Hobson's view, writing in the 1890s, lay in comprehensive government measures. The philanthropists' approach to unemployment – the careful investigation of individual cases – was

flawed because it did not deal with causes. Personal qualities were not
the most important cause of unemployment; they merely determined
who suffered it. Lack of work must be tackled by increasing consumption and to this end the purchasing power of the rich must be redistributed. Labour bureaux, which became popular in the twentieth
century, Hobson thought of limited value; they merely matched
labour to existing jobs without creating new ones. Labour colonies
might usefully remove tramps and beggars and offer rehabilitation,
but they did not deal with the causes of mass unemployment either.
Both labour bureaux and farm colonies were more to do with human-
ising the poor laws and the treatment of criminals than with tackling
unemployment, and both raised the difficulty of producing goods
that competed with those supplied by free labour. Nevertheless,
Hobson saw a need for carefully organised public works when jobs
were scarce to avoid the 'degradation of industrial character' and the
misery of long periods out of work. But such arrangements were
temporary expedients and must not divert attention from the primary
need for economic measures to increase consumption throughout the
community which alone could guarantee more industry and more
employment[15]

This was the critical social problem for Hobson; unemployment was
a denial of citizenship, a waste of work and of life. It left men idle and
resources unused. One part of the solution was education and training
to allow the power of each citizen to be used for social purposes. But
steps must also be taken to improve the organisation and conditions
of work. Hobson pointed to the social waste arising out of competition, evident in the 'alarming growth' of 'agents, canvassers, touts,
and other persons "pushing" trade', and determining not what goods
should be made or sold but who should make or sell them – a matter
of social indifference. This was not to deny any value from competition, but merely to recognise the waste in keeping twelve competing
grocers in one street instead of two.[16] Another form of waste was
represented by the upper class unemployed – a quarter of a million
men, Hobson reckoned, in 1891. And this was a subject that fuelled
growing antagonism. 'Poverty in a poor country is one thing; poverty
in a rich country another', Hobson remarked, joining Morris and
many others and anticipating Townsend's insistence on the importance of relative deprivation in *Poverty in the United Kingdom* in 1979.
In modern towns the luxury of the rich mocked the misery of the poor,
sowing the seeds of new wants without supplying the opportunities to
satisfy them.[17]

Furthermore, and again in the tradition of the nineteenth century critics of political economy, Hobson insisted that the wealth of nations was not to be measured by the market value of their products. The human value of a growing national income must be calculated he declared, echoing Ruskin, in terms of the pains and pleasures attached both to production and to consumption. The character of work, its distribution, the strength, sex, age, skill and race of the worker must all be considered. And so must the nature of the product be referred to some standard of wealth or 'illth'. True work must be judged in terms of its life sustaining and improving qualities.[18] The value of goods and services depended on who received them and on the use that was made of them.

His desire for the proper ordering of production and consumption to advance the well-being of all citizens led Hobson to contemplate the role of the state in social affairs, and the distinction between physical, or essential, and moral, or intellectual, needs. Often, he said, the two were confused. The state, as well as private charity, had sometimes attempted to supply 'higher' before 'lower' wants. This was misconceived and little else than irresponsible misdirection of reform energy, 'attempts to grow the ripe flowers of civilisation before we have grown the stalk, or even furnished the soil out of which the stalk may grow!'.[19] Such mistakes arose partly from the contention that the 'higher' things of the mind and soul were more important and should receive priority, and partly from reluctance to face drastic reforms of the economy. The priority of economic problems must be recognised. Although occasional individuals might be able to improve their position, this represented a 'moral miracle'; the majority could not alter their circumstances.

Such arguments raised the persistent question as to how individual and collective interests might be reconciled in the search for full citizenship for all. Individual rights, Hobson claimed, derived from the supreme obligation of society to protect and promote social well-being. Luxuries for some while others lacked necessities represented social waste or disutility – unless it were deemed desirable that some should starve. But it was dangerous to emphasise 'duty' rather than 'rights', to substitute 'mercy' or 'charity' for justice and 'claim merit for some defective act of restitution'.[20] The first duty of society was to provide everyone with work and adequate payment for it, for 'to consume without producing, to enjoy without effort at once lessens the quantity and lowers the quality of life'.[21]

Insistence on justice rather than charity underlay Hobson's demand for state rather than individual action. The Christian Socialists, shocked by the immorality of the economic order and the stark contrasts of wealth and poverty, should yet realise, he thought, that attempts to solve economic problems by appealing to the moral conduct of individuals were doomed to fail. To suppose, with Ruskin and Carlyle, that individual employers could improve working conditions was fatuous. The 'moralisation' of employers or workers could not resolve social ills. And, moreover, to receive as a gift what should be earned as a right injured character and damaged self-respect.[22]

The fundamental problem for Hobson, as for all who try to define the proper entitlements of citizenship, was how to determine a just distribution of resources and opportunities. Opportunities should be available in proportion to the advantage society would gain from individuals' use of them. This, Hobson asserted, did not imply conflict between individual and state. Individuals only existed within society, and individual ends were organically related to and determined by social ends.[23] Rewards should be related to effort and to need and to productivity, but it was impossible to decide how far productivity reflected individual effort and how far it was the outcome of cultural and economic and social endowment. So, goods and services should be related to needs; not those bringing private satisfaction, but those that raised the capacity for service to society. This austere pronouncement was part of the rationale behind the advocacy of a minimum wage.

The manifest dangers inherent in the assumption of the unity of individual and collective interests were modified in Hobson's further discussions of liberalism and of democracy. While society, he argued, was properly regarded as a moral and rational organism, having a psychic life, character and purpose which could not be resolved into the life and purpose of its individual members, yet liberalism was distinct from socialism in taking the chief test of policy to be the freedom of the individual rather than the strength of the nation. Liberalism should not be hostile to state intervention and public enterprise for this was the way to greater equality of opportunity; but the enlargement of state authority must always be justified by the enlargement of personal liberty.[24] Public services, moreover, had a routine character; officialdom crushed great achievement; so the finer skills and art must be private. 'Originality of thought and experiment, new ideas and impulses, will continue to be more freely generated and to flourish better in an unofficial atmosphere'.[25]

The crux of democracy lay in ensuring that public bodies were fit instruments for social reform. Like Samuel Barnett, Hobson believed that this depended on the intelligence and goodwill of private citizens informing public life, and on similar qualities and sentiments in public servants who would see the welfare of the community, not the running of an official machine, as the leading motive for their work. In these circumstances, where ordinary men and women were ready and able to exercise their influence on public affairs, the conditions for citizenship would be realised and the forms and institutions of society would be shaped and sized to make it possible. It is notable that Richard Crossman's much later disillusion with state welfare through the 1950s and 1960s reflected the failure to develop public services responsive to the wishes of the people as Hobson had wished.[26]

The preoccupation with freedom, equality and opportunity and concern for the proper balance between the state and individual powers and liberties which defines citizenship, is central to the writing of Hobson's contemporary, Hobhouse, and also in the later work of Tawney. In his long essay on liberalism published in 1911[27] Hobhouse grapples with the questions of freedom and control; with the entitlements and responsibilities of citizens in the governance of their society, in relation to work and maintenance and in the distribution of income and wealth. In all these matters Hobhouse is at pains to distance the New Liberalism – his own political creed – from the older *laissez-faire* liberalism and also from socialism. In an earlier work, *Democracy and Reaction*, he spelt out the distinction. Liberals stood for freedom; the inheritors of a long tradition of men who fought for liberty where law and government restricted human development. Socialists stood for solidarity and the obligations of the strong to the weak. In the New Liberalism these two ideals were not in conflict but complementary, it being recognised that not all talents should have freedom to develop, but only those that contributed to the harmonious working of an ordered society. Both liberalism and socialism might be and had been distorted: liberalism to countenance commercial competition where merit was measured by money-making capacity and mutual help scorned as saving the feckless; socialism when it shed its liberal and democratic elements, adopting the trappings of an authoritarian state, concentrating on the machinery of government and appointing 'experts' to prescribe to men and women how they should be virtuous and happy.[28]

Hobhouse, with Hobson, propounds an organic view of society where the rights and duties of individuals are defined by the common good, and where the common good implies and requires free scope for the development of the personality of each member of the community.

Concern for the common good, however, necessarily limits individual freedom, which can only be legitimately exercised in ways that do not injure anyone else. True liberty depends on restraint, by law or custom or individual feelings, from actions that may harm others.

Hobhouse's understanding of freedom implies a substantial measure of equality. If citizens are to be free to develop their personality – always bearing in mind that similar rights be accorded to others and that development must be consistent with the common good – they must have equal rights before the law and equal opportunities. 'Freedom to choose and follow an occupation, if it is to become fully effective, means equality with others in the opportunities for following such occupation.'[29] Thus, *laissez-faire* as a principle of government founders because state intervention may be necessary to establish sufficient equality of circumstances to permit, for example, 'free' bargaining between individuals:

> The weaker man consents as one slipping over a precipice might consent to give all his fortune to one who will throw him a rope on no other terms. True consent is free consent, and full freedom of consent implies equality on the part of both parties to the bargain.[30]

Such a conception of equality did not imply, Hobhouse pointed out, as Tawney after him, either equality of treatment or equality of powers: 'An absurd misconception fostered principally by opponents of equality for controversial purposes'.[31]

True liberty, then, meant opportunities for individual choice, subject to similar opportunities being assured for all, to pursue objectives consistent with the common good. Restraint was indispensable but it was only a means to an end – the enlargement of liberty. Thus Hobhouse attempted to resolve the problem of opposition of interest between state and citizen by denying its existence. The state was one of many associations for maintaining and improving social life; government intervention or 'restraint' involved no conflict with personal liberty but was necessary for its effective realisation.[32]

There was an essential condition, however, for the successful joint pursuit of individual freedom and the common good that turned on the character of the state. The 'full fruits of social progress' would only appear where the generality of men and women were contributors as well as recipients; where the rights and responsibilities of citizens were 'real and living' and extended as widely as the conditions of society allowed. This echoes Hobson's and Barnett's insistence that democracy required that the intelligence and goodwill of private citizens inform public life. In Hobhouse's words, if restraint were to be just it must reflect the wishes of the people; if individual freedom were curtailed, it should be for the common good; and the common good rested on the enlargement of mind and development of character in the whole community.[33]

This view of the state enabled Hobhouse to support government intervention. It was a very different matter, he argued, in Cobden's day when government was run by the aristocracy 'tempered by middle-class influence' so that it was natural for the leaders of democratic thought to oppose it. But when government represented the people opposition was neither necessary nor appropriate. Instead, 'there arises a stronger sense of collective responsibility and a keener desire for the use of the collective resources and organised powers of the community for public needs'.[34] This was not to suppose that social progress was automatic, nor that the state alone could ensure it. It depended also on co-operative effort and voluntary association and individual choice. Advance was not a mechanical affair but a liberation of 'living spiritual energy' and good government was that which allowed such energy free expression, so 'expanding and ennobling the life of the mind'.[35]

Nevertheless, absence of legal restraint might impair true freedom – as in bargaining where the stronger could coerce the weaker. Moreover, as the common good included the good of every member, even self-inflicted injury was matter for common concern. It was perfectly legitimate for the state to coerce a man for his own good, a view contrary to Mill's belief that intervention was not justified where a person's conduct affected only himself. Hobhouse illustrates his argument by pointing to the insane, restrained for social reasons as well as for their own benefit. The latter reason alone, he argued, would be sufficient to justify coercion, as it would for anyone incapable of rational choice, such as drunkards who are victims of an impulse grown beyond control. Liberty went with self-restraint; where that failed the state should act.

There were, however, limits to what coercion could achieve. In particular, and here Hobhouse parts company with Mrs Webb and follows the teaching of Green, legislation could not make people moral; what Acts of Parliament could do was create the conditions in which morality could grow.[36] The only enduring good for individuals lay in the development and fulfilment of personality, and this came only through the exercise of the individual's will and sense of right to overcome bad impulses. Where there was coercion there could be no moral development; liberty and self-control were preconditions of spiritual growth.[37]

For Hobhouse the problem of politics was to secure liberty and the right to personal development while containing the 'ubiquitous encroachment' of state authority. It was wrong to define liberty as the absence of state control; but government power must be directed to the maintenance and development of individual rights and away from attempts to control opinion and dictate private morality.[38] If it were the state's job to secure the conditions in which mind and character could develop and where citizens could equip themselves for full civic life by their own efforts, then the 'normal man' must be able to feed, house and clothe himself and his family through useful labour. This implied the right to work and also the right to a living wage – both just as valid as rights of person or property and integral to a good society.

Hobhouse elaborates and defends the right to work in detail. A society in which any man was unable to find work was defective. Workmen were not responsible for the failure of the economic system, but it was they who bore the cost, and this was an offence against justice. The claims of justice might be hard to meet but they could not be denied: 'the workman who is unemployed or underpaid through economic malorganisation will remain a reproach not to the charity but to the justice of society as long as he is to be seen in the land'.[39]

Such views, Hobhouse believed, were coming to prevail, partly through a greater sense of collective responsibility, and partly as a result of experience. But although living standards had risen through the nineteenth century in response to government measures and to trade union and co-operative effort, the prospect of complete and life-long independence for the average worker remained exceedingly remote. Education brought new needs but the increase in wages was not proportionate to the general increase in wealth, and Booth and Rowntree had shown that many workers could not earn enough for the bare physical necessities for their families. The industrial system thus failed to meet the ethical demands embodied in the concept of a living wage, for opportunities for work, as Hobson had also asserted, were beyond the control of individual workmen and could only be secured, if at all, by the organised action of the community. To the charge that this implied socialism, not liberalism, Hobhouse retorted that socialism could be liberal as well as illiberal, democratic and founded on freedom rather than depending on mechanical and dictatorial state power.

It is noteworthy that Hobhouse extends his discussion of the rights attaching to work to activities outside the formal economy, anticipating the debates of the later part of the century. His conception of a living wage included the idea of a pension without any means test to encourage thrift and permit independence. He sought to avoid destitution rather than rescue the destitute. Furthermore, mothers should receive payment to look after their children rather than being obliged to work. Such payment should be regarded not as a dole, but as recompense for civic service to enable women to bring up children in health and happiness with no degradation attached to receiving public money.[40] The recognition of the crucial social importance of what is generally women's work was only one aspect of the wider conception of social and economic justice espoused by the New Liberals. In a country as rich as the UK, Hobhouse declared, every citizen should have the chance of work offering a healthy and civilised life or, failing work, maintenance from the state as of right, not through charity.

Furthermore, the distribution of wealth needed review. Hobhouse proposed a general and universal right to property. It was wrong that the laws of inheritance and bequest perpetuated vast inequalities so that some were born to nothing but what they could earn and some to more than any individual could possibly deserve. Property had become a means to power over others rather than to personal security. Some part of the national wealth, Hobhouse argued, with Hobson, should be regarded as social, being the creation of society rather than of any individual. Society protected property owners against theft, maintained law and order and thus safeguarded possessions. It was also indispensable in the creation of wealth for in production men used the 'available means of civilisation'. Society provided opportunities and the different use made of them represented the personal element in production and the basis of claims to reward. The function of taxation should be to remove the element of wealth that was of social origin and bring it into the public coffers to be used for the common good.[41] Such redistribution involved no injustice, Hobhouse claimed, pursuing his attempts to reconcile individual and collective interests. Much expenditure directed to the poor also benefited everyone else; not only sanitary and educational policies but also the prevention and relief of poverty, for the existence of avoidable suffering diminished general well-being.

Returning to income and the concept of a living wage, Hobhouse insisted that earnings should be sufficient to provide against all risks for an average family, meeting not only the cost of food and clothing and shelter but of sickness, accident, unemployment, education and old age. They should also, however, be related to function. It should be a central object of liberal economics, Hobhouse declared, to equate social service and reward:

> every function of social value requires such remuneration as serves to stimulate and maintain its effective performance; . . . everyone who performs such a function has the right, in the strict ethical sense of that term, to such remuneration and no more; . . . the residue of existing wealth should be at the disposal of the community for social purposes.[42]

Such a doctrine would seem to bear hardly on those whose 'social function' had little market value. But Hobhouse resolved the problem by proposing that unskilled workers, as citizens, should be accorded property rights, representing a share in the social inheritance, to supplement their low earnings – an early statement of the case for what in the 1990s is called a basic or citizen's income.

Overall, Hobhouse's idea of liberalism is a large one. He envisaged a society where citizens were free to pursue their personal affairs according to their own preferences, but also acknowledged the economic sovereignty of the state, for liberty depended on control. On the other hand, liberalism, like some brands of socialism, could not be confined to one country; it was not a local but an international movement bound up, Hobhouse asserted grandly, with the advance of civilisation. The manner in which the state exercised control would have to be learned through experience. The lessons of history, Hobhouse believed, taught that progress was more secure when men were content to deal with problems piecemeal.

At the same time, the authority of the state, if it were to respect individual freedom, must depend on the 'willing, convinced, open-eyed support of the mass'.[43] Hobhouse recognised that 'whole-hearted absorption' in the public interest was rare, but he was confident that the masses would respond and assent to things forwarding the moral and material welfare of the country. Nevertheless, intelligent interest in public affairs could not be created by democratic forms of government alone. The modern state was highly complex, and individuals would need encouragement and direction to join fellow workers in trade unions, chapels or local government, organisations small enough to allow the development and exercise of responsibility. Social interest depended not only on adult suffrage but on a range of institutions intermediate between government and people. No amount of political democracy, however, could guarantee social rights and liberties; the organisation and experience of work remained a fundamental element in the experience of citizenship: 'People are not fully free in their political capacity when they are subject industrially to conditions which take the life and heart out of them.'[44]

It fell to Tawney, through the 1920s and 1930s and reviewing the state of the nation after the Labour government of the early post-War years, to gather together the threads of what he called 'The Radical Tradition' into a cogent and powerful critique of British industrial society. Tawney wrote about socialism rather than liberalism, evincing a commitment to democracy and to equality that would have shocked Ruskin, the self-styled conservative. But Tawney's socialism also involved a criticism of social and economic life, and a distinction between wealth and 'illth' which Ruskin would have heartily applauded. The revolt against capitalism, Tawney suggested, was the expression of resentment against an economic system that dehumanised existence by treating the mass of mankind not as responsible partners but as instruments to be manipulated for the pecuniary advantage of a minority of property owners.

Tawney described his ideal socialist society as 'a community of responsible men and women working without fear in comradeship for common ends, all of whom can grow to their full stature, develop to the utmost limit the varying capacities with which nature has endowed them.' The emphasis is on the free actions and intercourse of ordinary people. Government might extend its activities but there would be no deification of the state which was properly regarded not as master but as 'serviceable drudge'. The conscience of individuals was the ultimate tribunal by which all forms of policy would be tried.[45] The end of social organisation was:

> to ensure that limited resources are used in the general interest to meet social needs in the order of their relative importance, and that the crucial decisions . . . shall be taken not by persons responsible to no-one but themselves . . . but by public authorities who can be called to account.[46]

These words, written in 1952, contain the essence of Tawney's conception of the good society founded on freedom, equality and solidarity. The three principles were inextricably linked and interdependent. The supreme political good was the guarantee of freedom of opportunity for all citizens to become the best of which they were capable, the promoting of 'the growth towards perfection of individual human beings'.[47] But, with Hobson and Hobhouse, Tawney recognised that the liberties of individuals were limited in that they must be consistent with the common good; men must regard themselves not as owners of rights but as trustees for the discharge of functions, instruments of a social purpose.[48]

Also with Hobhouse, Tawney insisted that if governments were to secure liberty for their people they would need also to secure more equality; not 'to reduce the variety of individual character and genius to a drab and monotonous uniformity', but to 'cultivate those powers in all men, not only in a few'.[49] This did not mean equalising individual incomes; rather it called for pooling surplus resources through taxation and using them to provide for everybody, irrespective of income, occupation, or social position 'the conditions of civilisation which, in the absence of such measures, can be enjoyed only by the rich'.[50] Here was the commitment to solidarity, or fraternity in the older terminology. All citizens would receive a 'social income' over and above their earnings, not in the form of money but of social well-being. A sensible society would use its surplus first to raise general standards of health, second to equalise educational opportunities and third to provide for the 'contingencies of life', that is, to alleviate the insecurities of sickness and old age and unemployment.

The contrasts in the general levels of economic security were more fundamental and more damaging, Tawney maintained, than the contrasts in income. He agreed with Hobson that unemployment represented social breakdown and that society should bear the cost. Benefits for the unemployed must be adequate and a matter of right not grace. Nor must social provision disguise the need for more radical measures. 'The central problem of unemployment, however, is obviously different. It lies in the region of financial and industrial policy, with which the social services are not directly concerned.'[51]

In his writing on industrial policy Tawney vividly brings together his three guiding principles. He considered the extension of liberty from the political to the economic sphere among the most urgent tasks of industrial societies, but liberty must go along with equality and co-operation. The proper organisation of industry turned on the obligations attaching to property and on the rights and duties of workers in relation to managers and the owners of capital. Like Hobhouse, Tawney claimed that the possession of property was only morally acceptable when it was conditional on the performance of some function. Property that yielded income without any social obligation was a disaster that destroyed social unity. But in modern industrial societies, Tawney pointed out, most property consisted of rights in royalties or rents or shares, irrespective of service by their owners. This was better regarded, as Hobson had suggested, as 'Improperty'[52] and could be put to far better use:

> Turned into another channel, half the wealth distributed in dividends to functionless shareholders could secure every child a good education up to 18, could re-endow English universities, and . . . could equip English industries for more efficient production.[53]

Property in things, moreover, became sovereignty over persons; the wage earner could lose his livelihood if he were dismissed from his job. Control of a large enterprise gave a degree of power over the lives of workers that Tawney, in 1921, likened to 'industrial feudalism':

> It is not easy to understand how the traditional liberties of Englishmen are compatible with an organisation of industry which, except in so far as it has been qualified by the law or by trade unionism, permits populations almost as large as those of some famous cities of the past to be controlled in their rising up and lying down, in their work, economic opportunities, and social life by the decisions of a Committee of half-a-dozen Directors.[54]

The solution that Tawney had proposed in 1918, in 'The Conditions of Economic Liberty', was industrial democracy. The workers, not the capitalists, should become the centre of industrial authority with power and influence extending beyond the fixing of hours and wages to industrial policy and workshop organisation. 'The employer would cease to be a capitalist or "master", and would become an organiser . . . The workman would cease to be a "hand", and would become a citizen of industry, who . . . had a voice in industrial policy and organisation.'[55] The workers, Tawney believed, were best placed to hold industry to its proper character as a social function. The reorganisation of industry would offer 'conditions of corporate freedom', but it would also improve the quality and efficiency of service. It should be conducted in full publicity with regard to profits and costs; and all payments should be proportionate to service rendered, for 'No man will work harder to make necessaries, if he sees that another obtains comforts without working at all'.[56]

The arrangements that Tawney envisaged, echoing Ruskin, required that industry be regarded as a public service and organised as a profession. Building a house or making boots was no more degrading than curing the sick or teaching the ignorant – just as necessary and therefore just as honourable. Manual work should be equally bound by rules designed to maintain quality of service and equally free of the 'vulgar subordination of moral standards to financial interests'.[57] Professional organisation thus involved not only the abolition of functionless property but the active co-operation and goodwill of all workers, not just a select class, in seeing that work was performed effectively. But the development of professional feelings of collective responsibility for maintaining high standards, the alternative source of the discipline that capitalism had exercised in the past, posed problems among workers who were frequently hostile or apathetic. The apathy and torpor might be lifted, Tawney hoped, if socialism could develop as an 'inspiring force'; a socialist government, he wrote in 1952, must 'persuade men to be free'.[58] While no change of system or machinery of government could destroy the egotism, greed and quarrelsomeness of human nature, it could create an environment that discouraged those qualities.[59]

Trade unions must also change their role from that of 'an opposition that never became a government'. This might be unavoidable while they were absorbed in defending workers from capitalists intent on maximising their profits. But if the abolition of 'functionless property' transferred the control of production to bodies representing workers, trade unions need no longer merely oppose; they would have a duty to advise and initiate and 'to force upon their own members the obligations of their craft'.[60] So far as wages were concerned, Tawney followed the Hobsonian doctrine and the logic of his own distaste for functionless property, insisting that rewards be enough for efficient production and no more.

> No-one has any business to expect to be paid 'what he is worth,' for what he is worth is a matter between his own soul and God. What he has a right to demand, and what it concerns his fellow-men to see that he gets, is enough to enable him to perform his work.[61]

The severity of this pronouncement is modified by Tawney's equal insistence on the 'social income', the guarantee of collective provision for well-being over and above what might be purchased with individual earnings. Writing in 1952 on 'British Socialism To-day', he proclaims the aim to be 'a complete divorce between differences of pecuniary income and differences in respect of health, security, amenity of environment, culture, social status and esteem'.[62] This is linked to warnings of the dangers of pursuing equality of opportunity, which may well turn into equal opportunities to become unequal. Better to emphasise solidarity than mobility, Tawney declared, with high standards of civilisation for the mass of mankind who 'cannot perform athletic feats in scaling social heights'; better to concentrate on raising the quality of universal provision rather than 'enlarging the meshes of selective sieves'.

NOTES

1   Webb and Webb, 1963, Part II vol 2, pp. 640–57.
2   Morris, in *Commonweal* 1890, cited in Thompson, E. P., 1955, p. 666.
3   Webb, 'Historic' in Shaw, 1889, p. 35.
4   *Ibid.*, p. 47.
5   Besant, 'Industry under Socialism' in Shaw, 1889, p. 168.
6   Shaw, 'Transition' in Shaw, 1889, pp. 200–1.
7   Bland, 'The Outlook' in Shaw, 1889, p. 202.
8   Hobson, 1895, chapter 2.
9   *Ibid.*, p. 33.
10   *Ibid.*, p. 135.
11   *Ibid.*, p. 118.
12   *Ibid.*, p. 169.
13   *Ibid.*, p. 177.
14   Hobson, 1896, p. 16.
15   *Ibid.*, p. 160.
16   Hobson, 1909 (II), p. 11.
17   *Ibid.*, p. 13.
18   *Ibid.*, p. 44.
19   *Ibid.*, p. 83.
20   *Ibid.*, p. 91.
21   *Ibid.*, p. 116.
22   *Ibid.*, p. 135.
23   *Ibid.*, p. 223.
24   Hobson, 1909 (I), p. 93.
25   Hobson, 1909 (II), p. 245.
26   Crossman, 1973 in Halsey (ed.), 1976.
27   Hobhouse, 1945.
28   Hobhouse, 1904, p. 228.
29   Hobhouse, 1945, p. 32.

30   *Ibid.*, p. 91.
31   *Ibid.*, p. 131.
32   *Ibid.*, p. 134.
33   Hobhouse, 1922, p. 90.
34   Hobhouse, 1904, p. 221.
35   Hobhouse, 1945, p. 137.
36   *Ibid.*, p. 143.
37   Hobhouse, 1922, p. 71.
38   *Ibid.*, p. 82.
39   Hobhouse, 1945, p. 160.
40   *Ibid.*, p. 180.
41   *Ibid.*, p .189.
42   *Ibid.*, p 209.
43   *Ibid.*, p. 231.
44   *Ibid.*, p. 249.
45   Tawney, 'British Socialism Today' in Tawney, 1964 (II), p. 168.
46   *Ibid.*, p. 174.
47   Tawney, 'Inequality and Social Structure' in Tawney, 1964 (I), p. 85.
48   Tawney, 1982, p. 48.
49   Tawney, 'Inequality and Social Structure' in Tawney, 1964 (I), p. 86.
50   Tawney, 'The Strategy of Equality' in Tawney, 1964 (I), p. 122.
51   *Ibid.*, p. 148.
52   Tawney, 1982, p. 57.
53   *Ibid.*, p. 76.
54   *Ibid.*, p. 130.
55   Tawney, 'The Conditions of Economic Liberty' in Tawney, 1964 (II), p. 110.
56   *Ibid.*, p. 115.
57   Tawney, 1982, p. 92.
58   Tawney, 'British Socialism Today' in Tawney, 1964 (II), p. 177.
59   Tawney, 1982, p. 176.
60   *Ibid.*, p. 152.
61   *Ibid.*, p. 174.
62   Tawney, 'British Socialism Today' in Tawney, 1964 (II), p. 179.

8 Beveridge and After

Work is central to our lives . . . It is the heart of wealth and welfare.

(Commission on Social Justice)

For two or three decades after the Second World War discussion of the right to work and the organisation, conditions and rewards for employment slipped out of political debate. This was natural enough, for the depression of the 1920s and 1930s had been dissipated by the war, and economic growth, bringing jobs for nearly all who wanted them, continued into the 1970s. Furthermore, it was supposed that governments, following Keynesian precepts, would be able to avoid severe and protracted unemployment by balancing fluctuations in markets with public spending to maintain demand and secure jobs. Moreover, some old battles over working conditions and the organisation of industry seemed to have been won. Improvements in hours and pay and holidays were evident; wages councils were established for occupations where trade unions were weak; and some industries where relations between workers and employers had been particularly bad – notably the coal mines – had been 'nationalised' and came under the supposedly benevolent protection of the state.

The high hopes engendered in the 1940s, however, resting on assumptions of steady economic growth which would not only guarantee jobs but also provide the wherewithal for increasing state welfare for all citizens, in and out of work, did not survive the leaner years after 1974. Nor was the optimism ever universal. The liberal fear and distrust of an expanding state that threatened freedom, undermined moral character, sapped initiative and encouraged dependency – and which, moreover, would be unable to fulfil its promises – expressed, for instance, by Friedrich von Hayek and Milton Friedman were reflected in the claims of right-wing critics that much public welfare spending was unnecessary, damaging and wasteful.

The views of the economic liberals shaped the social and economic policies of the Conservative governments in office after 1979, but challenges to state welfare had already come from the left.[1] Not only were public services seen to be failing to achieve their aims, but the recognition of their limitations re-awakened the old debate about the proper division of responsibilities between government

145

and individuals. The vital importance for a civilised society of voluntary action and of the duties and responsibilities, as well as the rights,
of citizens received renewed emphasis.

These questions had also preoccupied Beveridge, the political liberal. They recur throughout his writing and form a central theme
in his famous plan for social security. His proposals for income
maintenance, designed to abolish poverty and make want 'forever
unnecessary', were intended as one element only in a much wider
programme of government action to tackle not only Want but
the other four giants barring the way to social advance – Idleness,
Ignorance, Squalor and Disease. So comprehensive a conception
of collective responsibility immediately raised familiar questions
about the limits of the authority of the state and the rights
and obligations of its citizens. These were matters of great moment
for Beveridge, and his writings reflect the dilemma of a liberal convinced that government must guarantee basic security for people
in distress but also fearful of the invasion of individual liberties by
state power. In *Social Insurance and Allied Services*, in *Full Employment in a Free Society*, and in *Voluntary Action*, Beveridge sets out
to balance the demands of increasingly intrusive government, albeit
acting in the interests of its people, with the claims and rights of
citizens to be left alone.[2]

The conception of citizenship that emerges is a delicate mixture of
rights and duties and responsibilities, but the rights are essentially
contractual, grounded in work, and thus distinct from the rights of
citizenship grounded in status as understood by T. H. Marshall. Work
was fundamental to Beveridge's notion of the social rights of citizenship in two ways. First, his whole scheme of protection against poverty could only survive in conditions of full employment. Return to
the mass unemployment of the years before the war would destroy it.
Here Beveridge was insisting that social and economic policies are
inseparable, and that social provision can only develop within a
healthy economy. Second, insurance benefits, the payments 'as of
right' to deal with poverty due to the interruption or failure of earning
power that Beveridge saw as the major hazard, were conditional on a
record of contributions during paid work. People with no history of
paid employment would rely on national assistance, receiving benefit
only after detailed enquiries into their needs. Such arrangements not
only undermined citizenship rights to privacy and independence, they
also discouraged saving and work and encouraged dishonesty and
concealment, as many writers have pointed out.[3] Lady Rhys Williams,

a contemporary of Beveridge spoke particularly vehemently against means tests:

> Nothing is more calculated to break down the proud spirit of a British workman, or to induce a whining, slavish outlook, than this intolerable instrument of mental torture . . . The establishment of the principle that the state owes maintenance to the individual *as a right*, and not out of pity, coupled with the corresponding assumption that the individual owes to the state the duty of maintaining the wealth of the community and contributing all he can to the well-being, not merely of his own family, but of all his fellow citizens, should do much to develop the spirit of public service in every section of the nation which has already been so strikingly aroused during war'.[4]

While a full employment economy was essential to reduce dependency and sustain the social security scheme, the opportunity to work was also one of the most fundamental rights of citizenship. This is a view echoed fifty years later in the Social Justice report: 'Work is central to our lives . . . It is a source of personal identity and individual fulfilment, social status and relationships. It is the heart of wealth and welfare'.[5] Full employment did not mean no unemployment. Seasonal changes made some work impossible at some times; and changes in the demand for labour would mean periods out of work before moving into a new occupation. By full employment Beveridge meant that there should always be more vacancies than men to fill them, and that the jobs should be at fair wages, and of such a kind and in such a place that unemployed men could reasonably be expected to take them. While overall unemployment might run at three per cent, those losing jobs must be able to find new ones within their capacities without delay.[6] No one should be out of work for a longer time than could be covered by unemployment benefit without risk of hardship or demoralisation.

That the labour market should be a seller's, not a buyer's, market followed from Beveridge's view that society existed for the individual. Difficulty in selling had infinitely more harmful consequences than difficulty in buying labour. Difficulty in buying meant inconvenience or reduced profits, but a person who could not sell his labour was told, in effect, that he was no use. The one problem might cause annoyance; the other was a personal catastrophe.[7] The object, however, was not *any* kind of employment. The end of all human activity, Beveridge declared, as Ruskin before him, was consumption. Men must be able to do *useful* work that led to more leisure or higher living standards. Employment that was time wasting or destructive – digging holes and filling them up again, making war or preparing for war – served no useful purpose.

But government policies for full employment raised questions about the balance of power between the state and its people. Essential citizen liberties, Beveridge insisted, including choice of occupation, must be preserved and this was a more complicated matter in a free society than in a totalitarian regime. Job security, for instance, might reduce incentives to productivity in work. But a civilised society must find other ways than fear for preserving industrial discipline; there must be no fines or imprisonment as punishment for refusing to work or for inefficiency: 'It is an essential condition of freedom', Beveridge wrote, 'that in peace each individual should be able to choose between leisure and more earnings, as he may choose between available occupations'.[8] Problems of industrial discipline or work incentives could be tackled by good management, by encouraging workpeople to discuss their common interests and develop a sense of partnership in the enterprise so that conditions of employment would be seen to be just. Or, as Ruskin or Tawney would have it, by treating workers as professionals.

Inflation was a further possible consequence of full employment that Beveridge foresaw. If a seller's market strengthened labour's bargaining power to win a larger share of the products of industry, that was to be welcomed. But irresponsible demands leading to wage and price inflation would benefit nobody. The main responsibility for avoiding such developments and achieving a unified wages policy, Beveridge asserted, lay with the central organisations of labour – in particular with the General Council of the TUC. But wages should be determined by reason, not simply by bargaining power, so there should be provision for arbitration where agreement broke down. The state and employers would also have their responsibilities; government for pursuing stable prices and employers for disclosing all the financial circumstances of their industries to induce rational discussion over wage claims.

It would be possible, Beveridge supposed, to reach full employment in a largely free enterprise economy, but should experience indicate that abolition of private ownership was necessary, abolition there would have to be. The full employment policy he proposed had three elements; the maintenance of demand, control of the location of industry and organised mobility of labour.[9] Only the state had the power to establish a demand for goods that would mean work for all.

Only the state could control the location of industry and so avoid the evils of congestion, overcrowding, ill-health, bad housing and the destruction of rural and urban amenities; and it was less an interference with liberty to control business men in placing their enterprises than to require workpeople to move their homes for the sake of employment. Organised mobility of labour did not mean that people would be constantly moving home and jobs, but that they would be guided into new occupations when change was necessary. Beveridge left it open as to whether everyone should be obliged to use labour exchanges, but he thought it should be compulsory for under 18s so that young people could be wisely directed into work.

It is ironical that the strategy of linking entitlements to contributions during paid employment, which Beveridge saw as a guarantee that benefits could be claimed as a right and without any stigma of poor relief, emerged forty years later as a major problem in social security arrangements. The huge increase in the number of people subjected to means tested assistance, widely considered not only demeaning but inefficient, has demonstrated the limitations of social security payments depending on contributions. And the failure to offer security to women looking after their households or children, and without paid employment, has further weakened the appeal of contractual arrangements. One proposed remedy is some kind of universal 'citizens' income' financed from general taxation – Tawney's social income, though in cash.

But in the 1940s, the contributory scheme that Beveridge had fashioned offered hope of a future which protected and nurtured the sense and the reality of the solidarity, liberty and equality on which citizenship depends. Contributions were important as both tangible and symbolic evidence of membership of the community; although without an actuarial relationship to benefits, they established the right to receive them in defined circumstances. They demonstrated the active part played by all workers in providing for a common future which could not be secured by individuals alone. They thus underlined the value of both independent and collective effort.

Beveridge was always anxious to preserve personal liberty and leave room for voluntary action. He avoided means tests as far as possible and set insurance benefits at a level intended to be adequate for essential needs but no more, leaving people 'free' to make their own arrangements for whatever higher standard of living they might desire – a rather spurious freedom, perhaps, for the poor. But meagre benefits, Beveridge supposed, protected liberty in another sense by reducing the need for tax transfers and higher taxation which would interfere with the right of higher earners to dispose of their incomes as they wished.

Apart from the desire to encourage solidarity and safeguard liberty, the insurance system also expressed a rather curious understanding of equality. Contributions and benefits were set at a flat rate, levied irrespective of earnings and paid without enquiry into income. All were to 'stand in on the same terms', contributions being low enough to avoid hardship for the lowest paid workers, and benefits sufficient for all 'normal' needs available without discrimination for people in the defined categories of risk.

But, however meagre, cash benefits without stigma were vulnerable to abuse so respect for individual liberties had to be balanced against the risk of 'free riding'. Perhaps more important, Beveridge regarded idleness, even with a guaranteed income, as demoralising. After a certain period, therefore, unemployment benefit should be conditional on attendance at a work or training centre.[10] Existing sanctions against people who had been dismissed for misconduct or had left a job without just cause or who refused the offer of suitable work should remain and would involve disqualification from unemployment benefit and transfer to national assistance. This latter scheme was subject to a means test, and to any conditions that might restore earning capacity. While adequate for subsistence, it was intended to be less desirable than unemployment benefit, thus emphasising the advantages of the contributory system. Even so, Beveridge acknowledged the need for measures to deal with those who might abuse the arrangements. In the last resort, a man refusing to comply with the conditions and failing to maintain his family could be imprisoned.[11]

Such a notion of citizenship, embodying the right but also the duty to work, survived without much challenge for thirty years or so after the Second World War. In the White Paper on employment policy of 1944, heralded by Beveridge as a milestone in political and economic history, the government accepted the maintenance of high and stable levels of employment, which would require policies for maintaining expenditure, as a primary aim. Even at the time, however, and despite his welcome for the White Paper, Beveridge criticised the inadequacy of the practical proposals to put the policies into effect. There was insufficient recognition, he thought, of the past failure of the unplanned economy; and a wrong sense of values in treating private enterprise as sacrosanct and in regarding a balanced budget as equally important as full employment.[12] During the 1970s, however, as full employment and stable prices slipped out of the government's grasp, and as unpaid work in families and communities, traditionally the responsibility of women, slowly won more status and recognition, the whole question of the rights and responsibilities of citizens in relation to paid employment began to be considered afresh.

THE REAWAKENING

There were two significant developments that fashioned the new debate. First was the insidious spread of tolerance for higher levels of unemployment along with the shift in political priorities to give more weight to controlling inflation and encouraging a competitive economy. Second, in response to the growing numbers of people out of work and challenging the apparent public and governmental complacency, a growing volume of research literature began to appear using sophisticated sociological analysis to examine the nature of unemployment, its causes and its consequences for people without jobs.

For twenty years or so after the war the average unemployment rate was under two per cent. Through the 1950s, however, British policies failed to reconcile full employment with stable prices[13] and at the end of the 1960s unemployment began to rise. By 1980 it was over six per cent, affecting one and a half million people, and was to rise still further to reach nearly three million in 1987 and again in 1993, a rate of over 12 per cent. By the late 1980s, it has been claimed, unemployment was a 'forgotten issue'; not because it had diminished, but because it had been redefined as an individual and residual problem for which an enterprising free market economy had no responsibility.[14]

The changing significance of unemployment in post-war politics and the acceptance of relatively high levels remain to be explained. In the optimistic war years of planning and reconstruction it was widely supposed that democratic institutions could not survive the return of the mass unemployment of the 1930s.[15] The social and economic distress of the Depression had failed to produce theories or policies to relieve it. But Keynes' adding of 'involuntary' to the frictional and voluntary unemployment recognised by the classical economists, and his support for government intervention to increase demand through stimulating consumption and investment, seemed to offer a solution. Beveridge also, viewing lack of work as a personal catastrophe, had insisted that governments could and should regulate the economy to maintain demand and that in a tight labour market government, trade unions and employers must work together to preserve industrial discipline and control wage inflation.

While the number of people out of work had remained at about half a million there had been little concern about malingering or pressure to reduce benefits. In 1956 the National Assistance Board concluded, after interviewing 32 000 men and women under 60 claiming unemployment benefit, that only one-third could be considered reluctant to work and that three-quarters of those were handicapped in some way. But as the numbers rose public opinion tended to harden against those without jobs, and the growing acceptance of free market economics encouraged the view that unemployment lay beyond government control. Many economists writing in the 1970s argued that full employment could no longer be the main objective of government policy as the danger of inflation was too great. In 1974 Sir Keith Joseph, for instance, who had great influence on Conservative politicians, declared that unemployment would not be cured by increasing demand. In any case, he suggested, its true extent was exaggerated; over 30 per cent of people out of work, he asserted, were either voluntarily unemployed or unemployable, others were merely changing jobs or waiting for retirement, and at least 10 per cent of claims were fraudulent. Genuine unemployment, Sir Keith claimed, was concentrated in a few parts of the country and among particular groups of workers; the best way to deal with it was to seek stable prices, encourage labour mobility, expand training and improve incentives to work.[16] Two years later, the Labour Prime Minister, Mr Callaghan, told the party conference that to spend your way out of a depression was no longer an option.

The rejection of demand management for supply-side policies was strengthened with the advent of Mrs Thatcher's administration in 1979 and continued during the succeeding Conservative governments. The persistence of this approach, in the face of official unemployment rising at times to around three million (and with many claiming a more realistic figure of four million) has provoked some economists to challenge the new orthodoxies. They point to the economic and social costs of maintaining people out of work and insist that unemployment is a crisis for the economy as well as for the individuals who suffer it. Meanwhile, the continuing high levels have stimulated the interest of sociologists in its causes and nature and consequences for people without jobs.

Unemployment had begun to emerge again as a political issue by the early 1970s with governments anxious to increase productivity and concerned about inefficiency and overmanning but facing a shortage of skilled labour even with over half a million unemployed. A central question of research studies of the time was how far such a level of employment was acceptable; how far it reflected people changing jobs, or people not keen on or not able to find them. In 1974 a national survey of the unemployed[17] found half the sample had been energetically but unsuccessfully looking for work for over three months. Only 22 per cent had no or little interest in finding a job, recognising that a combination of personal characteristics and market opportunities meant that their chances were poor. The report emphasised the handicaps of age, disability and long-term unemployment in job-seeking, and found no indication that benefits discouraged the search for work. Indeed, those with higher benefits, which were however low in relation to their needs, tended to be the keenest to find employment. More people were interested in retraining (31 per cent) than there were vacancies available for them, and over a quarter had considered moving to find a job but were deterred by the associated costs. The report concluded that insurance and assistance benefits for the unemployed were inadequate and should be raised, pointing out that only seven per cent received redundancy payments and that this group was constituted of those already better off.

Similar findings came from other enquiries. Through the 1970s and 1980s empirical research provided exhaustive accounts of the characteristics and attitudes of unemployed people and the economic, social and personal consequences of their experiences. One thing to emerge very clearly was the involuntary nature of nearly all unemployment and the peculiar vulnerability of particular groups. Men and women were out of work for the most part because they could not find jobs, not because they had not looked or did not want them or were satisfied with life on the dole.

During the 1970s, however, as unemployment rose to one million yet with inflation as high as an annual rate of 25 per cent, the latter came to be feared as the greater evil. As Showler and Sinfield point out, unemployment has a limited impact but inflation affects everyone.[18] Also, unemployment began to be seen as an international problem that individual governments could do little about. Attention shifted to controlling abuses, deterring 'scroungers', strengthening incentives to work and restraining wages. The emphasis on scroungers and 'supply-side' policies generally is perhaps a substitute for new jobs as a way of dealing with unemployment; it suggests it is a problem for individuals rather than for society, thus stigmatising the victim and diminishing the responsibility of everyone else. Both Labour and Conservative governments assumed that full employment could only be manageable with a change in trade union attitudes and, especially in the case of Conservatives, a lessening of trade union power.

In a volatile political and intellectual climate, the findings of research studies substituted evidence for conjecture. It has gradually become accepted that most people who are unemployed would prefer to be in work, and that there are some whose chances of jobs are particularly poor. These are the old and the young, people in poor physical or mental health, the unskilled, women and people belonging to certain ethnic minorities. The effect of high unemployment is to worsen further the opportunities of people already at a disadvantage, for definitions of unemployability depend on the strength of the demand for labour.[19] Apart from personal characteristics, geography and work history significantly affect the risk of unemployment. Jobs are scarce in some parts of the country and a poor employment record reduces the chances of finding work.

THE EXPERIENCE OF UNEMPLOYMENT

The experience of unemployment exacts a heavy price from those who suffer it in relative poverty, ill-health and strained family and social relationships.[20] While the real value of unemployment benefit almost doubled between 1948 and the early 1990s, its value relative to average incomes fell by nearly 25 per cent. Protection through insurance has dwindled over recent years and the majority of people out of work rely on means-tested income support, now also less generous.[21] Meagre state benefits do not seem to encourage successful job seeking, any more than generous ones seriously inhibit it. Andrew Dilnot suggests that levels of benefit may have a marginal influence on length of unemployment but that 'enormous' cuts would be needed for any significant effect.[22] As it is, people on the lowest benefits seem no more ready to take work at low wages nor to move house to find it than those who are slightly better off.[23] Overall the desire to work is higher among the unemployed than among the employed population. But there is little evidence that attitudes have much to do with job chances. Local labour market opportunities and access to informal information networks matter more.[24]

As we have seen, unemployed people have suffered a steady deterioration in their cash benefits, particularly through the 1980s.[25] Studies of unemployment have also emphasised its psychological consequences. Work gives a structure to the day, offers social relationships and the chance of joining in a collective purpose, and requires regular activity. Unemployment deprives people of these experiences and their psychological health is consequently poorer though sociability outside the household may lessen the sense of deprivation. Women appear less affected than men perhaps because they can more readily occupy themselves with domestic work.[26]

The consequences of mass unemployment in the 1930s – the psychological distress, loss of self-esteem, family tension and social withdrawal – have been well documented. But the apparent tolerance of its return in the 1970s and 1980s may have reflected a different kind of experience in the later years. Shorter working hours perhaps enabled people to develop other activities and interests which could be maintained when out of work, and better welfare arrangements perhaps made unemployment more tolerable. However, Gallie and Marsh found heightened psychological stress among unemployed men in the 1980s which lessened when they returned to work.[27] And unemployment was only the extreme form of more general job insecurity that had profound implications for people's sense of well-being. While it seemed that it no longer meant retreat into inactivity, as in the 1930s, it still affected the nature of sociability. Unemployed people mixed with other unemployed people and were therefore more vulnerable, with fewer acquaintances who could provide psychological support or financial help or assistance in finding a job.[28]Unemployment was also associated with poor relationships within the household and with increased risks of marriage failure. Broken marriages were more likely for individuals who had previously been out of work, and unemployment after marriage brought substantially higher risks of dissolution. However, cause and effect are not straightforward. People appear at greater risk of unemployment if their marriages fail, so it may be that some people have the characteristics that leave them vulnerable to both events.[29]

There has been much renewed discussion in the 1980s of the notion of an underclass, a term varyingly used to denote long-term dependency, persistent poverty, perhaps delinquency, and often implying a rejection by its members of the values of the wider society. Members of the underclass are sometimes supposed to belong by choice, unwilling to work and careless of stable family relationships. Sometimes, by contrast, they are regarded as the victims of circumstance.[30] As Gallie and Marsh point out, the term can be descriptive or evaluative, referring to people who have similar repeated experiences and become identifiable as a group, or labelling them as inadequate. The underclass does exist, they suggest, as a distinctive group who experience recurrent problems, but there is no evidence of fault either in them or in the welfare system. Rather, unemployment may result in a 'spiral of disadvantage' of social isolation, depression and family breakdown that makes it difficult to get back into work. The most important predictor of unemployment is a past record of unemployment. 'After the event we may identify a group with a distinct lifestyle at the bottom of the heap, but they were not destined to be there, and under different labour market conditions . . . they would not have been there'.[31]

THE GOVERNMENT RESPONSE

If unemployment is widespread, largely involuntary, involves severe personal distress and also wider social and economic costs there is a strong case for public intervention if any of the entitlements of citizenship are to be salvaged. Full employment has eluded governments since the 1970s. Some argue that it is a past dream, no longer attainable given the development of a global economy and sophisticated technology; others insist that political will or knowledge have been lacking and that priorities have lain elsewhere. Whatever the truth of the matter, the problem has proved so intractable as to divert discussion to supply-side policies – conceived albeit as second-best and short-term measures to alleviate the damage until full employment is regained.

It is the unskilled, the old and the young who are most at risk during recession and as technology changes. But placement and training services have a dismal record since before the First World War, meticulously analysed by Desmond King. Falling prey to essentially non-interventionist governments and attracting the suspicion of both employers and trade unions, who tended to see them as suppliers of inadequately trained cheap labour, they were further undermined and stigmatised by their additional responsibility for dealing with and policing claims for unemployment benefit.[32] Labour exchanges were established in 1909 but got off to a bad start. After 1911 they were given the job of distributing unemployment benefit and thenceforth their responsibilities for organising the labour market had to compete with handing out benefits and regulating claims. This earned them the distrust of the trade unions: they might supply strike breakers; they might fail to enforce union rates of pay and they were seen as relief agencies primarily concerned with the unskilled. Skilled men turned to their unions for help in finding jobs. After 1921, as unemployment rose and the insurance base of benefits collapsed, the exchanges were called upon to distinguish people without adequate contributions and establish whether they were genuinely seeking work. In *Actively Seeking Work?*, King points to the 'devastating' effect; the emasculation of the exchanges, initially set up to help the unemployed to find work but failing to provide jobs and transformed into punitive agencies for distributing benefits after intrusive enquiries. They were regarded by the unemployed as enemy territory. Through the 1930s the exchanges filled only about one-fifth of vacancies. Employers preferred to make their own arrangements for recruiting labour and mistrusted the exchanges as suppliers of poor quality workers.

All this King sees as reflecting the British liberal political tradition, respecting individual freedom, preferring market to government in organising economic activity and leaving government to provide a minimal safety net expressive of the suspicion and wrath directed to able-bodied mendicants. After 1945 full employment and the continuing voluntarist approach to training emphasised the role of the exchanges as dealing only with the most marginal workers, a placing service for the unemployed, but with neither trade unions nor employers nor government much interested in the needs of the small though persistent group of workers failing in the market. During the years of full employment the development of training policies had perhaps seemed less urgent, but in the 1960s the comparatively poor economic performance of the UK led to more attention to promoting economic growth and thus to training. Industrial training boards with compulsory levies on industry were established to increase the supply of skilled workers and in the early 1970s the Manpower Services Commission was set up as a national body to formulate training policy.

Any aim to develop a comprehensive manpower policy, however, was undermined by the growth of unemployment among young people, a problem that overshadowed training for those in work. In the 1980s, with little support from trade unions or employers for comprehensive training policies the new programmes were directed to the young and the long-term unemployed. Even the attempt to revitalise placement and training services by establishing Job Centres had begun to flag by the 1980s as the centres ceased to focus exclusively on placement and reverted to dealing with unemployment, resuming historic policing functions with the reintegration of placement and benefit work. In 1988 the Manpower Services Commission was scrapped, having barely altered the voluntarist approach to training through apprenticeships. The long-term government neglect of manpower policies proved difficult to reverse as unemployment rose through the 1970s and the old preoccupation with unemployment and possible malingering re-emerged more strongly in the work welfare programmes of the 1990s.

Support for such programmes had been growing for some years under the impetus of new ideologies that distinguished clearly between the deserving and the undeserving and emphasised the duties of citizenship rather than the entitlements, linking rights to benefit to work or training. King notes the abandonment by government of social democratic pretensions, and the return to liberal principles that went along with diminishing labour influence, signifying the political weakness of the unemployed despite their increased numbers. The trade unions opposed compulsory training, fearing a poor quality of experience that would lead only to unsatisfactory jobs, but their power was declining after 1979. The Manpower Services Commission also opposed compulsion, but it too grew steadily weaker under successive Conservative governments. The 1990s then, displayed liberal market-oriented policies that failed to deal adequately with training needs, that aimed to control unemployment and dependency rather than provide significant training programmes. They emphasised the distinction between deserving and undeserving recipients of assistance with a corresponding distinction between contributory and non-contributory benefits and required the unemployed to demonstrate their search for work and take part in training arrangements.

In the Queen's speech in 1997 the new Labour government reaffirmed its pledge to tackle unemployment. It intended to remove 250 000 young people from the dole, offering them a choice of subsidised private or voluntary sector jobs, full-time study on an approved course, or work with a new Environment Task Force. The government also proposed a rebate for employers taking on the long-term unemployed. The schemes are to be funded by a 'windfall' tax on privatised utilities. The plans suggest greater readiness to contemplate demand-side policies to reduce unemployment. It remains to be seen whether they prove more successful than earlier 'welfare to work' programmes.

The research literature provides considerable evidence of the limitations of increasingly rigorous 'supply-side' policies. Studies from the early 1970s found little understanding or use of government training schemes but also more people interested in such programmes than were vacancies locally available.[33] The enquiries emphasised the inadequacy of unemployment benefit and the disastrous consequences of unemployment, especially for middle-aged men with dependants. They also emphasised the vulnerability of older people who were actually in jobs and the need for more effective protection against unfair dismissal. The best way to guarantee jobs for the insecure, it was pointed out, was to pursue policies of full employment, but early retirement arrangements including the early award of pensions might avoid some of the stigma of being out of work.

Another point of criticism was the collapse of insurance protection for the unemployed and the consequent dependence on means-tested allowances. By 1980 less than half of people who registered as unemployed were receiving insurance benefits. If unemployment of two million were to be permanent, Sinfield argued, it was essential to give decent support to those who suffered it. Full employment policies were being abandoned too easily and uncritically, he claimed. Lack of protest stemmed perhaps from beliefs that jobs were available, that the unemployed were malingerers or unemployable, that welfare state benefits were generous or that the 'informal economy' provided opportunities for work. All these beliefs were false, Sinfield asserted. Without an adequate demand for labour there was little hope of bringing the 'hard to employ' back to work on any significant scale.[34] A full employment economy, moreover, offered wider advantages than easing the lot of people without work. It reduced inequalities in making it easier for vulnerable workers – the old, the young, people from ethnic minorities, and the disabled – to find jobs but it also reduced fears of unemployment among working people which might lead to restrictive practices and resistance to change.[35]

The costs of a 'workless state' then, went far beyond the devastating effects on the unemployed and the loss of the production that might have improved general well-being. Discussing 'work for all' as a social policy, Showler and Sinfield insist on the importance of the quality of the experience of employment.[36] Following Ruskin and Morris, they argue that work should be enjoyable, useful and educative. Too many jobs are unproductive, unpleasant and unsatisfying. There should be more consideration of the kind of work a modern democratic society should aim to provide and of how technological change might be controlled. Furthermore, there should be attempts to remove obstacles for those not actively seeking work but who might welcome opportunities for part-time jobs such as women with children or older people. And there should also be discussion about the distribution of existing work as well as about the treatment of those without it.

While acknowledging that without a strong demand for labour measures to help the unemployed will have limited success, the need for adequate compensation becomes specially urgent as policies move in the other direction and evidence of poverty accumulates. Higher benefits for people out of work do, however, present problems if they also reduce the financial incentive for low earners to take jobs. This is particularly likely with means-tested benefits that disappear as earnings rise, and has helped to stimulate renewed interest in some form of basic income scheme which would, among other things, allow easier movement in and out of employment.[37]

A BASIC INCOME?

Cash grants from the state to guarantee a minimum standard of living when other income is deemed inadequate or is non-existent are familiar enough in the various social security arrangements of industrial countries. Benefits are generally tied to contributions during employment or depend on a means test or relate to groups who are thought to merit special support. So far as unemployed people are concerned, they are usually carefully policed to make sure that the claimant is not malingering. Payments cease on return to work.

A 'basic income', by contrast, would be a universal and unconditional payment as of right to all adults, and to parents in respect of dependent children, regardless of marital status and continuing through employment and unemployment alike. Such an arrangement has been gaining wider support and publicity over the past ten years. The Basic Income Research Group was established in 1984 (renamed Citizen's Income Research Group in 1992) to urge the case for a guaranteed minimum income and to draw attention to the growing research literature and to the lively international debate. Arguments for some kind of basic income scheme are not new. Stephen Quilley points to Tom Paine as an early exponent of a Citizen's Income. Paine urged the right to support of those 'thrown out of their natural inheritance' by the development of private ownership of land. Every proprietor of cultivated land, he claimed, owed the community a ground rent which could generate an income to pay fifteen pounds to every person reaching 21 years of age as part compensation for the loss of their 'natural inheritance' and a further ten pounds a year for the rest of their lives to those reaching the age of fifty.[38]

Similar insistence that society has a just claim on all forms of capital is, as we have seen, a familiar theme in socialist writing. Hobson distinguished the 'conscious socialists' who recognised the social property inherent in all capital in that a large part of any individual's work was due not to his solitary effort but to the assistance lent by the community that educated him.[39] It was not possible to determine the proportion due to individual effort or to society, so the only limit to society's claim was expediency. Such 'conscious socialism', Hobson admitted, was seldom explicit in England but it explained the 'unconscious socialism' underlying much of the social legislation of the nineteenth century.

Hobhouse developed a similar position. His 'liberal socialism' required the state to guarantee 'useful labour' to enable citizens to equip themselves for full civic life and to provide maintenance as a right, not a charity, if work failed. Furthermore, Hobhouse asserted a general and universal right to property. Some part of wealth should be regarded as the creation of society rather than of any individual and taxation should redistribute it for the common good. More specifically, and tackling the problem of reconciling the dual and sometimes incompatible functions of wages as rewarding work and as providing a decent livelihood, Hobhouse proposed that all unskilled workers, as citizens, should have property rights to provide an independent income to supplement low earnings.

The argument is continued by Tawney. His ideal society was one where all could grow to their full stature or, in the language of T. H. Green and his followers, develop their 'best selves'. This meant that government must use surplus resources to provide security for everyone. There must be a 'social income', not in the form of money but in well-being. Payments to the unemployed must be a matter of right, not of grace. Payments to people in work should be enough only for efficiency but low wages should be supplemented by the social income aiming at common standards of health, security, amenity, culture, social status and esteem. These things should be universally available, totally divorced from individual earnings.

In his more recent description of Agathotopia, J. E. Meade is determinedly realistic.[40] His mythical island is not utopia because imperfect individuals cannot produce a perfect society. But it is, the

Agathotopians claim, a good place to live, the economy combining the best features of socialism and capitalism. A crucial part of their arrangements is an assured basic income, essential to allow the introduction of flexible wages which are necessary for economic efficiency and for maintaining full employment. A secure fixed income in addition to earnings would equalise income distribution, and by reducing the danger that variable wages would cause personal hardship it would help to make flexible pay politically acceptable. The inhabitants of Agathotopia, Meade tells us, recognise that a secure income independent of work might lead some to choose idleness, but they dismiss this danger for four reasons. First, the assured income is too small to tempt many to rely on it. Second, it would only take effect when it became necessary to reduce wages to increase the demand for labour, so the consequent fall in involuntary unemployment would balance any rise in voluntary idleness. Third, work incentives for most people would be maintained as the secure income would continue in employment. And, finally, in any event, Agathotopians disdain unlimited growth and unnecessary consumerism and willingly accept some reduction in total output for the sake of a fairer distribution.[41] Meade elaborates this last point in Galbraithian terms when he suggests that in highly populated, rich industrial countries increases in economic activity tend to produce luxuries rather than necessities (for which demand has to be created by wasteful competitive advertising) and that increased production incurs social costs in greater congestion and greater damage to the environment which individual producers and consumers would not consider. In such circumstances more leisure may well be preferable to more employment.

Proposals for a restricted basic income – payments for children – stretch back to the nineteenth century. They have had various aims: to alleviate poverty, to encourage population growth and healthy child rearing, to recognise the importance of women's work, to preserve incentives to employment and to redistribute income from men to women and in favour of families. Ruskin advocated grants from the state to young men and women for the first seven years of marriage to enable them to 'teach and maintain their children honourably' and also so that rich and poor should not be 'sharply separated in the beginning of the war of life'.[42] Hobson wished to discourage the industrial employment of women in order to protect men's jobs and to free women for the vital business of rearing children, so laying a 'firm physical foundation for the progress of the race,'[43] but did not suggest any payment! Others proposed more practical inducements.

Hobhouse's liberal socialism involved payments to mothers for looking after their children so that they would not be obliged to work, the
payments being regarded as recompense for civic service, not as a
dole. And for Tawney, support for children was part of his wider
conception of a 'social income', collective provision for the health and
well-being of adults and children alike.

The most sustained arguments for child allowances, however, came
from Eleanor Rathbone, a persistent campaigner from the 1920s until
Beveridge introduced family allowances in his report of 1942.
Miss Rathbone believed the payments were vital for the welfare of
children and so for the health and happiness of future generations.
Men's wages were unreliable for supporting a family and in any case
women's work as housewives and mothers was so important and so
skilled that it should be publicly acknowledged and rewarded:

> the work that a woman does in her own home in bearing and
> rearing children is not only so much more important to society,
> but so much more skilled, varied and interesting than nine out of
> ten of the jobs done by working women, or for the matter of that
> by working men, that only crass bad management on the part of
> society made it seem more distasteful than tending a loom or
> punching a tram ticket.[44]

In the 1940s Beveridge recommended universal state grants for children for two main reasons: to meet family poverty, recognising that
the costs of dependants could not be a charge on wages, and to
preserve the gap between relief and employment income (by adding
allowances to earnings) and so maintain incentives to work.[45] Meanwhile Keynes had pointed out that a flat rate payment for all children
would make it easier to restrict wages and limit consumption in time
of war by protecting the poorest families.[46]

Nevertheless, the family allowances introduced in 1945, for all but
the first child, aroused little public interest, and over the next twenty
years their value was allowed to decline during a period of complacency about the effectiveness of welfare state measures. Neither of the
main political parties paid much attention to them in their election
campaigns between 1945 and 1970, being more concerned to develop
policies for old age. After 1965, however, the Child Poverty Action
Group led a movement to restore the value of the allowances, aiming
not only at more generous grants but also at simpler and better
integrated tax and welfare policies. The aims were partially met by
the introduction of the universal flat rate child benefit scheme to

replace the existing family and tax allowances for children. The campaign for universal payments for children can be seen as one element in the proposals for a basic income for all citizens.

The Citizen's Income Research Group presently defines its aims as 'For every citizen the inalienable right regardless of age, sex, race, creed, labour market or marital status to a small but guaranteed income unconditionally'.[47] There is some disagreement over details among its supporters. Different proposals may be differently financed and involve more or less generous benefits. Some, like A. B. Atkinson, prefer a 'participation' income conditional on some kind of socially useful activity as more politically acceptable than an universal handout. But whatever the variations in particular aspects of the plan, the essential features and purposes remain.

First, it is to provide a guaranteed and reliable income for people both in and out of work who have to depend on a highly volatile labour market where increasing numbers of jobs are insecure or temporary, and which offers little prospect of a return to anything like full employment in the foreseeable future. Second, it is an addition to earned income to produce a more reasonable standard of living for those on low wages or for people who can only work part-time. Third, it is an acknowledgement of the social importance of work that is presently unpaid, such as child rearing or looking after other dependants or, for those who favour an unconditional grant, the assertion of the right of every citizen to a fixed minimum income in all circumstances.

From a rather different point of view, a basic income scheme can be seen as a possible remedy for the ailing social security arrangements. Means tested benefits, on which these arrangements increasingly depend, are now widely regarded as unsatisfactory; they fail to reach many people who are eligible for them, they are expensive to administer, they stigmatise their recipients and they penalise personal savings. Moreover, they may encourage dependency. People who subsequently take a job will lose their own or their spouse's income support, so there will be little financial incentive to work if wages are low or employment is part time or if 'in work' costs – the need to buy child care, for example, or the obligation to pay tax – are high.[48] Frank Field believes that means tests provoke dishonesty in so far as receiving benefit depends on concealing other earnings or resources.[49] On all these counts means tests neither meet the entitlements nor encourage the duties of citizenship.

A basic income would reduce the need for means tested benefits, though to what extent would depend on the value of the grant. It now seems agreed that a payment adequate for subsistence, however stringently defined, would be too costly and require tax rates that would not be politically viable. In 1972 J. E. Meade took a more sanguine view, arguing – in anticipation of the Agathotopians – that a basic income, or social dividend as he then named it, should be set at the current supplementary benefit level, and that any consequent voluntary idleness or loss of production could be well afforded and might, indeed, count as social gain.[50] His successors of the 1990s are more cautious. They contemplate a more generous citizen's income, as T. H. Marshall saw the aim of social policy generally, as a guide and spur to political action; a statement of an ideal to be pursued and attained, perhaps, in the future rather than immediately realised.

NOTES

1   See, for example, Crossman 1973 in Halsey (ed.), 1976.
2   Beveridge, 1942, 1944, 1948.
3   Parker, 1995; Field, 1995.
4   Rhys Williams, 1943, p. 157.
5   Commission on Social Justice, 1994, p. 151.
6   Beveridge, 1944, p. 29; pp. 124–31.
7   *Ibid.*, 1944, p. 128.
8   *Ibid.*, 1944, p. 198.
9   *Ibid.*, 1944, p. 29.
10 Beveridge, 1942, p. 163.
11 *Ibid.*, 1942, p. 142.
12 Beveridge, 1944, pp. 261–74.
13 Showler, 1981.
14 McLaughlin, 1991, p. 2.
15 Deacon, 1981, p. 181.
16 Cited in Deacon, 1981, p. 77.
17 Daniel, 1974.
18 Showler and Sinfield, 1981, p. 231.
19 Sinfield and Showler, 1981.
20 Gallie and Marsh, 1995.
21 Hills, 1993.
22 Dilnot, 1991.
23 Gallie and Marsh, 1995.
24 *Ibid.*, 1995, p. 151, 1995.
25 Atkinson and Micklewright, 1989.
26 Gershuny, 1995.
27 Gallie and Marsh, 1995, p. 15.

28 Gallie, Gershuny and Vogler, 1995.
29 Lampard, 1995.
30 See, for example, Murray, 1990, 1994; Field, 1989; Smith, 1992; Morris, 1994; Wilson, 1987; Jencks, 1992.
31 Gallie and Marsh, 1995, p. 30.
32 King, 1995. The following discussion of the history of labour exchanges is based on King's study.
33 Hill *et al.*, 1973; Daniel, 1974.
34 Sinfield, 1981, p. 105.
35 Showler, 1981.
36 Showler and Sinfield, 1981.
37 Hakim, 1991; Deakin and Wilkinson, 1991.
38 Citizen's Income Research Group, Bulletin, no. 17, January 1994.
39 Hobson, 1895, p. 198.
40 Meade, 1993.
41 *Ibid.*, 1993, p. 91.
42 Ruskin, 1867, p. 128.
43 Hobson, 1895, p. 169.
44 Rathbone, 1924, p. 247.
45 Beveridge, 1942, paras. 411, 412.
46 Keynes, 1940.
47 Citizen's Income Research Group, Bulletin, no. 16, July 1993 and later.
48 Parker, 1995.
49 Field, 1995.
50 Meade, 1972.

III Citizenship and Welfare

9 All for One and One for All?

The discussion of citizenship and work and welfare has particular resonance at the end of the twentieth century. Economic and demographic and social trends have weakened both the market and the family, the most important sources of social well-being and economic opportunity. The decline of old industries and the rise of new technology have brought higher unemployment – especially for the unskilled – and more casual, intermittent and low paid work. Families are smaller, less durable and likely to be geographically scattered. So more people are more insecure in employment and in family attachments. This would suggest a larger role for state welfare if economic and social well-being is to be protected. But although there have been important developments in policy to widen the social rights of citizenship, governments are now increasingly reluctant to meet the mounting costs of dependency. The resurgence of economic liberalism has brought renewed insistence on family and individual responsibility and on the dangers of an interventionist state. This bodes ill for the future of citizenship. In a time of economic and social instability and increasing inequality careful government planning and high quality public services are critical for public well-being.

The problem, as Ralf Dahrendorf expresses it, is how to include people in their society; about how 'provisions' can be transformed into 'entitlements.'[1] As countries grow richer their 'welfare effort' also tends to grow; or at any rate it did before 1975.[2] But the process is neither automatic nor irreversible. Economic development opens up opportunities for redistribution but it may also bring greater inequality. Automation attracts capital and concentrates it in fewer hands but reduces the demand for labour, bringing high earnings for fewer workers in capital intensive industries but leaving more people in labour-intensive and poorly paid jobs or without any employment at all. 'What shall we all do when output per man-hour of work is extremely high but practically the whole of the output goes to a few property owners, while the mass of the workers are relatively (or even absolutely) worse off than before?'[3] Writing in the 1960s, J. E. Meade was anticipating developments that have become more marked 30 years later with the spread of highly sophisticated information technology. In *Efficiency, Equality and the Ownership of Property* he considered various strategies for avoiding such outcomes, including a Welfare State where taxes on the incomes of the rich would subsidise the incomes of the poor. This would involve problems, however, as high taxes would necessarily have some effect on incentives to work, to save, to innovate and to take risks. Moreover, taxes on incomes would do little to equalise the ownership of property. This was a matter of crucial significance, Meade pointed out, as property brings bargaining strength, security, independence and freedom; an unequal distribution would involve inequalities of power and status even though income were reasonably evenly spread.[4] Later, following the New Liberals, he proposed a scheme for full employment which included redistribution of capital.[5]

Furthermore, there is a political problem. Although rich societies have more resources, as they grow richer, to enable them to develop welfare states, they may not wish to do so. Redistributive policies may well be resisted in countries where most people feel themselves comfortably off and where a 'culture of contentment' inhibits the transfer of resources to the poor.[6] In democracies even governments that would like to extend citizenship rights and entitlements are restrained by the need to win and maintain the support of their electors.

However, the quality of citizenship is not just a matter of what governments do, any more than it is entirely dependent on employment opportunities and the character of work – fundamental though these be. If Marshall's understanding of citizenship status in terms of civil, political and social and economic rights is extended to encompass the idea of 'inclusion', other institutions than government and the market become highly significant, partly as independent sources of welfare but also because they are crucially important in determining how people use both public services and personal incomes. Families, local communities, churches and voluntary organisations can all contribute to – or, in their absence deny – opportunities for social exchanges and for participation in social affairs.

Such an approach to citizenship that goes beyond the state and the market to emphasise the importance of other social institutions and different kinds of voluntary association for people's well-being, exposes further problems that face governments that wish to guarantee entitlements for their populations. Perhaps most significant are demographic changes. An ageing population raises questions about how to arrange for the economic and social welfare of increasing numbers of old people. The decline in fertility means fewer workers to provide cash transfers for pensions and health and welfare services for those who are retired, and it also means fewer children to provide social and family care.

Furthermore, social changes in women's roles and opportunities and aspirations, associated – be it as cause or effect – with a falling birth rate, add to the problems of governments. As more women seek paid employment outside their homes to escape poverty or in pursuit of wider interests or in search of independence, pressure grows to shift responsibility for child rearing and the care of other dependants from families to public bodies. And women themselves expect, along with independent earned incomes, social security benefits in their own right rather than by virtue of their marital status. Families become less reliable providers as they get smaller and as their members adopt new activities, and most fragile are the growing proportion headed by lone parents, reflecting the rapid increase in divorce and separation and in births out of marriage. Family welfare is, of course, heavily dependent on economic resources. In Britain the growth in inequality since the 1970s has left a higher proportion of children than of adults in poverty, in families made especially vulnerable by low earnings and meagre benefits.

Finally, as wider educational and employment opportunities lead to more geographical mobility, local connections wither. The exchange of sociability and services in long settled communities and the conviviality, authority and discipline emanating from familiar individuals and institutions fades. Advanced capitalist economies tend to bring greater freedom for more people. But they also weaken familial and communitarian links and leave individuals more isolated. Marshall defined the social element in citizenship as including 'the right to share to the full in the social heritage and to live the life of a civilized being according to the standards prevailing in the society'.[7] However the 'life of a civilized being' be defined, it seems fair to assume that if it is to be realised governments must find ways of enabling people in a more atomised society to establish social relationships and take part in communal enterprises. As Mary Douglas remarks, in modern industrial societies people need goods 'in order to commit other people to their projects'.[8]

Marshall also observes in *Citizenship and Social Class* that the status involves duties as well as rights, and that these require that 'acts should be inspired by a lively sense of responsibility towards the welfare of the community'.[9] Duties are also much emphasised by the modern communitarian movement and by British governments

– especially since 1979. How far governments can foster such attitudes and activities through various forms of bureaucratic and professional intervention is uncertain. Economic and demographic and social change alter people's circumstances and expectations to a degree that makes the achievement of both the rights and responsibilities of citizenship a formidable and wide-ranging task, which we shall now consider.

IN AND OUT OF WORK

As we have seen, the growing interest in some form of basic income in Britain and more generally in Western Europe is an acknowledgement of the failure of the market and of traditional state welfare policies to guarantee an adequate standard of living for all citizens. If an economy cannot provide work for a significant number of people, and if a substantial number of jobs are insecure, temporary or badly paid, governments face pressing questions about the degree of protection they should offer and how it should be organised. Whether the advanced countries, now linked in the 'global economy' and dependent on increasingly sophisticated technology, will be able to restore the high levels of reliable employment that Beveridge and others took for granted in the 1940s, remains a matter for debate. The problem is twofold: how to spread employment and how to find ways of distributing the product more equally. The task is daunting and the strategies controversial.[10] In Britain unemployment has fluctuated between two and three million through the 1980s and 1990s. As long as it remains at this level, government social security arrangements for the well-being of people without jobs assume the greatest importance.

If people out of work are to retain their status as citizens their first requirement is for 'a modicum of economic welfare and security'. This means adequate benefits that are readily available for people who need them. Nobody should be deterred by ignorance of entitlement or by excessively complicated claiming procedures or because the receipt of benefit is regarded as stigmatising. But, on the other hand, generous benefits may raise problems if they undermine – or are thought to undermine – incentives to work. Beveridge hoped to avoid this difficulty when he proposed 'minimum but adequate' insurance payments and introduced child allowances to increase the incomes of working families. More recent efforts to strengthen work incentives have adopted the opposite strategy of reducing the incomes of families out of work!¹¹ So the rich have lower taxes and the poor lower benefits. In the years since the war, and especially over the past two decades, the fall in the value of child benefit relative to average earnings and the increase in intermittent and low paid jobs has underlined the vulnerability of growing numbers of employed as well as unemployed families, and brought the complex and sometimes destructive interaction of relief and earned incomes, and of benefit and taxation policies into sharper focus.

By the late 1990s British social security arrangements had become badly flawed – not only in excluding many people from ordinary social life, but in failing to protect minimum standards of physical health and material welfare. As economic and demographic trends have brought more dependants and more demands for state benefits, governments' attempts to control social security spending by cutting entitlements have provoked mounting unease. The public income maintenance programmes of the 1990s are a feeble and unreliable guarantee even of basic social necessities. They are very far indeed from the kinds of policies designed in Ruskin's phrase to make people 'do right'. Any such aim for government intervention is and always has been contentious. Some argue that the state cannot and should not attempt to influence moral behaviour directly. But such arguments have a hollow ring. Government intervention in social matters necessarily either enlarges or restricts opportunities for individuals or groups to behave in particular ways. The arguments are more properly about the range of choices people should have to do what sort of things; about who should have their opportunities expanded and about the most effective strategies to that end.

The policies emerging through the 1980s and 1990s have not been responsive to pressure to extend the entitlements of poor people. In many ways social security arrangements are pale shadows in the cave that bear little resemblance to any ideal plan. They are more about strengthening incentives to work and to independent living than about meeting the claims of citizens to be included in their society. And the inducements to independence are punitive and negative; they have tended to mean cutting benefits rather than providing education and training and jobs. To this extent the 1834 Poor Law principles retain their power; they appeal both to those who want to reduce public spending and to those who see dependence on the state as a preferred and attractive option for the poor – a dependency culture that must be discouraged.¹²

Although governments have refused to define a poverty line, in 1992 nearly five million people were living *below* the government's own income support level, 27 per cent in families with a full time worker.[13] Official figures suggest that in the same year roughly two billion pounds of income-related benefits were unclaimed.[14] The average incomes of the poor were about one quarter below income support, with pensioners moving up to 80 or 90 per cent and younger people falling to 60 or 70 per cent of the supposed minimum standard. These five million people living below the *de facto* poverty line are the submerged tenth of the 1990s – the casualties of the market and of government welfare policies. And their numbers have been rising. At the end of the 1970s just over three million people fell below the then supplementary benefit level, compared with the five million below the state minimum in the early 1990s.

One of the main causes of this most acute poverty is that people do not claim the benefits to which they are entitled. There are many reasons: stigma inevitably attaches to means tested payments when detailed investigation of personal circumstances effectively destroys any sense of right; excessive time and effort may be required to complete lengthy and elaborate application forms; complicated rules of eligibility and inadequate publicity may leave people ignorant of entitlement; or the sums of money available may be too small to make claiming worth the trouble. Whatever the explanation the gap between entitlement to and receipt of benefit stands as a measure of government failure to honour the most minimal requirements of citizenship that it has itself defined in legislation.

However, any poverty line is contentious. A more generous standard of 50 per cent of average income is now widely used in the UK and in international studies and sets poverty firmly in its social context. On this measure, 14 million people – a quarter of the population – are poor in the UK at the close of the twentieth century. This points to a further weakness in social security arrangements as a response to claims of citizenship. It is not only that they fail to guarantee that everyone entitled to benefits receives them and that means tests undermine any sense of right and are liable to humiliate people. It is also that the value of payments is widely considered inadequate.[15]

Everything turns on definitions. When Rowntree found a tenth of the population of York in primary poverty a hundred years ago, he was pointing to people who lacked the income to buy the necessities to maintain bare physical efficiency; his calculations of essential expenditure which determined the poverty line made no concessions to ignorance or popular tastes or social conventions. The austerity of Rowntree's poverty line reflected his desire to establish a definition that was uncontentious and that could be used to devise a research tool that would allow precise measurement of 'absolute' poverty. It was not, even in the 1890s, a standard recommended to governments that might wish to develop a social security programme, and in the 1990s a subsistence level as a sufficient indicator of poverty is increasingly dismissed. But to to take a more generous view and think in terms of 'exclusion' means that opportunities for a greater variety of consumption and social activity have to be considered. While this may bring a better understanding of the predicament of poor people and of the nature of social deprivation in rich countries, it opens the way to endless debate as to where the poverty line should be set.[16] Failing agreement and failing any concerted pressure of public opinion, governments have evaded the question, refusing to define a poverty line, denying even that a definition is possible, keeping benefits to a minimum and, over the past two decades in Britain, watching inequalities increase.[17] And it is not only that inequalities have widened; real living standards have fallen for the poorest over recent years.[18]

THE THIRD AGE

We live now in the oldest society in recorded history. Increasing longevity and declining fertility have produced a novel family structure – thin and elongated with fewer brothers and sisters and cousins and more grandparents and great grandparents. In any society, and particularly in industrial countries, people over retirement age face a diminution in their status as citizens in the sense of their opportunities to take part in social exchanges and activities. The loss of formal employment means loss of income and of occupation – the attachment to a common enterprise that can give a sense of purpose and provide companionship.[19] In times of high unemployment and rapid technological change older workers, as we have already seen, are especially vulnerable. They are among the first to lose jobs and among the last to find them.[20]

Quite apart from less likelihood of employment, however, demographic trends and changing family habits reduce the occasions for social interaction. There are fewer children available for sociability and support; the growing number of younger women taking paid jobs and following careers may interfere with family care of older people;

and increasing geographical movement nationally and internationally scatters family members and reduces the support they can give. These same trends combine to weaken local neighbourhood and community ties that at any rate in some places have sustained social relationships and mutual aid – even though such exchanges depend heavily on the obligations and reciprocities of kinship[21].

The uncertainty of the market, the fragility of the family and the fading of local communities – vital sources of economic security and social welfare – mean greater responsibilities for government if the entitlements and opportunities of citizenship are to be assured for older people. During the 1980s and the 1990s, however, attempts to control public spending have led successive administrations to emphasise the threat to liberty and independence and enterprise posed by an interventionist state and to proclaim the virtues of a deregulated market, self-help, family responsibility and voluntary effort. In an increasingly fragmented society it is extremely hazardous to rely on those institutions for individual well-being. It is paradoxical and unfortunate that the powers of local government have been steadily reduced when strong local bodies accountable to local people as well as to central government are badly needed.

The voluntary sector has a crucial part to play – in supplementing state services, in pointing to new needs and pioneering new ways of meeting them, in criticising official arrangements, offering alternatives and campaigning for higher standards. But voluntary bodies have limited resources and they are not democratically accountable. In the end they are irresponsible. Only government can guarantee or require any particular set of rights or opportunities and make the appropriate provision for them – either directly or through agreements with non-state organisations. Government may not wish to do anything of the kind, of course, and prefer retrenchment and a smaller role, as has been the recent trend in Britain. But it is a dangerous mistake to imagine that the voluntary sector is sufficiently powerful or reliable or even-handed to act in its stead. The challenge for governments in regard to older people is to secure enough redistribution from the younger population to those no longer working and from the relatively wealthy to the relatively poor to provide decent incomes and medical and social services. It is also a matter of finding ways of strengthening families and local communities and encouraging a variety of informal social exchanges. And finally it is a question of developing opportunities for third agers who so wish to move into paid employment or voluntary work.

Transferring resources to finance decent services becomes more of a problem as there emerge a growing number and proportion of old and of very old people who are likely to be heavily dependent. There were 9 million people over 60 in the UK in 1961, 12 million in 1994, and it is estimated that there will be 18 million in 2031. Over the same period the number of people over 80 is expected to rise from two million to four million. In 1994 the population over 60 represented 20 per cent of the total but over the next 40 years it is forecast to grow to nearly 30 per cent, with the most highly dependent, people over 90, increasing nearly five-fold.[22] Between 1980 and 2040 the support ratio (the number of people of working age, 15–64, to those of 65 and over) is expected to fall from just over four to three, though, as Hills notes, this would represent a more favourable balance than for any other industrial country except Ireland. For the present, however, if the total dependent population is considered (people over 60 and children under 16), the UK appears with the third highest proportion of dependents in the European Unions, after the Irish Republic and Sweden.[23]

In the 1960s the British government reacted to evidence of persisting poverty among old people, many of whom failed to apply for national assistance,[24] by proposing more generous pensions linked to both average and individual earnings.[25] A state earnings related pensions scheme was subsequently introduced but only to fall victim to the the demand for cuts in government spending that was mounting through the 1970s. Nearly half of public spending on benefits is absorbed by elderly people so it is not surprising that these payments should be vulnerable to calls for economy.

The present debate revolves around the old issues – levels of benefit and the extent of means testing. But it is also increasingly about methods of finance; about whether the state scheme should be revived and made more generous or whether arrangements for privatised individual funded pensions might accord better with the ideology of government and the preferences of the electorate.[26] In the meantime, A. B. Atkinson points out that although the average incomes of retired people have risen slightly more than for the rest of the population through the 1980s, yet inequality among them has increased. The proportion of pensioners living below the 'decency' standard of 50 per cent of the national average doubled to reach 30 per cent by 1990.[27] This represents the reality of Titmuss' prophecy of two nations in old age, delivered in the 1960s and referring at that time to the division between those with occupational or private pensions and those who were obliged to rely on the state. The reduction of state support since the 1970s has hastened and hardened the division and threatens to exclude one third of old people from normal social activity.

The necessity for so gloomy an outcome for substantial numbers of people after retirement has been challenged by many and particularly by Peter Laslett in his delineation of 'societies of the third age'. Third Age societies have both economic and demographic characteristics; they are those relatively rich countries with a GNP at least three times the world average, with at least 10 per cent of their populations over 65 and where people of 25 have a better than even chance of living beyond retirement.[28] Third age individuals are those who have passed through a first age of childhood dependency and a second age of more or less productive work and reached a time of leisure and freedom to do the things they want to do – realise old ambitions or take a larger part in social or political life. This happy outcome is a possibility because people are not only living longer but are surviving in better health. Laslett's fourth age is one of increasing dependency and decline but which he supposes would be brief.

Such a scenario for old age seems to offer high hopes of a period of retirement and independence when people can pursue individual interests or join in community activity or public service; a time when the privileges and responsibilities of citizenship can be savoured to the full. But the reality is more elusive. In the first place the development of such an enviable state of affairs requires that a long life be also a healthy life, and while there have been dramatic improvements in life expectancy in Western societies it is less clear what is happening about morbidity. Failing conclusive research, Markides considers that the weight of evidence indicates that people are living longer but with more disability and impairment.[29] Moreover, as Laslett pointed out, governments must supply adequate income and social services if a third age is ever to emerge for most people as a time of leisure and achievement and sociability. In the UK at any rate, as the proportion of old people has grown so has the reluctance of government to spend public money on them.

Laslett supposed that a larger elderly population might form a voting block sufficiently powerful to persuade politicians to divert resources to their ends, especially as they might be supported by younger people whose own expectations of survival beyond retirement would give them a direct interest in generous arrangements. Phillipson, however, points out that the interests of older people are very diffuse, and determined less by age than by position in the social structure – by class, religion, race, occupation and so forth. He notes (citing the *Sunday Times*, 12 April 1992) that Conservative support among women over 64, the poorest group of old people, increased between 1987 and 1992.[30] The two nations remain in old age and among younger people, as we have seen, and government would have to be determinedly interventionist if citizenship entitlements and opportunities were to be a common experience.

If government were to take seriously the extension and guarantee of citizenship rights for older people, the most important things to attend to would be adequate personal income and the chance of useful activity. When Laslett wrote about third age societies he defined them in relation to the proportion of the population over 65. But in much recent discussion the qualifying age has been lowered to include people over 50 in recognition that increasing numbers of younger men and women are no longer in full time work – be it through choice or lack of opportunity – nor, given current fertility trends, engaged in full time child rearing. They have thus entered a period of life whose main characteristic, as the Carnegie Inquiry into the Third Age puts it, is the increasing freedom that it offers.[31]

If freedom is to be of value, however, people must have the wherewithal to enjoy it and to pursue their chosen interests. They must also have the respect of others. The Carnegie Inquiry emphasised the widespread stereotyping and denigration of older people, commonly regarded as dependents and represented in policy discussions as a 'burden' making inexorably mounting demands on national resources. The element of truth in this is the expected survival of more people into very old age – the fourth age – when the need for medical care and social support is bound to increase. But the other side of the picture is the growing number of third agers who can count on 20 or more years of active and healthy life. It seems that on balance most of the years gained through greater longevity are free of any major disability.[32] Moreover, some handicaps of old age arise out of 'extrinsic' or environmental and lifestyle factors – poor diet, lack of exercise, isolation – rather than the inevitable physiological processes of ageing. Governments might usefully attempt to modify the effects of growing old by tackling such damaging experiences. It is in this sense that the well-being of the old requires attention to the young. Prevention would benefit both society and individuals, for the longer disability is delayed, the shorter it lasts.[33]

INCOME AND RETIREMENT

Appreciation of this new demographic phenomenon is beginning to shift policy discussion beyond problems of coping with dependency to questions of how older people, as citizens, might be offered more chances to contribute to and take part in economic and social and political affairs. Foremost among the material resources required for citizenship is money. Substantial employment income is no longer an option for most third agers, personal wealth is the possession of only a minority, and cash transfers within families tend to go from parents to children rather than the other way round. So most old people rely heavily on the state. But, as we have seen, although the basic pension may have increased its value in real terms, its relation to earnings has fallen steadily. At the end of the 1970s it was worth 20 per cent of average male earnings; in 1996 15 per cent; and by 2030 it is estimated that it will fall to 9 per cent.[34]

Moreover, as we have also already seen, inequalities among older people are growing. Those obliged to rely on state pensions are the poorest; those who have had well paid and continuous employment, and belonged to occupational or private pension schemes, may move into the third age with considerable assets. While inevitable constraints on public spending may make it desirable to encourage individual saving to avoid too sharp a fall in living standards on retirement it is also the case that some private schemes are unsatisfactory, and proper regulation is essential for a reliable income in old age. But the first priority for government must be adequate state support for the poorest. The Carnegie Inquiry points out that the worst off are unemployed people in their 50s with a history of low or part time earnings and periods out of work, and that women, people from ethnic minorities and those who are unskilled are especially likely to fall into this group. Government action – or inaction – has consigned increasing numbers of these poorest people to means tested benefits – themselves very doubtfully adequate – as the relative value of pensions has dropped. The continuance of such policies, which involve increasing polarisation of income, without any discussion of consequences and without public debate are not, the Carnegie report declares, an 'acceptable option'.[35]

Criticism of the readiness of government to preside over increasing disparity between the living standards of the poor and the rest come from many sides, but prescriptions for action vary. Some temper a desire for social justice with scepticism about the willingness of the majority to pay more to support other people in old age despite their avowed good intentions.[36] Frank Field has asserted that one of the most powerful of human motives is self-interest so that pension schemes will be most acceptable and most successful if people can see a personal return for their own investment.[37]

Recognising the political difficulties of raising taxation to finance a universal increase in the basic pension, A. B. Atkinson has advocated a scheme whereby people whose pension income fell below a defined adequacy level would receive a supplement on retirement to make up the difference. This would involve a means test but one that would be less humiliating and simpler to administer than the existing arrangements.[38] It would honour the status of citizen and ensure that everyone received their entitlement. It would avoid an alternative strategy of raising the basic pension and restoring the link with earnings which would not only cost more money but would distribute most of it to the better off.

The report from the Retirement Income Inquiry makes a similar proposal. Adequate pensions, it insists, must involve a national minimum related to earnings. Present arrangements depending on the basic pension and income support fail because the pension is derisory and income support unsatisfactory. The report suggests introducing an 'Assured Pension' whereby income from pensions or any other savings would be made up to a defined adequacy level on retirement.[39] Some employment income and some income from savings would be disregarded in calculating the Assured Pension to avoid discouraging work or thrift. Everyone would be covered. People with a history of low earnings or irregular work and lacking National Insurance contributions would still qualify. This would do something to redress the disadvantages of women, who frequently have a broken employment record, and of old people living alone (generally women) who tend to be among the poorest as they have had less opportunity of belonging to generous private schemes, and more years of retirement to watch their meagre state pensions fade to insignificance.

Although the Retirement Income Inquiry assumes that the first priority in pension reform would be a decent income for the poorest, it also considers some kind of 'second tier' is needed to relate pensions to past earnings for the better off. There is some controversy as to whether the second tier should be run by the state – through a revived earnings related scheme – or should rely on private arrangements. But it is generally reckoned desirable that contributions towards an additional pension should be compulsory up to a minimum; enforced savings for those who can afford it to prevent their being eligible for means tested benefits in old age. The Retirement Income Inquiry proposes that the existing state earnings related scheme be abolished but that a national funded scheme be set up as an alternative for people without satisfactory private arrangements.

WORK AND RETIREMENT

If money is crucial for civilised living in the third – as in any other – age, the opportunity for occupation, be it paid employment or some kind of voluntary activity, is hardly less important. The Carnegie report emphasised the danger, both for elderly people and for everybody else, of assuming old age to be a time of dependency and of physical or mental incapacity. The shifting population balance makes it financially prudent to increase opportunities for people who have moved out of full time work to remain active. The experience and leisure of old age may be a valuable resource for voluntary organisations and for children and young people inside and outside the family group.

Only a very small proportion of the income of pensioners comes from earnings – overall 7 per cent – and a mere 15 per cent of people of pension age, concentrated in the richest 30 per cent, have any employment income. The economic activity rates for younger men have been falling over recent years, though they have been rising for women. By 2006 it is expected that only 74 per cent of men between 55 and 59 years old and only 45 per cent of those between 60 and 64 will be in work. It is this trend to finish regular employment earlier that persuaded the Carnegie Inquiry to regard the third age as starting at 50. However, the move out of full time work may be involuntary. According to the DSS Survey of 1992[40] nearly 40 per cent of men retiring early did so because of ill health and a further 14 per cent were made redundant or urged to leave by their employers. The 50 per cent or so who chose early retirement were encouraged by adequate pensions or the desire for a better quality of life or dislike of their job.

Public policies aiming to strengthen citizenship status in old age would have to guarantee not only adequate income when work ceased but some choice in deciding when that should be. While retirement brings leisure and opportunity for some, for others it brings poverty, boredom and isolation. In their study *Life After Work*, Young and Schuller found two-thirds of their sample of retired people unable to create satisfactory lives for themselves. Mostly manual workers, earlier disadvantages had accumulated and left them ill-fitted for retirement; the work that had structured their lives had also incapacitated them and left them unable to take advantage of their new freedom. A satisfactory third age depends on people's earlier experiences.[41]

In modern economies, older workers are at a disadvantage in the competition for jobs. Rapidly changing methods of production and technology put a premium on education, training and qualifications, and the demand for unskilled labour shrinks. But education and qualifications are more common among the young. So older people are vulnerable to redundancy and if they lose a job have difficulty finding another. The question of the efficiency of older workers is controversial, but should be considered in relation to occupation. Age may be a handicap in heavy manual work or in tasks requiring fast and precise responses. But it may be an asset in jobs depending on long experience. By and large, 'age is not a good discriminator of the ability to work and learn'.[42] Despite this judgement, the Carnegie Inquiry found widespread discrimination against older people in recruitment, training opportunities, promotion, and selection for redundancy and early retirement.[43] Such policies are damaging not only for the individuals who suffer from them but also for the economy and for society as the potential contribution of older people is lost.

What might government do to offer third agers more choice over work and retirement? Here is an immediate dilemma in that in times of persistent high unemployment measures to enable older people to stay in work may cost the jobs of younger people, and there are strong arguments for giving priority to the young. However, by the 2020s the population of working age will be smaller as the children of the postwar 'baby boom' move into retirement so it is prudent to consider how the future 'burden' of dependency might be reduced.

A first step would be to create more chances of employment. The Carnegie Inquiry found a considerable number of people out of work in 1990 who would have preferred a job: half the men and 20 per cent of the women between 55 and 59; 30 per cent of the men and 11 per cent of the women between 60 and 64; and 12 per cent of the men between 65 and 69. Very few found one. Among men and women out of work in 1989, only one tenth of those in their late 50s and four per cent in their early sixties had re-entered employment a year later. Over half of those searching for work said they wanted to be with other people and over a third wanted the money.[44]

If there is to be more choice to work or not to work jobs must be available and pension arrangements and retirement age must be flexible. People may need or wish to switch to a different occupation as they grow older. The increase in casual, part-time and service sector employment may suit older men and women provided they have the necessary skills. This points to the great importance of preparation for retirement. Employees entering the third age – at 50 or so – should be encouraged to anticipate the move out of regular work. They should have time to learn about other possible jobs, opportunities for training, and the chance to become involved in the voluntary sector and develop new interests. Such measures might alleviate the trepidation, loss of occupation and loss of self-esteem that often attend the move out of full time work.[45]

In the end, as Young and Schuller point out, the quality of life of older people depends greatly on what happened to them when they were younger. Education, and training in appropriate skills for work, and the chance to develop other interests and activities in the first and second ages are crucial for contentment in the third – just as proper diet and sufficient exercise are important for younger people if they are to stay healthy and active. Many of the disabilities of old age, as we have seen, are environmentally determined. But the risks of poverty, unemployment, poor health and poor education in earlier years are strongly linked to class position and to inequality, which has intensified over the past two decades. If the position of older people is to be substantially changed for the better, government will have to invest heavily in the health and education of the young.

FAMILIES AND HOUSEHOLDS

There is one area of human experience that governments seem to have little power to touch but that is fundamental for the well-being of old and young alike – family structures and relationships. Trends in fertility and marriage and divorce proceed for the most part independently of legislation. They reflect the complex interaction of the changing values and aspirations of new generations responding to new economic and social circumstances and new opportunities. Governments may hesitate to intervene in family affairs that tend to be seen as matters for private rather than public decision making. Where fear of a declining population has led countries to attempts to increase the birth rate, they have been notably unsuccessful. Births outside marriage have become common without any public encouragement and despite what might be considered the deterrent effects of meagre public financial and welfare support for lone parents. And the escalation of divorce can hardly be regarded as a response to more liberal divorce laws. It is rather the other way round; the legislation is better seen as an accommodation to the growing rate – and intolerance – of marriage failure. Nevertheless, if government cannot dictate demographic trends nor substantially affect fertility and marriage behaviour, it can certainly modify their consequences. It is important to be aware of changes in family structures and family roles if vulnerable individuals are to be protected and appropriate decisions made about the responsibilities of public authorities.

It is well known that the great majority of older people rely on their families and, to a lesser extent and for different things, on friends and neighbours for assistance as they grow frailer. The state plays a very small part indeed. Help generally comes from a spouse or, less often, from a daughter. Married people have better physical and emotional health than the single and widowed who, if they have any severe disability, rarely survive in the community unless they can join the household of a child. Public domiciliary services are very thin on the ground; inadequate, unreliable and inflexible, despite the supposed development of 'community care' since 1993. So people living on their own, and without children who can help, are likely to have to enter an institution when they can no longer look after themselves.

There has been a marked increase in the number of people over 65 living alone in England and Wales over the past century. Between 1921 and 1981 the proportions for men rose from 6 to 17 per cent and for women from 11 to 42 per cent.[46] The trend accelerated after 1962, showing a 15 per cent increase in solitary old people during the subsequent 20 years, a rate of increase similar to that which before 1962 had taken several centuries to accomplish since mediaeval times. Widowed and single people are most vulnerable to isolation; one fifth lived alone in pre-industrial times, but two thirds of the men and nearly three quarters of the women by 1982.[47] The preponderance of women on their own reflects their greater longevity and, as those who marry tend to choose men several years older than themselves, their greater probability of outliving their spouse. Re-marriage is rare as a way of coping with loneliness, and in any case more common for men than for women. Nevertheless, the steepest increase in living alone since 1971 has been among men under 65 – a consequence of decline in marriage and the increase in divorce. This group is expected to form the largest proportion of one person households within about 10 years – outstripping women of 60 and over.[48]

The explanation for the growth in single person households is not entirely clear, nor is it certain what the trend bodes for the future. The residence of elderly parents with their children was unusual in pre-industrial England, though census information is very patchy before 1900. The preference seems to have been for independent living, and sharing a response to economic necessity – the poor law alternative was very unpleasant – or to failing health or shortage of dwelling places. Michael Anderson has shown how older women might join their daughters' households to look after grandchildren while the younger women worked, but also how adolescents would move out of the parental home if wages were high enough for them to support themselves.[49] It is not clear how the introduction of old age pensions in 1908 affected habits of residence. They may have enabled old people to live independently or have meant that they were more welcome in their children's households. In fact they had little visible impact on living arrangements.[50]

The greater proportion of people on their own also reflects the drop in the number living with non-relatives. Households in the past more commonly included lodgers or servants or might comprise collections of paupers supported by the poor law authorities, arrangements that rising standards of living and more dwelling space have made less usual. If the existence of a spouse in the same household or an available daughter are the best protection in old age, then the widowed and the unmarried and the childless are most at risk. And although successive generations reaching old age after 1945 have been wealthier and healthier than their predecessors, and thus more able to stay independent until they are very old, changes in fertility and marriage habits and in migration weaken support networks.

It seems that old people share households more easily when sharing is a long-term arrangement, when care of a highly dependent spouse or parent is rarely resented. Resentment is more likely in recent marriages or when sharing is the response to the need for care.[51] It is rather probable, however, that the number of people who are vulnerable in these respects will grow. In the past, higher fertility and wider spacing of births meant that it was common for women to continue child bearing for twenty years or so and into their forties, and this made it more likely that in old age there would still be an adult child in the household. Lower marriage rates also meant more unmarried daughters – traditionally responsible for the care of older relatives. The fall in fertility and increase in marriages through this century have reduced the number of available young women. David Eversley has calculated that a couple married in 1920 and aged 80 and 85 in 1980, would then have 42 female relatives alive, 14 not working. By contrast, a couple married in 1950 and 80 years old in 2005 would have only 11 female relatives alive, and only three not working.[52] On the other hand, more marriages also mean that more people will move into old age sharing a household with a spouse. However, the more recent decline in marriage and the exponential increase in divorce and separation suggest that fewer shared households will survive in future. And not only will ties between spouses be weakened; younger women estranged from their partners will be less likely to take on the care of parents in law.[53]

Thus, on balance the demographic picture of the long thin family implies weaker kin support for frail old people and fewer close relatives to help to maintain independent living. But, as we have noted, two further developments threaten the 'support networks ' of third agers. One is the move of younger women into the labour market so that paid employment competes with elderly relatives for their time. While some studies suggest that children in full time work are less likely to provide care,[54] a finding that accords with common sense, the Carnegie Inquiry did not regard growing employment among women as incompatible with care giving.[55] Nevertheless, efforts to combine the two responsibilities will inevitably make heavy demands on younger people.

The other threat to family care for the elderly is the geographical mobility characteristic of modern societies. Support is most secure if a spouse or child shares a household or a daughter lives nearby. The migration of younger people following jobs or careers leaves their parents without local kin, and although friends and neighbours may be important for assistance and sociability at low levels of dependency, long-term personal help is generally only available from close relatives. Failing local family support, people with serious disabilities will have to rely on private arrangements or statutory services which, given the severe shortage of domiciliary workers, may well mean entering an institution.

THIRD AGE CITIZENS?

For older people, as for everyone else, social citizenship requires security, independence, respect, opportunities to contribute to the general well-being through paid or voluntary work, and recreation and sociability. It seems, however, from the research literature and from common experience, that ill-founded prejudice among employers and prevailing social attitudes and behaviour frequently stigmatise old age in a way that denies these basic entitlements. Elderly people are widely perceived as disabled or incompetent or worse. This is reflected in the media and the press. BBC research shows that older people are under-represented by one third on television in relation to their numbers in the population (ethnic minorities appear roughly proportionately and women are under-represented by one half).[56] Where they do appear the image, as in advertisements, is often unfavourable or caricatured. And similar attitudes are apparent, as we have seen, in discrimination in employment in both the statutory and voluntary sectors.

Demographic trends create fears of growing numbers of frail old people who will make increasing demands on public resources. But while arrangements must be made for the care of highly dependent people, by far the greater number of third agers are fit and active. Recent research discounts the common belief that old people gain more from the welfare state than they contribute over their lifetime.[57] An alternative prospect to the gloomy predictions of a heavy burden of dependency points to the substantial contribution of active and healthy third agers in paid and voluntary work and in familial exchanges. The challenge for public policy is to provide opportunities for them, not services.

The Carnegie Inquiry emphasised the significant contribution older people already make to the support of the very old, and of younger people with disabilities; half of all care givers are between 50 and 74, and one fifth of this age group provide care for another person.[58] But the contribution might be enhanced if statutory and voluntary organisations took steps to encourage and recruit older people by publicising opportunities for useful activity, arranging training, supporting inexperienced newcomers, providing expenses, and not assuming any particular age to be a bar to service.

Nevertheless, while 'useful activity' may be important for self-esteem and for the common good, citizenship also demands the chance to develop individual interests and join others in social and recreational pursuits. It calls for more informal educational opportunities to attract people who lacked such opportunities when they were young; two thirds of men and women between 50 and the statutory retirement age left school by the time they were 15, compared with one third of younger adults. Peter Laslett has described the growth of the 'university of the third age' throughout Europe, everywhere a rapidly expanding part of education systems. He writes graphically of the huge potential for further expansion, not only for training and re-training, but for learning, teaching and research among older people.[59]

Freedom to join in activities of all kinds – in work, education and leisure – along with other people is what gives substance to the notion of 'inclusion' and social citizenship. And it is all the more important as the chances of third agers being included in family exchanges diminish. Most present day families are small and scattered and the women, traditional guardians of family solidarity, have other preoccupations. In his study of Bethnal Green in the 1950s, Peter Townsend described a long settled working class community bound together by kinship and poverty and propinquity and common employment. The old people were absorbed into familial and neighbourhood exchanges, a pattern of reciprocal services and sociability whereby they traded the help that they gave to their daughters in domestic management and child rearing for assistance and care when they themselves grew frail. Old people in Bethnal Green lived close to their families; most of them, 78 per cent, saw a son or daughter daily.[60] But this was unusual in England, even in the 1950s. Although there is little comparable information, later local studies suggest children were more remote, between 15 and 51 per cent of parents having the nearest child beyond the parish boundary.[61] And a national survey in the 1970s found only one third of people over 65 having several visits a week from relatives, and 20 per cent receiving fewer than one a month. Single and divorced people were most isolated, with far fewer visits than those who were married or widowed; one fifth of those who were divorced had no living relatives outside the household compared with five per cent of all the elderly respondents.[62]

Distance does not, of course, destroy family affection or sense of responsibility. But it does mean that they are differently expressed – by letter or telephone or overnight visits or gifts of money rather than through daily exchanges of services and conviviality. As older people are left more solitary it becomes the more important for the public authorities to find ways of developing and strengthening civic and community life.

Townsend noted the significance of reciprocity in family exchanges in Bethnal Green and the degree to which older people were providers as well as receivers of services. This was an important way of preserving self-respect and enabling people to accept help more readily when they needed it, and it led Townsend to ask how far familial exchanges might be extended beyond the kin group, with third agers helping with the care of other people's children. Such arrangements to provide various kinds of supervision for children and young people have been hailed recently as a vital contribution to family well-being, a benefit to old and young alike Older people, for instance, might take responsibility for children beyond the limits of the normal school day where both parents were in full time work.[63] Whether old people may wish to spend their time with young children, especially if they have not had any of their own, is another matter. The Carnegie Inquiry found third agers far more likely to be visiting other old or sick people than to be looking after children.[64] This may have been due to lack of opportunity, but the most common volunteering activities of older people were raising money, sitting on committees or helping to organise various events.

The most vulnerable people, however, are the very old who are highly dependent. Wenger estimates that personal long-term care, that only families provide in the community, is probably available for less than half of those who need it. The success of family arrangements in any case depends on the nature and quality of earlier relationships. Some people may not wish to rely on their daughters, just as some may resist any intrusion into their homes by public authority workers. If people are to retain autonomy and control over their lives in advanced old age they must be able to choose between family care and public services. Attempts to 'legislate family piety are doomed to failure'.[65] Where families are involved a very large increase in professional and financial support for care givers would be needed to make the task tolerable. At present statutory services are frequently inadequate and of poor quality.[66]

Arber and Ginn have argued that people retain a sense of independence and control in so far as they are able to maintain familiar roles and customary activities that express their 'personal identity'.[67] Thus, if statutory help is to preserve autonomy and self-esteem it must be designed to allow older men and women to take part in the various domestic tasks and activities, rather than merely supplying services for them.[68] Such sensitive and flexible public arrangements are rare, but as family resources diminish only a substantial expansion of domiciliary services will allow the more fragile third agers the choice of independent living.

The alternative is institutional care, but it is here that the loss of autonomy and control is clearest. For very disabled people institutions may be unavoidable, and some may welcome the security they offer and the relief from the responsibility of managing their own affairs. For others, however, they bring apathy and despair. Policies to extend people's command over their lives should encourage institutions to offer residents opportunities to take part in running the establishments, and to involve local people in the life of the homes.

More 'community care' might reduce admissions to costly institutions but it should not be seen by government as a convenient way of controlling public spending by shifting responsibility to families and friends and neighbours; they may not be available or may not be the preferred helpers of older men and women. The organisation of appropriate and reliable support for people in their own homes calls for careful co-ordination of many different types of formal and informal care in the light of individual circumstances and needs. The cost is likely to be high, though whether it would exceed the cost of residential places would, of course, depend on the adequacy and quality of the respective domiciliary and institutional arrangements.

If older people are to receive proper recognition of their entitlements and responsibilities as citizens, and be able to join in the life of their society, they must have the chance of work and leisure, of education and recreation, of offering services to others and the assurance of care for themselves when they need it. This is not only a matter for government. Popular attitudes and understanding and tolerance also need to change. An ageing population has fostered prejudices about infirmity and dependency which are misconceived and damaging. Third agers are contributors to the well-being of everyone else as well as recipients of services. There is, of course, the inescapable dilemma of how to reconcile the competing claims of young and old on public resources and on private benevolence or, in nineteenth-century terms, of how to reconcile the individual and the common good. It is not always the case, unfortunately, that the two necessarily coincide, as some writers have claimed. But to argue for more consideration for third agers is no special pleading; it is to point to the part that older people play in social, economic and cultural life, and to ways in which their opportunities might be extended to the benefit of themselves and everybody else. As Young and Schuller have remarked, 'The ageless society is just as noble a cause as the classless society'.[69]

NOTES

1   Dahrendorf, 1988.
2   Wilensky, 1975.
3   Meade, 1964, p. 26.
4   *Ibid.*, p. 39.
5   Meade, 1995.
6   Galbraith, 1992.
7   Marshall and Bottomore, 1992, p. 8.
8   Douglas, in Halsey (ed.), 1976, p. 205.
9   Marshall and Bottomore, 1992, p. 41.
10 Nickell, 1994; Meade, 1995; Grieve Smith, 1997.
11 Atkinson and Micklewright, in Atkinson, 1989.
12 Murray, 'The Emerging British Underclass', 'Underclass: the Crisis Deepens', in Lister (ed.), 1996.
13 Oppenheim and Harker, 1996, pp. 30–2.
14 *Ibid.*, p. 32.
15 Oldfield and Yu, 1993; Bradshaw and Lynes, 1995.
16 Atkinson, in Barker (ed.), 1996.
17 Barclay, 1995; *The Archbishop of Counterbury's Commission*, 1985; Hutton, 1995.
18 Crafts, 1997.
19 Young and Schuller, 1991.
20 Laczko and Phillipson, 1991.
21 Townsend, 1957; Abrams, 1985; Bulmer (ed.), 1986; Roberts,   1984; Finch, 1989.
22 Central Statistical Office, 1996; Hills, 1993.
23 Central Statistical Office, 1996, p. 40.
24 Cole and Utting, 1962.
25 Department of Health and Social Security, 1969.
26 Townsend and Walker, 1995; Field, 1995; Falkingham and Johnson, 1993; Johnson, 1994.
27 Atkinson, 1995, p. 315.
28 Laslett, 1987.
29 Markides, in Atkinson and Reid, 1993.
30 Phillipson, in Walker (ed.), 1996.
31 The Carnegie Inquiry, 1993, p. 90.
32 Hodkinson, in Grimley Evans (ed.), 1993, p. 52.
33 Grimley Evans, 1993, p. 8.
34 *The Retirement Income Inquiry, 1996*, p. 10.
35 The Carnegie Inquiry, 1993, p. 47.
36 Brook, in Jowell *et al.*, 1996.
37 Field, 1995.
38 Atkinson, 1995, p. 320.
39 *The Retirement Income Inquiry, 1996*, p. 25.
40 Cited in the Carnegie Inquiry, 1993, p. 127.
41 Young and Schuller, 1991, p. 124.
42 The Carnegie Inquiry, 1993, p. 23.

43   See also Laczko and Phillipson, 1991.
44   The Carnegie Enquiry, 1993, p. 27.
45   *Ibid.*, p. 29.
46   Wall, in Kertzer and Laslett (eds), 1994.
47   Wall, 1984.
48   Office for National Statistics, 1997.
49   Anderson, 1971.
50   Wall, in Kertzer and Laslett (eds), 1994.
51   Wenger, 1992, p. 203.
52   Cited in Bulmer, 1987, p. 2.
53   Qureshi, in Walker (ed.), 1996, pp. 113–5.
54   *Ibid.*, pp. 115–6.
55   The Carnegie Inquiry, 1993, p. 75.
56   Cited in the Carnegie Enquiry, 1993.
57   Falkingham and Hills, 1995.
58   The Carnegie Inquiry, 1993, p. 77.
59   Laslett, 1989, pp. 159–77.
60   Townsend, 1957, p. 37.
61   Wall, in Marsh and Arber (eds), 1992, p. 75.
62   Hunt, 1978, p. 95.
63   Young, 1991; Young and Halsey, 1995.
64   The Carnegie Inquiry, 1993, p. 81.
65   Wenger, 1992, p. 204.
66   Glendinning and McLaughlin, 1993, pp. 20–1.
67   Arber and Ginn, in Marsh and Arber (eds), 1992.
68   Wenger, 1992, p. 117.
69   Young and Schuller, 1991, p. 165. Note also the proceedings of a
     Discussion Meeting on Ageing: Science, Medicine and Society, organ-
     ised jointly by the Royal Society and the British Academy in 1997.
     Publication is forthcoming.

Conclusion

The arguments about citizenship and work in Britain over the past 200 years traced in this study represent only one strand in a much larger debate. But it is a strand of fundamental importance in that employment, or the lack of it, is central for individual well-being and for the good of society. The discussion has become more complex in the second half of the twentieth century. National labour markets are increasingly exposed to competition from other parts of the world, and industrial decline and technological change alter the character of work, creating new jobs, transforming others and removing some altogether. Moreover, quite apart from changes in employment prospects, changes in social expectations and aspirations raise new questions about the position of women, of people from ethnic minorities and of older people who have tended to exist on the fringes of the labour market, peculiarly vulnerable to dismissal, poor working conditions and low pay. For all of them the questions are about their entitlements and responsibilities as citizens; about how the entitlements might be honoured and the responsibilities discharged.

In some senses the questions remain the same. They are about the nature of the good society and the place of work within it. The colourful tradition of social criticism of the nineteenth century, discussed in earlier chapters, attacked the damaging nature of industrial labour that left the workman 'scant of life' and the merciless industrial system that led to the social, economic and geographical divisions between the classes that represented the 'social problem' of the two nations. The social criticism of the twentieth century tackles similar questions about conditions of employment, the right or duty that people may have to work, the responsibility that government may have to provide it and the problems of a society in which income and opportunities are increasingly unequal.

To some extent the answers, too, remain the same. Canon Barnett and Ruskin and Morris all wanted work to be pleasant and educative and useful. Fabians and New Liberals and Beveridge and those who came after had similar hopes, regarding employment as fundamental for personal and social well-being and insisting on the duty of government to provide it. During the 1990s the Social Justice Commission has again re-asserted the central importance of work: 'Paid or unpaid, it is the way in which we meet needs, create wealth and distribute

194

resources ... a source of personal and individual fulfilment, social status and relationships'.[1] And most recently the Council of Churches for Britain and Ireland has proclaimed that 'enough good work for everyone' should be a national aim, a way to fashion a society with a sense of common purpose.[2] Both bodies are ready to contemplate higher taxes and a minimum wage as strategies for achieving their ends.

Although the questions and answers are familiar, however, they are now discussed in a very different social and economic milieu. First, the country is very much richer; the gross domestic product has multiplied by five since 1900.[3] For much of the nineteenth and early twentieth centuries the problem for Christian Socialists and New Liberals was how best to secure minimum standards of material welfare for everyone. In citizenship terms, T. H. Marshall regarded civil and political rights and a 'modicum' of social and economic welfare as the crucial requirements. Present arguments move the discussion beyond basic entitlements to the idea of 'relative poverty' and 'inclusion', emphasising the significance not only of possessions or services but of relative standards of living and of the quality of relationships. Citizenship then comes to involve the chance of joining with others in political and economic and social affairs. Such matters however, have tended to elude the attention of governments and they certainly escape the conventional indicators of prosperity in estimates of GNP. The European Union experiments in developing more sophisticated 'quality of life' indicators are an effort to find a better measure of poverty and progress and well-being. They suggest a wider understanding of citizenship to include social exchanges and relationships, and they also point to the importance of the physical environment in quality of life measures, a move that would have been welcomed by Ruskin and Morris.

The widening of the concept of poverty and of citizenship in no way detracts from the significance of work. As we have seen, the experience of employment and of unemployment is of vital importance for most people. But the shift from an 'absolute' to a 'relative' approach means that the political task of translating the more generous notions and entitlements into social arrangements becomes more daunting. Questions about redistribution are more pressing and more contentious. The increase in national wealth has brought higher expectations – for the rich as well as for the poor – so greater resources are no guarantee of support for egalitarian policies.

There is another development that challenges the ingenuity of advanced societies in securing the entitlements of citizenship for all their people, and that is the emergence of the third age. As the country has grown richer, the population has grown older. Old people were much rarer in the nineteenth century and so made comparatively light demands on national resources and on the time and energy of their children. Britain is now an older society than it has ever been. As the retired population approaches 20 per cent, the need for transfers of goods and services is substantial. As we have argued, employment or at any rate occupation is often an important part of the lives of older people, but it tends to give place, as age advances, to social and recreational activities rooted in communities and families. The 'conceptual shift' towards the importance of relationships as well as material circumstances in interpreting deprivation or evaluating citizenship is especially pertinent for third agers.

This study has attempted to give some account of the way that different writers have conceived the rights and responsibilities of the state and of individuals in fashioning a just society. In the nineteenth century great emphasis was placed on personal moral obligation to strive for self-improvement or for the welfare of others in face of the harsh conditions imposed by unregulated industrial development. By the end of the century there was increasing emphasis on the responsibility of government to provide minimum living standards and employment for the casualties of the market. After the Second World War politicians committed themselves to the pursuit of a 'welfare state' that involved a collection of universal services in education, health and welfare that went far beyond any notion of minimum standards, and at the same time accepted responsibility for maintaining full employment. By the 1970s, however, state welfare and full employment policies were coming under attack as governments struggled with economic and industrial and demographic change and with the revival of old ideologies favouring more responsibilities for individuals and a smaller role for the state.

During the past 20 years, as Britain has grown richer but as social and economic inequalities have widened, old controversies and old protests are again emerging. Canon Barnett thought luxury as great an evil as pauperism and an insult to the poor. And a near destitute class of workers or workless men and women was a threat to everyone else; 'starvelings', Morris declared, could only riot. In a similar way contemporary discussion of citizenship is beginning to insist on the need to include everybody in a common way of life. 'We need to learn to assess society's "wealth" as its well-being as a whole, and not merely some average well-being but that (so far as we can) of each individual'.[4] The Labour Party came to power in 1997 after a campaign that put great emphasis on such sentiments. It remains to be seen whether they retain the power and the will to shift a growing wealth of 'provisions' into an increasingly diverse collection of 'entitlements' which all can share in a society which is a 'good place to live'.

NOTES

1   Commission on Social Justice, 1994, p. 151.
2   Council of Churches for Britain and Ireland, 1997, chapters 1 and 4.
3   Dilnot, 'The Economic Environment' in Halsey (ed.), 1988, p. 146.
4   Council of churches for Britain and Ireland, 1997, p. 7.

Bibliography

Abel, E. K. Canon Barnett and the First Thirty Years of Toynbee Hall, unpublished PhD thesis. University of London, 1969.

Abrams, P. 'Policies to Promote Informal Informal Social Care', *Ageing and Society*, 5(1), March 1985.

Aitken, W. F. *Canon Barnett Warden of Toynbee Hall.* Partridge, 1902.

Anderson, M. *Family Structure in Nineteenth Century Lancashire.* Cambridge University Press, 1971.

Anthony, P. D. *John Ruskin's Labour.* Cambridge University Press, 1983.

Arber, S. and Ginn, J. 'In Sickness and in Health: Care Giving, Gender and the Independence of Elderly People' in Marsh and Arber (eds) 1992.

The Archbishop of Canterbury's Commission on Urban Priority Areas. *Faith in the City.* Church House, 1985.

Arnold, M. *Culture and Anarchy.* Thomas Nelson, 1869.

Ashbee, C. R. *The Building of Thelema.* Dent, 1910.

Atkinson, A. B. (ed.) *Poverty and Social Security.* Harvester Wheatsheaf, 1989.

Atkinson, A. B. *Incomes and the Welfare State.* Cambridge University Press, 1995.

Atkinson, A. B. 'Promise and Peformance: Why We Need an Official Poverty Report' in Barker (ed.) 1996.

Atkinson, A. B. and Micklewright, J. 'Turning the Screw: Benefits for the Unemployed 1979–1988' in Atkinson (ed.) 1989.

Atkinson, A. B. and Reid, M. (eds) *Age, Work and Social Security.* Macmillan, 1993.

Baines, E., Oastler, R. and Cawood, J. *New Lanark, A Failure!* Report of a Deputation of the Guardians of the Poor of Leeds to Visit and Inspect New Lanark. Leeds, 1819.

Balls, E. and Gregg, P. *Work and Welfare.* Institute for Public Policy Research, 1993.

Barclay, P. (Chairman) *Inquiry into Income and Wealth.* Joseph Rowntree Foundation, 1995.

Barker, P. (ed.) *Living as Equals.* Oxford University Press, 1996.

Barnett, H. O. *Canon Barnett: His Life Work and Friends.* John Murray, 1918.

Barnett, S. A. *Universities' Settlement in East London.* 1888.

Barnett, S. A. *The Service of God.* Longmans Green, 1897.

Barnett, S. A. *Religion and Progress.* Adam and Charles Black, 1907.

Barnett, S. A. *Religion and Politics.* 1911.

Barnett, S. A. *Worship and Work.* Letchworth Garden City Press, 1913.

Barnett, Canon and Mrs S. A. *Towards Social Reform.* Fisher Unwin, 1909.

Basic Income Research Group (BIRG) *Bulletin*, nos. 1–15, 1984–1992.

Berg, M. *The Machinery Question and the Making of Political Economy 1815–1848.* Cambridge University Press, 1980.

Beveridge, W. H. *Unemployment, a Problem of Industry.* Longmans Green, 1909.

Beveridge, W. H. *Social Insurance and the Allied Services*. HMSO, 1942.
Beveridge, W. H. *Full Employment in a Free Society*. Allen and Unwin, 1944.
Beveridge, W. H. *Voluntary Action*. Allen and Unwin, 1948.
Beveridge, Lord, *Power and Influence*. Hodder and Stoughton, 1953.
Booth, General. *In Darkest England and the Way Out*. McCorquodale, 1890.
Bradshaw, J. *Household Budgets and Living Standards*. Joseph Rowntree Foundation, 1993.
Bradshaw, J. and Lynes, T. *Benefit Uprating Policy and Living Standards*. Social Policy Research Unit, University of York, 1995.
Braithwaite, W. J. *Lloyd George's Ambulance Wagon*. Methuen, 1957.
Briggs, A. (ed.) *William Morris: News From Nowhere and Selected Writings and Designs*. Penguin, 1986.
Brook, L. 'Public Spending and Taxation' in Jowell *et al.* (eds) 1996.
Bulmer, M. (ed.) *Neighbours: The Work of Philip Abrams*. Cambridge University Press, 1986.
Bulmer, M. *The Social Basis of Community Care*. Allen and Unwin, 1987.
The Carnegie Inquiry into the Third Age. *Life, Work and Livelihood in the Third Age*. Carnegie UK Trust, 1993.
Central Statistical Office *Social Trends 26*. HMSO, 1996.
Chadwick, E. *The Sanitary Condition of the Labouring Population of Great Britain 1842*, edited and with an introduction by M. W. Flinn. Edinburgh University Press, 1964.
Citizens' Income Research Group (CIRG) *Bulletin*, nos. 16–22, 1993–1996.
Clarke, P. *Liberals and Social Democrats*. Cambridge University Press, 1978.
Cole, D. and Utting, J. E. G. *The Economic Circumstances of Old People*. Occasional Papers on Social Administration 4. Codicote Press, 1962.
Collingwood, W. G. *The Life and Work of John Ruskin*. Methuen, 1893.
Collini, S. *Liberalism and Sociology: L. T. Hobhouse and Political Argument in England 1880–1914*. Cambridge University Press, 1979.
Commission on Citizenship. *Encouraging Citizenship*. HMSO, 1990.
Commission on Social Justice. *Social Justice: Strategies for National Renewal* (Chairman Sir Gordon Borrie). Vintage, 1994.
Council of Churches for Britain and Ireland *Unemployment and the Future of Work*. Delta Press, 1997.
Crafts, N. *Relative Decline of the British Economy 1870–1995*. Social Market Foundation, 1997.
Crossman, R. 'The Role of the Volunteer in the Modern Social Service', Sidney Ball Memorial Lecture 1973 in Halsey (ed.) 1976.
Dahrendorf, R. *The Modern Social Conflict*. Weidenfeld and Nicolson, 1988.
Daniel, W. W. *A National Survey of the Unemployed*. Political and Economic Planning, 1974.
Deacon, A. 'Unemployment and Politics in Britain Since 1945' in Showler and Sinfield (eds) 1981.
Deakin, S. and Wilkinson, F. 'European Integration: The Implications for UK Policies on Labour Supply and Demand' in McLaughlin (ed.) 1991.
Dennis, N. and Halsey, A. H. *English Ethical Socialism*. Oxford University Press, 1988.

Department of Health and Social Security. *National Superannuation and Social Insurance.* Cmnd 3883. HMSO, 1969.

Dilnot, A. 'Social Security and Labour Market Policy' in McLaughlin (ed.) 1991.

Dilnot, A., Disney, R., Johnson, P. and Whitehouse, E. *Pensions Policy in the UK: An Economic Analysis.* Institute for Fiscal Studies, 1994.

Douglas, M. 'Relative Poverty – Relative Communication' in Halsey (ed.) 1976.

Falkingham, J. and Hills, J. (eds) *The Dynamic of Welfare.* Prentice Hall, Harvester Wheatsheaf, 1995.

Falkingham, J. and Johnson, P. *A Unified Funded Pension Scheme (UFPS) for Britain.* Discussion paper WSP/90, Welfare State Programme, London School of Economics, 1993.

Field, F. *Losing Out: The Emergence of Britain's Underclass.* Blackwell, 1989.

Field, F. *Making Welfare Work: Reconstructing Welfare for the Millennium.* Institute of Community Studies, 1995.

Finch, J. *Family Obligations and Social Change.* Polity Press, 1989.

Freeden, M. *The New Liberalism.* Oxford University Press, 1986.

Friedman, M. and Friedman, R. D. *Capitalism and Freedom.* Chicago University Press, 1962.

Galbraith, J. K. *The Affluent Society.* Hamosh Hamilton, 1958.

Galbraith, J. K. *The Culture of Contentment.* Penguin, 1992.

Gallie, D. and Marsh, C. 'The Experience of Unemployment' in Gallie *et al.* (eds) 1995.

Gallie, D. and Vogler, C. 'Unemployment and Attitudes to Work' in Gallie *et al.* (eds) 1995.

Gallie, D., Gershuny, J. and Vogler, C. 'Unemployment, the Household, and Social Networks' in Gallie *et al.* (eds) 1995.

Gallie, D., Marsh, C. and Vogler, C. (eds) *Social Change and the Experience of Unemployment.* Oxford University Press, 1995.

Gell, P. L. *Work for University Men in East London.* Fall and Tyler, 1884.

Gershuny, G. 'The Psychological Consequences of Unemployment: An Assessment of the Jahoda Thesis' in Gallie *et al.* (eds) 1995.

Glendinning, C. and McLaughlin, E. *Paying For Care: Lessons From Europe,* Social Security Advisory Committee. HMSO, 1993.

Green, T. H. *Liberal Legislation and Freedom of Contract.* Simpkin Marshall, 1881.

Greengarten, I. M. *Thomas Hill Green and the Development of Liberal Thought.* University of Toronto, 1981.

Grieve Smith, J. *Full Employment: a pledge betrayed.* Macmillan, 1997.

Griffith, R. *Community Care: Agenda for Action: A Report to the Secretary of State for Social Services* (the Griffith Report). HMSO, 1988.

Grimley Evans, J. (ed.) *Health and Function in the Third Age,* papers prepared for the Carnegie Inquiry into the Third Age. Nuffield Provincial Hospital Trust, 1993.

Grimley Evans, J. 'Human Ageing and the Differences between Young and Old' in Grimley Evans (ed.) 1993.

Hakim, C. 'Unemployment, Marginal Work and the Black Economy' in McLaughlin (ed.) 1991.

Halsey, A. H. (ed.) *Traditions of Social Policy*. Blackwell, 1976.
Halsey, A. H. *Change in British Society*, 3rd edn. Oxford University Press, 1986.
Halsey, A. H. (ed.) *British Social Trends Since 1900*. Macmillan, 1988.
Harris, D. *Justifying State Welfare*, Basil Blackwell, 1987.
Harris, J. *Unemployment and Politics: A Study in English Social Policy, 1886–1914*. Clarendon Press, 1972.
Hayek, F. A. *The Road to Serfdom*. Routledge, 1944.
Hayek, F. A. *The Constitution of Liberty*. Routledge and Kegan Paul, 1960.
Hill, M. J., Harrison, R. M., Sargeant, A. V. and Talbot, V. *Men Out of Work*. Cambridge University Press, 1973.
Hills, J. *The Future of Welfare: A Guide to the Debate*. Joseph Rowntree Foundation, 1993.
Hills, J., Ditch, J. and Glennerster, H. (eds) *Beveridge and Social Security*. Clarendon Press, 1994.
Himmelfarb, G. *The Idea of Poverty: England in the Early Industrial Age*. Faber and Faber, 1984.
Hobhouse, L. T. *Democracy and Reaction*. Fisher and Unwin, 1904.
Hobhouse, L. T. *The Elements of Social Justice*. Allen and Unwin, 1922.
Hobhouse, L. T. *Liberalism*. Oxford University Press, 1945 (first published 1911).
Hobson, J. A. *Problems of Poverty*, 2nd edn. Methuen, 1895.
Hobson, J. A. *The Problem of Unemployment*. Methuen, 1896.
Hobson, J. A. *John Ruskin Social Reformer*. James Nisbet, 1898.
Hobson, J. A. *The Crisis of Liberalism: New Issues of Democracy*. P S King & Son, 1909 (I).
Hobson, J. A. *The Social Problem*. James Nisbet, 1909 (II).
Hodkinson, M. 'Active Life Expectancy and Disability' in Grimley Evans (ed.) 1993.
Hunt, A. *The Elderly at Home*, OPCS Survey. HMSO, 1978.
Hutton, W. *The State We're In*. Jonathan Cape, 1995.
Jencks, C. *The Underclass*. Brookings Institution, 1991.
Jencks, C. *Rethinking Social Policy: Race, Poverty and the Underclass*. Harvard University Press, 1992.
Johnson, P. *The Pensions Dilemma*. Institute for Public Policy Research, 1994.
Johnson, P., Conrad, C. and Thomson, D. (eds) *Workers versus Pensioners: Intergenerational Justice in an Ageing World*. Manchester Univesity Press, 1989.
Jowell, R. *et al.* (eds) *British Social Attitudes: The 13th Report*. Social and Community Planning Research, 1996.
Kertzer, D. I. and Laslett, P. (eds) *Ageing in the Past: Demography, Society and Old Age*. University of California Press, 1994.
Keynes, J. M. *How to Pay for the War*. Macmillan, 1940.
King, D. *Actively Seeking Work?* University of Chicago, 1995.
Laczko, F. and Phillipson, C. *Changing Work and Retirement*. Open University Press, 1991.
Lampard, R. 'An Examination of the Relation between Marital Dissolution and Unemployment' in Gallie *et al.* (eds) 1995.
Lansbury, G. *My Life*. Constable, 1928.

Laslett, P. 'The Emergence of the Third Age' *Ageing and Society*, 7, pp 133–160, 1987.

Laslett, P. *A Fresh Map of Life: The Emergence of the Third Age*. Weidenfeld and Nicolson, 1989.

Laurie, A. P. *Pictures and Politics*. International Publishing Company, 1934.

Lister, R. (ed.) *Charles Murray and the Underclass*. Institute of Economic Affairs, 1996.

McBriar, A. M. *An Edwardian Mixed Doubles: the Bosanquets versus the Webbs: A Study in British Social Policy 1890–1929*. Clarendon Press, 1987.

Macdonald, R. 'Labours of Love: Voluntary Working in a Depressed Local Economy', *Journal of Social Policy*, 25(1), 1996, 19–38.

Mackail, J. W. *Life of William Morris*, 2 volumes. Longmans Green, 1907.

Macnicol, J. *The Movement for Family Allowances 1918–45*: A study in Social Policy Development, Heinemann, 1980.

McLaughlin, E. 'A Crisis of Unemployment' in McLaughlin (ed.) 1991.

McLaughlin, E. (ed.) *Understanding Unemployment*. Routledge, 1991.

McLaughlin, E., Millar, J. and Cooke, K. *Work and Welfare Benefits*. Social Policy Research Unit, 1989.

Mansbridge, A. *Arnold Toynbee*. The Pioneer Biographies of Social Reformers, no. 5. London, n.d.

Mansbridge, A. *Fellowmen: A Gallery of England, 1871–1946*. Dent, 1948.

Markides, K. S. 'Trends in the Health of the Elderly in Western Societies' in Atkinson and Rein (eds) 1993.

Marsh, C. and S. Arber (eds) *Families and Households: Divisions and Change*. Macmillan, 1992.

Marshall, T. H. 'Citizenship and Social Class' in *Sociology at the Crossroads: and other Essays*, Heinemann, 1963.

Marshall, T. H. and Bottomore, T. *Citizenship and Social Class*. Pluto Press, 1992.

Meacham, S. *Toynbee Hall and Social Reform 1880–1914: The Search for Community*. Yale, 1987.

Meade, J. E. *Efficiency, Equality and the Ownership of Property*. Allen and Unwin, 1964.

Meade, J. E. 'Poverty in the Welfare State', *Oxford Economic Papers*, 24, 1972.

Meade, J. E. *Liberty, Equality and Efficiency*. Macmillan, 1993.

Meade, J. E. Full Employment Regained? An Agathotopian Dream, Department of Applied Economics, University of Cambridge, 1995.

Middlemiss, J. T. *A Modern Prophet and His Message: John Ruskin*. Smith and Taylor, 1896.

Milner, A. *Arnold Toynbee: Address to Members of Toynbee Hall*. London, 1895.

Morris, L. *Dangerous Classes: The Underclass and Social Citizenship*. Routledge, 1994.

Morris, W. 'News from Nowhere' in Briggs, (ed.) 1986.

Murray, C. 'The Emerging British Underclass' 1990 in Lister (ed.) 1996.

Murray, C. 'Underclass: the Crisis Deepens' 1994 in Lister (ed.) 1996.

Nettleship, R. L. *Memoir of Thomas Hill Green*. Longmans Green, 1906.

Nickell, S. 'Can Unemployment in the UK be Reduced?' unpublished paper for 'Options for Britain' Conference, Nuffield College, Oxford, 1994. Institute of Economics and Statistics, University of Oxford, 1994.

Norman, E. *The Victorian Christian Socialists.* Cambridge University Press, 1987.

Office for National Statistics *Social Trends 27.* The Stationery Office, 1997.

Oldfield, N. and Yu, C. S. *The Cost of A Child.* Child Poverty Action Group, 1993.

Oppenheim, C. and Harker, C. *Poverty: The Facts.* 3rd edn. Child Poverty Action Group, 1996.

Owen, R. *The Life of Robert Owen* (written by himself). Effingham Wilson, 1857.

Owen, R. *A New View of Society and Other Writings*, edited by G. Claeys. Penguin, 1991.

Paget, S. (ed.) *Henry Scott Holland: Memoirs and Letters.* John Murray, 1921.

Parijs, P van (ed.) *Arguing for Basic Income.* Verso, 1992.

Parker, H. *Instead of the Dole.* Routledge, 1989.

Parker, H. *Taxes, Benefits and Family Life: The Seven Deadly Traps.* Institute of Economic Affairs, 1995.

Parker, J. *Women and Welfare.* Macmillan, 1989.

Phillipson, C. 'Intergenerational Conflict and the Welfare State' in Walker (ed.), 1996.

Podmore, F. *Robert Owen.* Hutchinson, 1906.

Popper, K. R. *The Open Society and Its Enemies.* Routledge and Kegan Paul, 1962.

Qureshi, H. 'Obligations and Support within Families' in Walker (ed.) 1996.

Rathbone, E. *The Disinherited Family.* Edward Arnold, 1924.

The Retirement Income Inquiry (Chairman Sir J. Anson) *Pensions 2000*, the Retirement Income Inquiry, 1996 (set up by the National Association of Pension Funds).

Rhys Williams, J. E. *Something to Look Forward To.* Macdonald & Co, 1943.

Richter, M. *The Politics of Conscience: T. H. Green and his Age.* Weidenfeld and Nicolson, 1964.

Roberts, D. *Victorian Origins of the British Welfare State.* Yale University Press, 1960.

Roberts, E. *A Woman's Place: An Oral History of Working Class Women 1880–1940.* Basil Blackwell, 1984.

Rogers, F. *Labour, Life and Literature: Some Memoirs of Sixty Years.* Smith Elder, 1913.

Room, G. (ed.) *Beyond the Threshold: The Measurement and Analysis of Social Exclusion.* The Policy Press, 1995.

Rowntree, B. S. *Poverty. A Study of Town Life.* Macmillan, 1901.

Ruskin, J. *Essays on Political Economy.* Routledge, n.d. (reprinted from Fraser's Magazine, June, September and December 1862 and April 1863). Subsequently *Munera Pulveris*.

Ruskin, J. *Unto this Last.* Allen and Unwin, 1960 (first published 1862).

Ruskin, J. *Time and Tide by Weare and Tyne: Twenty-Five Letters to a Working Man of Sunderland on the Laws of Work.* Smith Elder, 1867.

Ruskin, J. *Fors Clavigera: Letters to the Workmen and Labourers of Great Britain*. Bedford, Clarke, 1871.

Ruskin, J. *The Crown of Wild Olive*. George Allen, 1895.

Schuller, T. 'Learning Generations: Age and Education' in Walker (ed.) 1996.

Sen, A. 'Poor Relatively Speaking', *Oxford Economic Papers* 35, 1983.

Sen, A. 'A Sociological Approach to the Measurement of Poverty: A Reply to Professor Peter Townsend', *Oxford Economic Papers* 37, 1985.

Shaw, G. B. (ed.) *Fabian Essays in Socialism*. Fabian Society, 1889.

Showler, B. 'Political Economy and Unemployment' in Showler and Sinfield (eds) 1981.

Showler, B. and Sinfield, A. 'A Most Unequal Tax' in Showler and Sinfield (eds.) 1981.

Showler, B. and Sinfield, A (eds) *The Workless State*. Martin Robertson, 1981.

Sinfield, A. 'Unemployment in an Unequal Society' in Showler and Sinfield (eds) 1981.

Sinfield, A. (ed.) *What Unemployment Means*. Martin Robertson, 1981.

Sinfield, A. and Showler, B. 'Unemployment and the Unemployed in 1980' in Showler and Sinfield (eds) 1981.

Smith, D. J. (ed.) *Understanding the Underclass*. Policy Studies Institute, 1992.

Spender, H. *The Fire of Life*. Hodder and Stoughton, 1926.

Tawney, R. H. *Equality*. Allen and Unwin, 1964 (I) (first published in 1931).

Tawney, R. H. *The Radical Tradition*. Allen and Unwin, 1964 (II).

'R. H. Tawney's Commonplace Book' *Economic History Review*, Supplement 5, Cambridge, 1972.

Tawney, R. H. *The Acquisitive Society*. Wheatsheaf Books, 1982 (first published 1921).

Taylor, P. and Walker, A. 'Intergenerational Relations in the Labour Market: The Attitudes of Employers and Older Workers' in Walker (ed.) 1996.

Thompson, E. P. *William Morris: Romantic to Revolutionary*. Lawrence and Wishart, 1955.

Thompson, P. *The Work of William Morris*. Heinemann, 1967.

Titmuss, R. M. *The Gift Relationship: From Human Blood to Social Policy*. Allen and Unwin, 1970.

Townsend, P. *The Family Life of Old People*. Routledge and Kegan Paul, 1957.

Townsend, P. *Poverty in the United Kingdom*. Allen Lane, 1979.

Townsend, P. and Walker, A. *The Future of Pensions: Revitalising National Insurance*. Fabian Society, 1995.

Toynbee, A. 'Industry and Democracy', in Toynbee, 1844.

Toynbee, A. *Progress and Poverty: A Criticism of Mr Henry George*. Kegan Paul, 1883.

Toynbee, A. 'Are Radicals Socialists?' in Toynbee, 1884.

Toynbee, A. 'The Education of Co-operators', in Toynbee, 1884.

Toynbee, A. 'Wages and Natural Law', in Toynbee, 1884.

Toynbee, A. *Lectures on the Industrial Revolution*. Rivingtons, 1884.

United Nations Development Programme. *Human Development Report 1996*. Oxford University Press, 1996.

Walker, A. (ed.) *The New Generational Contract*. University College London Press, 1996.

Wall, R. 'Residential Isolation of the Elderly: A Comparison over Time'. *Ageing and Society*, (4) 1984, 483–503.

Wall, R. 'Relations between the Generations in British Families Past and Present' in Marsh and Arber (eds) 1992.

Wall, R. 'Elderly Persons and Members of their Households in England and Wales from Pre-Industrial Times to the Present', in Kertzer and Laslett (eds) 1994.

Webb, B. *My Apprenticeship*. Longmans Green, 1926.

Webb, S. and Webb, B. *English Poor Law History, Part I, The Old Poor Law*. Frank Cass, 1963.

Webb, S. and Webb, B. *English Poor Law History, Part II*, Vols 1 and 2, *The Last Hundred Years*. Frank Cass, 1963.

Wells, H. G. *New Worlds For Old*. Constable, 1908.

Wenger, G. L. *Help in Old Age: Facing up to Change*. Liverpool University Press, 1992.

Wilensky, H. L. *The Welfare State and Equality*. University of California Press, 1995.

Williams, R. *Culture and Society 1780–1930*. Chatto and Windus, 1958.

Wilmer, C. (ed.) *John Ruskin: Unto This Last and Other Writings*. Penguin, 1985.

Wilson, W. J. *The Truly Disadvantaged*. Chicago, 1987.

Young, M. *The Rise of the Meritocracy 1870–2033*. Thames Hudson, 1958.

Young, M. *A Haven in a Heartless World: the Future of the Family*. Economic and Social Research Council, 1991.

Young, M. and Halsey, A. H. *Family and Community Socialism*. Institute for Public Policy Research, 1995.

Young, M. and Schuller, T. *Life After Work*. HarperCollins, 1991.

Index

Abel, E. K. 50
active citizenship xii, 9, 113
  Speaker of House of Commons
    appointed committee (1988) xii
adult suffrage 5, 93
Amnesty International 8
Anderson, Michael 186
Anthony, P.D.
  on Marx and Ruskin 83
Arber, S.
  independence and control for elderly
    people 190–1
Atkinson, A. B. 164
  on pensioners 177; pensions 181;
    participation income 164
Arnold, Matthew 50
  Culture and Anarchy 109
Ashbee, C. R. 51

Barnett, Henrietta 30
Barnett, S. A. xi, 29, 49, 76, 81, 104, 113,
  134
  Anglican Church 30, 46–8
  children's holiday scheme 51
  on class 32, 36
  denouncement of Charity Organisation
    Society 30–1, 40, 42
  on freedom 33
  in Whitechapel 33, 36, 37, 50, 51;
    campaigning for local
    amenities 38
  on Labour Party 35, 93
  on luxury as a danger 35
  on pauperism as fatal disease 36, 42
  on pensions 41
  on reform of poor laws 34, 42, 43, 44
  sketch of ideal city 31–2
  on slumming as fashionable
    amusement 50
  at St Jude's church 37
  Toynbee Hall *see* settlements
Bell, Andrew 68
Bentham, Jeremy 63
  pleasure-pain principle 104
Besant, Annie 125
Beveridge W. H. 7, 42, 51, 52, 65, 145
  General Council of the TUC 148
  National Assistance Board 152

plan for social security 146; *Full
  Employment in a Free Society;
  Social Insurance and Allied
  Services; Voluntary Action* 146
state grants for children 163
Social Justice report 147
view on unemployment 147–9, 150–3;
  White Paper (1944) 150; national
  survey (1974) 153
Bland, Hubert 126
Boards of Conciliation 25
  see also A. Toynbee
Booth, Charles 136
Booth, General William
  industrial settlements 128
Bottomore, T.
  approaches to citizenship 13
  human rights 8
  societal policies 13
Briggs, Asa
  on William Morris 118
Burke, Edmund
  industrial education 25
Burne-Jones, Sir Edward Coley 106

Callaghan, James, Labour Prime
  Minister 152
Carlyle, Thomas 9, 81, 109, 128, 132
  and the romantic revolt 105–6
Carpenter, Mary 17
Charities
  see organisations
Chartism 49, 65, 104
Child Poverty Action Group 163
Christian Socialism 49
  see also E. Norman
Christian Socialists 5, 17, 48, 104, 106,
  108, 131
co-operative associations
  see organisations
Co-operative Congress (1831) 72, 75–6
Cobbett, William, *Black Dwarf* 77
Cobden, Richard 135
Coleridge, Samuel Taylor 9
Collingwood, W. G.
  on Ruskin 81
Committee on the Poor Laws (1816)
  71